THE SCHOOL PORTFOLIO

SECOND EDITION

A Comprehensive Framework for School Improvement

VICTORIA L. BERNHARDT, Ph.D.

Executive Director
Education for the Future Initiative
SBC Foundation[1]

Professor
Department of Professional Studies in Education
College of Communication and Education
California State University, Chico, CA

[1] The SBC Foundation, along with the Southwestern Bell, Pacific Bell, and Nevada Bell Foundations, is the charitable foundation of SBC Communications and its family of companies, including Pacific Bell, Southwestern Bell, Nevada Bell, SNET, and Cellular One properties.

EYE ON EDUCATION
6 Depot Way West
Larchmont, NY 10538
(914) 833-0551
(914) 833-0761 fax

Library of Congress Cataloging-in-Publication Data

Bernhardt, Victoria L., 1952-
    The school portfolio : a comprehensive framework for school
improvement / by Victoria L. Bernhardt. -- 2nd ed.
        p.   cm.
    Includes bibliographical references (p.   ) and index.
    ISBN 1-883001-64-1
    1. School improvement programs--United States. 2. Portfolios in
education--United States. 3. School management and organization-
-United States. 4. Educational evaluation--United States.
    I. Title.
    LB2822.82.B47   1999
    371.2'00973--dc21   98-41529
                                                             CIP

10 9 8 7 6 5

Also Available from Eye on Education

DATA ANALYSIS FOR COMPREHENSIVE SCHOOLWIDE IMPROVEMENT:
by Victoria L. Bernhardt

PERFORMANCE ASSESSMENT AND STANDARDS-BASED CURRICULA:
The Achievement Cycle
by Allan A. Glatthorn with Don Bragaw, Karen Dawkins, and John Parker

TRANSFORMING SCHOOLS INTO COMMUNITY LEARNING CENTERS
by Steve R. Parson

RESEARCH ON EDUCATIONAL INNOVATIONS 2/E
by Arthur K. Ellis and Jeffrey T. Fouts

RESEARCH ON SCHOOL RESTRUCTURING
by Arthur K. Ellis and Jeffrey T. Fouts

THE PERFORMANCE ASSESSMENT HANDBOOK
Volume 1 Portfolios and Socratic Seminars
Volume 2 Performances and Exhibitions
by Bil Johnson

THE EDUCATOR'S BRIEF GUIDE TO THE INTERNET
AND THE WORLD WIDE WEB
by Eugene F. Provenzo, Jr.

EDUCATIONAL TECHNOLOGY:
Best Practices from America's Schools 2/e
by William C. Bozeman

THE DIRECTORY OF INNOVATIONS IN ELEMENTARY SCHOOLS
by Jane McCarthy and Suzanne Still

LEADERSHIP THROUGH COLLABORATION:
Alternatives to the Hierarchy
by Michael Koehler and Jeanne Baxter

TRANSFORMING EDUCATION THROUGH TOTAL QUALITY MANAGEMENT:
A Practioner's Guide
by Franklin Schargel

THE ADMINISTRATOR'S GUIDE TO SCHOOL COMMUNITY RELATIONS
by George E. Pawlas

THE REFLECTIVE SUPERVISOR:
A Practical Guide for Educators
by Ray Calabrese and Sally Zepeda

THE PRINCIPAL'S EDGE
by Jack McCall

The Principal as Steward
by Jack McCall

A Collection of Performance Tasks and Rubrics
Middle School Mathematics
by Charlotte Danielson
High School Mathematics
by Charlotte Danielson and Elizabeth Marquez
Upper Elementary School Mathematics
by Charlotte Danielson

School-To-Work
by Arnold H. Packer and Marion W. Pines

Handbook of Educational Terms and Applications
by Arthur K. Ellis and Jeffrey T. Fouts

Teaching in the Block
Strategies for Engaging Active Learners
by Robert Lynn Canady and Michael D. Rettig

The Educator's Brief Guide to Computers in the Schools
by Eugene F. Provenzo, Jr.

The Interdisciplinary Curriculum
by Arthur K. Ellis and Carol J. Stuen

Implementation
by Anita Pankake

Information Collection:
The Key to Data-Based Decision Making
by Short, Short, and Brinson, Jnr.

Problem Analysis:
Responding to School Complexity
by Achilles, Reynolds, and Achilles

Judgement:
Making the Right Calls
by James Sweeney and Diana Bourisaw

Written Expression:
The Principals' Survival Guide
by Podsen, Allen, Pethel, and Waide

ACKNOWLEDGEMENTS

There are many people who become involved in the writing of a book. This is, of course, how it is possible to write one while working full-time.

I owe gratitude first and foremost to the *Education for the Future Initiative* staff for their patience, understanding, and outstanding assistance throughout the entire book-writing process, with both the first and second editions. I know it was difficult at times. I hope you know how much I really do appreciate all that you did and do.

My very special thanks to my husband, Jim Richmond, who throughout the entire process of visualizing, traveling, researching, drafting, completing, and revising this book has given me his special brand of support and encouragement.

And my sincere thanks to the SBC Foundation[1] whose concern and support for public education is unmatched. I continue to say there hasn't been a day in eight years that I didn't wake up in the morning or go to bed at night thinking that I was the luckiest person on earth to have the greatest job in the universe. Thank you for your continued support for me and for the *Education for the Future Initiative*. It is very easy to dedicate the royalties from this book back to the Initiative.

Now, four years after the first edition was published, many of the same individuals are still helping to continuously improve the School Portfolio. Thanks again to Mary Leslie, Marlene Trapp, Brad Geise, Sally Withuhn, Lara Bunting, Sandy Flinn, Leni von Blanckensee, Mary Tribbey, Fran Rebello, Marcy Lauck, and George Bonilla. Special thanks to Lynn Varicelli for her talents with design and layout and her tireless dedication to learning new things, and to Jonni Davenport for her editing. A meaningful thanks to Bob Sickles, Publisher, Eye on Education, for his patience and diligent support.

I sincerely appreciate the selfless efforts of each and every one of you. I hope what follows exceeds your expectations. If it does, it is because of the continuous improvement that resulted from your insights and assistance.

---

[1] The SBC Foundation, along with the Southwestern Bell, Pacific Bell, and Nevada Bell Foundations, is the charitable foundation of SBC Communications and its family of companies, including Pacific Bell, Southwestern Bell, Nevada Bell, SNET, and Cellular One properties.

ABOUT THE AUTHOR

Victoria L. Bernhardt, Ph.D., is Executive Director of the *Education for the Future Initiative*, and Professor in the Department of Professional Studies in Education at California State University, Chico. In addition to the *Education for the Future Initiative*, Dr. Bernhardt directs a partner office of the Region XI Comprehensive Center. Dr. Bernhardt received a Ph.D. in Educational Psychology Research and Measurement, with a minor in Mathematics, from the University of Oregon in 1981. Her B.S. and M.S. degrees are from Iowa State University in the fields of statistics and psychology.

Dr. Bernhardt has directed the *Education for the Future Initiative* since 1991. While working with schools in the *Initiative*, she developed the concept of the school portfolio. In 1996, this work was named one of the top three Business-Education Partnerships in the World when it received the NOVA Corporation Global Best Award for Educational Renewal and Economic Development. Dr. Bernhardt was the recipient of the 1995 McKee Foods Corporate Award for Partnership Leaders. In addition to receiving two dozen other awards, she has made numerous presentations at professional meetings and has conducted over 300 workshops on the school portfolio and data analysis processes at local, regional, state, and national levels.

The author's first edition of *The School Portfolio: A Comprehensive Framework for School Improvement*, published by Eye on Education, was written to disseminate the research behind the school portfolio. It assists schools with clarifying the purpose and vision of their learning organizations. It measures and ensures congruence of all parts of the organization to enable the attainment of their vision. This second edition updates the original school portfolio book and incorporates the content of a workshop workbook that will assist learning organizations as they develop their school portfolios.

Dr. Bernhardt's companion books: *Data Analysis for Comprehensive Schoolwide Improvement* was written to help learning organizations use data analysis to inform them of where they are, where they want to be, and how to get there—sensibly and painlessly; and, *The Example School Portfolio*, written with Dr. Bernhardt's associates, shows what a completed school portfolio looks like and supports schools in developing their own school portfolios.

Dr. Bernhardt, and her associates, offer workshops on school portfolio and data analysis processes throughout the United States.

The author can be reached at—

Education for the Future Initiative
400 West 1st Street
Chico, CA 95929-0230
Tel: (530) 898-4482
Fax: (530) 898-4484
vbernhardt@csuchico.edu
http://eff.csuchico.edu

TABLE OF CONTENTS

FOREWORD

As a corporate philanthropic organization, the SBC Foundation[1]—through the work of the Pacific Bell and Southwestern Bell Foundations—is proud to be associated with Victoria L. Bernhardt and the *Education for the Future Initiative*, an organization that we have supported since 1991. Through our involvement, we have become convinced that technology and data can improve students' learning, as well as help contributors like Pacific Bell and Southwestern Bell make informed grantmaking decisions while making a real difference in the communities we serve.

This second edition of *The School Portfolio: A Comprehensive Framework for School Improvement* describes the exemplary work of the *Education for the Future Initiative* in helping schools re-examine their role in improving student learning. In this edition, Dr. Bernhardt explains how California schools, working with the *Education for the Future Initiative*, have integrated technology and data-based decision making into their school improvement efforts.

Her message is one of valuable lessons learned and we, at Pacific Bell and Southwestern Bell are proud to be a part of helping more educators benefit from her experience. Through the Pacific Bell-sponsored *Education for the Future Initiative*, Dr. Bernhardt has worked with more than 1,500 schools. The program has been credited with improving test scores, increasing parental involvement, and even prompting migrant families to make participating school districts a home base for their children despite seasonal moves for other family members.

Dr. Bernhardt advocates a results-oriented approach that pulls together the interrelated workings of a school to focus on student performance. It's a message that resonates with educators, parents, and businesses, including us at Pacific Bell and Southwestern Bell.

I'm sure you, like the growing number of personnel from schools and state departments of education who have selected Dr. Bernhardt to work with their school

---

[1] The SBC Foundation, along with the Southwestern Bell, Pacific Bell, and Nevada Bell Foundations, is the charitable foundation of SBC Communications and its family of companies, including Pacific Bell, Southwestern Bell, Nevada Bell, SNET, and Cellular One properties.

improvement efforts, will find this book a helpful guidepost as you work together with parents, teachers, and students to improve student learning. The small part we have played in helping students has been truly rewarding. Good luck in your efforts.

Gloria Delgado
President
SBC Foundation
San Antonio, Texas

PREFACE

On November 21, 1991, principals and restructuring coordinators from the eight original *Education for the Future Initiative* schools, representatives from their district offices, lay persons, researchers, funders, and staff met to design an evaluation process that would in part lead to understanding the impact of two years of restructuring.

The day began by brainstorming responses to questions such as: What is the purpose of evaluation? What do we want it to do for us? What are the purposes and expectations of the partnership between these schools and the Pacific Bell Foundation[1]? Who is the audience for the evaluation? What do they need to know and see? What kinds of evaluation are they used to seeing? What is restructuring? What are the desired outcomes? How can they be measured? How else can we measure student achievement besides standardized test scores? How can we measure the effectiveness of the *Initiative*? How do we establish a comprehensive evaluation process that will provide information for each audience? How can we also provide information to help the schools improve without inundating them with data-gathering requirements?

The school representatives were clear. They wanted an evaluation which would provide feedback on their process and progress, and help to improve—a process more "authentic and restructured" than standardized test scores. The funders wanted to see student achievement increases and to know that their dollars were being well-spent.

By the end of the day, butcher paper—covered with handwritten diagrams and words—encircled the huge meeting room.

Initiative staff took the butcher paper and began synthesizing the information. Before long, categories began to form and methods for assessing the categories became clear.

---

[1] Pacific Bell Foundation initiated the Education for the Future Initiative in 1989 and continues to support it with the SBC Foundation, its current corporate parent.

After about six months of working, reworking, drafting, reviewing, and redrafting, an innovative evaluation design evolved: a comprehensive school portfolio framework that would document plans, processes, progress, and products, and a set of rubrics—known as the *Education for the Future Initiative* Continuous Improvement Continuums. These continuums would be used to assess plans, processes, progress, and products while guiding the improvement efforts.

Since the schools began using the school portfolio and continuous improvement continuums, their continuous improvement efforts have progressed positively and impressively. The schools are now able to see—

- ◆ their many accomplishments which gives them the motivation to continue
- ◆ the interdependencies and interrelationships of the multiple dimensions of continuous improvement which help them understand how to leverage and implement multiple aspects simultaneously
- ◆ the impact of their efforts
- ◆ how to plan for the continuous improvement of all elements of the school organization

Additionally, the assessment process enables staff to shape and maintain a shared vision, to look for and maintain congruence of the elements with their vision and mission, and to lay out plans for next steps. Likewise, the funders are able to see and understand the complexities of school; the impact of the partnership at each school; and, the school's needs, efforts, and results.

The schools were so proud of their school portfolios and the progress they made with this approach that they decided a parallel process had to be developed for teacher improvement. This led each school to design its own set of rubrics that go deep into the student achievement continuum to describe a continuum of implementation for that school's specific vision. Teachers took the process two steps further by developing their own professional portfolios and conducting action research in their classrooms. With this key combination, teachers can now describe the impact of specific changes in their classrooms and student achievement increases. These teachers now truly understand the impact of their actions on students and student learning, and how their efforts impact the total learning organization. They also understand that improvement is forever and continuous, and that one cannot collect too much data when trying to understand phenomena.

The overall results of the portfolio and rubrics process has led to systemic change in these schools. It also led to extended support of the *Initiative* by the Pacific Bell Foundation—support beyond their original five-year commitment.

I encourage every school undergoing systemic improvement efforts to consider establishing a school portfolio around the *Education for the Future Initiative* Continuous Improvement Continuums, or around their own dimensions, as long as they are comprehensive and based on literature about systemic change. The process really helps focus schools' efforts as this incredible task unfolds.

The first step in the work is done—the development of the School Portfolio Framework and the *Education for the Future Initiative* Continuums. The next step is up to you . . .

August 1998

Four years later, all of the above still holds true. Since this was written, School Portfolio workshops have been offered to representatives of schools in every state of the United States. The School Portfolio continues to rival every approach to schoolwide change with its positive measurable results.

This second edition was designed in part by the users of the first edition of *The School Portfolio: A Comprehensive Framework for School Improvement* (1994). This edition combines the previously published workbook for school portfolio workshops with the content of the first edition of *The School Portfolio: A Comprehensive Framework for School Improvement*—and more. Specifically, new questions at the end of each chapter will help guide school personnel who are attempting to build a school portfolio on their own. In addition, each chapter has been updated, and a new chapter has been added at the end of the book with suggestions for updating and maintaining your school portfolio.

Further, this second edition is in a new 8.5″ x 11″ format that makes using it while you are building your school portfolio easier—another suggestion we appreciated from users of the first edition. We hope you like our new look and content.

To join in our efforts to promote comprehensive continuous improvement efforts with learning organizations, please visit our website or contact us by e-mail.

Victoria L. Bernhardt, Ph.D.
Executive Director
Education for the Future Initiative
Chico, California

Visit our web site for additional information:
http://eff.csuchico.edu

Chapter 1

INTRODUCTION
The Need for a Framework for School Improvement

Almost every school in America today is (or was) in the process of "restructuring." However, a large percentage of these schools will abandon their efforts before they complete their restructuring process. Why is this? Clearly, schools want to improve. There is certainly nothing lacking in any school's desire to improve. Why is restructuring—so needed and desired by schools—so hard to accomplish?

Further, many teachers believe that when efforts to restructure are implemented, it is an indicator that the school has set up a shared decision-making structure, i.e., teachers and principals would attend meetings, write a mission statement, create a new vision for the school, set goals, attend staff retreats, and participate in staff development activities that would enable them to implement a list of innovations in their classrooms.

restructure rethink rebirth improve better These words are exciting in the context of school—words designed to refute the kind of reports to which Americans have become accustomed for almost two decades. Why then, are teachers at many of the formerly restructured or restructuring schools so relieved to be back to "just being teachers and minding their own business"?

We have reached the point of diminishing returns . . . in continually reminding ourselves about the problems of education. And we've reached that refreshing point where we're talking about solutions.

Garrey Carruthers
Former Governor of
New Mexico

Why "Restructuring" is Not Working

Reasons that the positive energy and interest for restructuring gets derailed and visions crumble are varied. Most teachers say something like, "it was too hard; too much work for too little or no benefit; we needed to get back to focusing on the kids; we got too tired; the conflicts became too great; we don't want to make the decisions any more; the principal left; certain teachers left; the superintendent left; the district resented us for getting 'special treatment'; nothing was different; the 'wrong' people were in power; it wasn't what we thought it would be.... "

Some researchers say that restructuring efforts do not work in most schools because critical elements are missing in the process, such as a solid plan or direction for change, personal meaning, a shared vision, incentives for change, learning opportunities for educators, "possibility thinking," effective communication, and an evaluation or monitoring system—the latter tending to be the element most often missing.

These reasons imply that restructuring efforts are defeated early in the process because they probably *started* wrong. The sad fact is that schools usually have only *one* opportunity to launch a restructuring effort. It is next to impossible to begin such a gut-wrenching, time-consuming effort twice. When recognizing a false start, it is excruciating to back up and get on the *right* track.

Schools need help with the enormous challenge of restructuring. They need a framework to help them *start right* so they can get to the point of implementing and sustaining improved practices. A framework can help schools understand the overall process of school change, how to think through what to improve, how to improve, how to implement the improvement, and then how to know that the improvement is making a difference.

Starting Right

The manner in which schools think about the improvement or restructuring process as they begin determines their success. Schools wanting to restructure or improve systemically must thoroughly understand the overall process *before* they commit to begin that process. The process must be driven upward from the bottom and supported downward from the top. There must be a solid *commitment* to the process from every staff member, or, at a minimum, from a group of individuals, to not thwart colleagues' efforts. There must be a solid, shared definition and plan for restructuring.

Further, a committed school would perhaps benefit by dropping the word *restructuring* and, instead, talk about *rethinking* the process of school to improve learning and achievement on a never-ending—

or continuous improvement—basis. Too often, the word *restructuring* is misconstrued. School staff tend to believe that everything will be different, almost automatically more wonderful, when their school begins to restructure. They believe the restructuring process will be *fun*.

Staff at one school actually thought the corporation sponsoring their restructuring efforts would be sending them to Japan to study Japan's educational system. Unfortunately that was not the picture the corporation had in mind. Many other schools started their restructuring efforts by designing schools of the future that resembled space ships, complete with swimming pools, waterfalls, and theaters. A handful of others thought, "I can't wait until we are restructured so I can have my own office, my own secretary, and a teaching assistant in a beautiful new building. What will be neatest is that my class will be one-half the size, and I will have the entire afternoon to plan—everyday."

Regrettably, the *reality* of the process is enough to end some schools' dreams of ever working differently. Indeed, to learn that school improvement of any kind is difficult, extremely complex, and not something to start unless the school is ready to commit its energies to focusing on the students and their learning is a hard lesson. The schools described above could have profited from an overview of school improvement before they started dreaming. They either never would have started the process, or, at best, their efforts might have been grounded in reality.

Overview of the School Improvement Process

A framework for school improvement can help schools start their efforts by offering an overview of the process, followed by a comprehensive view of the elements within the process.

School staff must understand from the beginning that major elements of change are internal rather than external, requiring a transformation of all individuals' thinking about school, students, teaching, and learning. Schools must also acknowledge and reinforce the fact that a new way of thinking, communicating, and budgeting time is required of all individuals. New mental models developed with facts, data, and research must replace old agendas and assumptions. Needs of students and different approaches to teaching must be studied as if both were totally unknown. A true collegial school must be one in which students are the focus; where staff communicate effectively and continuously about student learning; and, where staff work together, developing a continuum of learning for students as their first priority.

For real and appropriate changes to be implemented, school staff must conduct comprehensive needs analyses of students, teachers, parents, and the school community. They must develop a shared vision, based upon the values, beliefs, and personal visions of the individuals in the school community. They must establish a governance structure to support the bottom-up approach. Then, utilizing this information, they must develop a comprehensive action plan to increase each teacher's repertoire of skills and understanding; include the community as true partners; evaluate the impact of new strategies; and, establish a plan for continuous improvement. These new ways of thinking and operating require strong teachers and principals who are capable of new levels of communication—who know from the start that there is no ending point, that the work is hard, and that school improvement is a continuous process.

The Purpose of this Book

This book provides a practical resource for school administrators and teachers. It describes a unique framework for school improvement that can assist schools in—

- thinking through the overall change process, enabling them to start the process right

- planning for improvements, with personal meaning for the individuals implementing the improvements

- determining what to improve in order to better meet the needs of the individuals they serve

- maintaining internal motivation during the process of improvement

- understanding the importance of establishing effective communication within the school, with parents, with the school community, with other schools in the district, and with the district

- guiding the concurrent implementation of multiple improvements

- assessing whether or not the school improvement effort is making a difference

- keeping the complex elements of the school congruent in order to create a whole, healthy, effective learning organization focused on students

This unique framework for school improvement takes the form of a portfolio—a *school portfolio*—with measurement rubrics that serve as the monitoring and guiding device for the school improvement process.

With the use of this book, schools will be able to develop their own school portfolios; assess their efforts using a framework of continuums; learn from examples provided about other schools' efforts; and, think through and plan their own improvement from the overview of the systemic school improvement process. Most of the information contained in this book is not new. The intent is not to provide the world with one more restructuring book. The intent, rather, is to provide an overview of the thinking behind the continuums and to share research findings. References and additional resources for further reading are noted in the References and Resources section of this book.

The Structure of this Book

The School Portfolio: A Comprehensive Framework for School Improvement, second edition, begins by describing the need for a framework for school improvement and continues with how the school portfolio can serve as an overview and framework for comprehensive schoolwide planning.

Chapter 1 examines the school portfolio as an effective, positive, and ongoing monitoring system that is able to reflect the multidimensionality of each unique school—a system that can simplify the improvement and evaluation of these complex organizations.

Chapter 2 discusses the structure, purpose, and the various uses for the school portfolio.

Chapter 3 illustrates how the effective use of a school portfolio depends upon the criteria used to monitor the processes, products, and progress of the improvement efforts. It sets forth guidelines for creating, adopting, and adapting criteria. It introduces the *Education for the Future Initiative* Continuous Improvement Continuums (CIC). These continuums are used to form the basis of the school portfolio and schoolwide improvement efforts described in this book. It also discusses how the criteria serve as assessment and monitoring tools for the evaluation process.

Each of the next seven chapters, chapters 4 through 10, are devoted to one of the *Education for the Future Initiative* Continuous Improvement Continuums. Each chapter displays a continuum, defines the desired outcomes and elements of the continuum it discusses, and provides examples and lists of items to include in that section of the school portfolio. The final section of each chapter includes a self-assessment tool for use in developing an outline for a school portfolio. A brief overview of chapters 4 through 11 follows.

Chapter 4, Information and Analysis, explains how school personnel who collect, analyze, and use information about the school community make better decisions about what to change and how to institutionalize systemic change. Chapter 4 discusses the use of demographic information, different ways to survey the school's clients, the use of student and teacher perceptions of the learning environment, disaggregating and charting standardized test scores and questionnaire results, problem analysis, and the effective use of synthesized data.

Chapter 5, Student Achievement, describes how to keep the focus of school improvement on students, with the goal of moving teachers from providers of information to researchers who can predict the impact of their actions on student achievement, and moving students from recipients of knowledge to goal-setting, self-assessors who produce independent, quality products. This chapter discusses using data to understand the unique needs of each student and the student population, identifying student learning standards, identifying critical processes to increasing student achievement, monitoring the implementation of new practices through the use of staff-developed rubrics and other data, and the value of teacher action research.

Chapter 6, Quality Planning, describes how all well-defined and well-executed school improvement efforts have a comprehensive, schoolwide strategic plan that provide a logical framework for clarifying and achieving a *shared* vision based upon collective values and beliefs, and the purpose, vision, and mission of the school. Quality schools have one plan and one budget, both of which focus on achieving one shared vision.

Chapter 7, Professional Development, describes how the process of school improvement requires systems thinking and a culture in which principals, teachers, and related staff are able to communicate clearly and effectively with each other, trust and respect each other's motives and actions, and build the capacity of individuals to share and collaborate to achieve a vision. The chapter also describes the need to establish a plan for professional development for new teaching strategies that incorporates the use of peer coaching, collaborative action research, and teacher portfolios as a means to support the implementation process and eventually replace traditional means of evaluating teachers.

Chapter 8, Leadership, describes how a leadership infrastructure that emphasizes the prevention of problems and encourages the active participation of all shareholders can assist schools in becoming effective learning organizations. The chapter discusses shared decision making, the roles of the participants, site-based management, and the keys to making all of these innovative structures work.

Chapter 9, Partnership Development, describes how to plan for establishing partnerships with businesses, the community, parents, and higher education to make instructional programs exciting, relevant, and conducive to developing students into capable workers and lifelong learners.

Chapter 10, Continuous Improvement and Evaluation, provides a comprehensive chronology of the school improvement process, discusses the continuous improvement and evaluation of the learning organization, and illustrates how ratings on the continuums must congruently focus on and commit to supporting the attainment of agreed-upon student learning standards.

Finally, Chapter 11, Putting It All Together, looks at issues and logistics related to creating and maintaining the school portfolio and the benefits of working with an external change agent, such as a school coach.

THE SCHOOL PORTFOLIO

garden

*A school portfolio is like a garden—
It takes planning and hard work,
requires the weeding out
of unnecessary elements,
and promotes positive feelings.
You're proud to show it off!*

photograph album

*A school portfolio
is like a photograph album—
It brings back memories
for the people involved,
shows changes over time,
and introduces people to thinking
in ways they have
never thought before*

master's painting

*A school portfolio
is like an old master's painting—
It captures the school's essence, and yet,
a closer look reveals
interesting details.
The more you study it,
the more you see.*

wise friend

*A school portfolio
is like a wise friend—
It listens, clarifies your ideas,
and is something
you don't want to lose.
Most of all, it provides insight
to help you create your future.*

Many People of Education for the Future, 1994

A school portfolio is a purposeful collection of work telling the story of the school. A school portfolio describes efforts to engender and maintain systemic and continuous school improvement; it exhibits the school goals, vision, plan, and progress. A school portfolio allows for the continuous collection and assessment of evidence and is always evolving, growing, improving, and enabling school personnel to make better decisions.

Chapter 2

A FRAMEWORK FOR SCHOOL IMPROVEMENT:
The School Portfolio

An Effective Framework for School Improvement

A comprehensive school portfolio is a uniquely appropriate and effective framework for describing current processes, and for planning, monitoring, and evaluating school improvement efforts. The school portfolio guides the improvement of what is most important to the overall school organization and is able to reflect the multidimensionality of each unique school organization. It simplifies the evaluation of schools—which are by nature complex organizations—by offering a means to monitor the parts and their interrelationships as they compose the whole.

A comprehensive school portfolio, used in conjunction with assessment criteria, has all of the characteristics common to measurements used to create successful business organizations (as defined by Tom Peters, 1987).

> *People support what they create.*
> Margaret Wheatley

- *A simple presentation*—easy to read and understand text, graphs, and charts with a hard copy available for viewing by all interested parties at any time
- *Visible measurements*—located in the portfolio, developed or adopted by staff
- *Everyone's involvement*—in the design and development, in activities described within, and in keeping it current
- *An undistorted collection of primary information*—such as historical student achievement and demographic data

- *A straightforward measurement approach*—using a combination of rubrics and outcomes that explicitly describe what is important to and what is to be measured by school staff

- *An overall feel of urgency and perpetual improvement*—which results from the discrepancy between where the school is and where the school wants to be, and from a sense of accountability on the part of the staff to move the school to where it wants to be (to show improvement) as measured against rubrics and outcomes

Purposes and Uses of the School Portfolio

Some of the most important purposes of the school portfolio include the need to—

- *establish one document that describes an overall school plan, and the school's mission, vision, beliefs, and rationale for improvement*

  Too often schools wrestle with many different school plans, each designed to meet the requirements of a particular regulatory agency, program, or grant. Until these plans are coalesced into one plan—understood and supported by staff—the school's vision will not be achievable. A school portfolio helps maintain one overall schoolwide plan congruent with the schoolwide vision and outcomes.

- *document efforts on a number of elements important to schoolwide improvement*

  A school portfolio is a flexible, physical entity which documents the depth, breadth, and growth of a comprehensive schoolwide improvement effort, allowing schools and programs to concentrate on important areas at different times while still keeping the schoolwide picture visible.

- *understand the complexities of the school organization*

  As they identify and document change related to the elements and processes of their school, school staff begin to understand the complex elements that make up the school and the interrelationships of these elements. This understanding is necessary to uncover root causes of problems, to discover solutions, and to ensure the congruence of all the elements within the whole.

- *provide readily accessible and necessary information for data-based decision making*

  A comprehensive school portfolio includes data about the school: population; facilities; resources; test scores; self-assessment results; and, the school's vision for the future. These data establish a context for all aspects of the schoolwide improvement effort.

♦ *reflect on progress and purpose*

One element important to the motivation of staff is a periodic review of the progress they have made. A school portfolio allows staff to see what they have achieved, illustrates the benefits of their hard work, and reminds them of where they were when they started and why they are making the changes they are working so hard to make.

♦ *trouble-shoot the continuous improvement efforts of the school*

The school portfolio visually chronicles the progress (or lack of progress) made in each element of the schoolwide improvement process in text, graphs, charts, and pictures. This information helps school staff decide where to focus efforts needed to increase the effectiveness of their actions. Additionally, the school portfolio can be used to identify elements incongruent with the school's vision, mission, outcomes, and plans which deter the progress of the school's improvement efforts.

♦ *assess and guide the school's unique approach to continuous improvement*

Using this approach, staff can monitor the improvement process against established criteria. These criteria are useful for self-assessment and as guides for determining next steps toward the outcome. The portfolio approach and use of criteria provide for the assessment of progress on the individual elements that make up a comprehensive school improvement plan. The assessment is multidimensional—like schools—flexible and, therefore, more extensive, relevant, and useful than relying solely on unidimensional product assessments such as test scores.

♦ *be accountable*

A comprehensive school portfolio documents action plans, efforts, and products which are assessed on a regular basis, demanding a high level of accountability.

♦ *communicate*

A comprehensive school portfolio effectively serves as a public record to communicate important information about the school—its purpose, mission, and vision; the values and beliefs held by staff; its plans for improvement; the reasons particular approaches have been chosen; and, the results of the schoolwide improvement efforts. The portfolio is an effective way to keep school district officials informed of school improvement efforts and progress and helps to maintain district support. To potential partners, the school portfolio also effectively communicates basic information about the school, the steps in the schoolwide improvement process, and how potential partners can contribute to the effort.

♦ *replace a local, state, or regional accreditation process*

Because school portfolios are comprehensive and focus on an inclusive plan for schoolwide improvement, they are being used successfully in place of traditional evaluation and accreditation processes. Accrediting agencies and state departments of education acknowledge that working with discrete elements of a school plan in program reviews can actually keep schools from making progress toward their vision. Alternatively, a school focused on implementing one schoolwide vision and one comprehensive school plan congruent with that vision is poised to achieve the vision.

Because school improvement is an ongoing, complex, and multifaceted process, the school portfolio is the most appropriate and authentic means to chronicle the multidimensionality of school improvement and its development over time. Schools that use a school portfolio benefit immensely from ownership and a shared meaning of the improvement process and its results. A school portfolio, combined with assessment criteria, allows for a deep understanding of the elements and processes of a school; what needs to be improved, and why; how the school plans to carry out the improvement efforts; the expected outcomes of the approach to improvement; the efforts to implement the plan; and, the results of the effort. A school portfolio provides a view of the big picture of all the elements and shows how they interrelate to make a whole. With a school portfolio, it is easy to see what needs to be altered to keep the efforts progressing.

Chapter 3

CRITERIA FOR ASSESSING SCHOOL IMPROVEMENT

A comprehensive school portfolio is an excellent organizer of all information necessary to make informed decisions about any part or all parts of a school. The school portfolio is useful to schools whether or not they are involved in systemic school improvement efforts. The school portfolio does not, however, stand alone. Ultimately, the success of its utility depends upon the categories or classifications used and the criteria applied to measure the process, product, and progress of the school's efforts with respect to these categories.

Assessment criteria can facilitate the process, keep staff focused on one vision and one overall plan, and keep them informed about how they and their processes are performing to guide next steps. The important thing is to do the assessing. Even imperfect measures provide an accurate strategic indication of progress, or lack thereof (Tom Peters, 1991).

> *What gets measured gets done.*
>
> Tom Peters

Choosing Criteria for Assessing School Improvement

Systemically improving the manner in which a school operates is a complex and multidimensional process. It requires a complete understanding and appreciation of the complexities and interrelationships of each of the components of the organization in order to alter the whole, or even a part of the whole, effectively. By understanding the underlying principles, processes, and paradigms of the parts of the whole, staff can better understand and plan for the magnitude of effort required by systemic school improvement. Criteria for assessing the improvement process and progress must provide for the simultaneous assessment of each changing part, as well as assessment of the whole. There are three basic routes available for choosing assessment criteria. A school can create its own criteria, adopt existing criteria, or adapt existing criteria.

Create Own Criteria

This is a very positive approach because it requires everyone within the organization to assist with the development of the criteria, leading to staff buy-in, commitment, personal knowledge, and personal meaning. The downside is that developing criteria is extremely difficult and time consuming, as any teacher who has developed comprehensive rubrics for student assessment can attest. The writing of comprehensive criteria will generally take a minimum of one year. An example of school-developed criteria appears in Appendix B.

Adopt Existing Criteria

This works best when certain conditions are upheld. Everyone on staff must—

- understand what the criteria are measuring, and why
- agree that the criteria are congruent with what the school needs and wants to measure
- understand how to use the criteria correctly
- commit to using the criteria thoroughly and completely
- acknowledge the creators

The *Education for the Future Initiative* Continuous Improvement Continuums are examples of criteria that can be adopted (see Appendix A).

Adapt Existing Criteria

Taking existing criteria and adapting them to include additional elements important to the school is also an accepted approach, with two cautions:

- Make sure the developers of the chosen criteria did an extensive amount of research and testing to ensure that the criteria work.
- Avoid diluting existing criteria to make it easier for the school to rate itself high on the assessment scale.

It is ideal when the users of any assessment criteria are also the developers of the criteria. For very practical reasons, this is not always possible. If creation is out of the question, there are quality criteria available to adopt. If considering adopting or adapting existing criteria, the users must understand, agree with, and commit to using the criteria, in total. Whether your school develops, adopts, or adapts assessment criteria for its school portfolio and school improvement efforts, the criteria must be—

- *focused on what is important—the students.* The purpose of systemic school improvement is to improve the preparation of students, the primary clients of the school, and to rebuild the school organization to serve students' needs. Any criteria for assessing comprehensive school improvement must focus on students.

- *simple to use.* The goal is to spend time reflecting on progress, implementing the "big picture," and discussing next steps, rather than conducting cumbersome assessments.

- *indicative of what needs to happen.* A straightforward measurement device must be unambiguous, must be direct, must assess the target, and be easy to understand. It makes clear the steps which need to be achieved to move forward.

- *set up for self-assessment.* For assessment to have maximum impact, the people whose progress is being assessed should do the assessing. Very few people external to the process can come in, judge the value of a school's progress, and then inspire those involved with the change to do more, or do things differently. Therefore, the criteria must be set up for self-assessment.

- *challenging, but achievable.* The objective is not only to make the outcomes against which progress is judged achievable (so there can be a true feeling of accomplishment), but also to make them challenging enough to effect real improvement.

- *a working contract, as opposed to a form-driven exercise.* Excellent assessment criteria encourage ongoing conversations about the things that are important, rather than demanding activities that require conforming to rules and paperwork.

- *comprehensive in scope.* If the overall concern is systemic school improvement, it does no good to measure only those elements on which the school wants to focus, ignoring the comprehensive learning organization. This does not lead to systemic improvement and is an error common to many unsuccessful improvement efforts. It is important to measure *everything* to see how changes and progress in any specific

Guidelines for Assessment Criteria

15

area effect the entire organization. Unless all parts of a school are considered simultaneously, the school's efforts will form circles around the whole issue and will never get to the real issue. Staff will end up tired, overworked, uninterested in further change and, like the teachers described in the Introduction (Chapter 1), glad to be "...back to minding their own business." For instance, many schools beginning systemic improvement efforts assume they know enough about their clients and do not need to analyze existing data or gather additional information on students, parents, or the school in general. However, one small rural school district in northern California learned why the information was important to gather.

Each year, for several years, the community watched 80 percent of their graduates go off to college in the fall, 40 percent return to the community by Christmas, and almost 95 percent return by the end of spring—for good. This recurring problem was discussed widely among teachers and the community. Their hypothesis was that their students lacked experience and social skills. Their students simply did not have the social skills to function in other environments. Everyone knew that these students did not interact positively with people they knew, so they could not possibly know how to interact positively with strangers. Based on this "knowledge," the school district began an extensive restructuring effort centered around working with all K-12 students to develop social and communication skills. At the request of a consultant brought in to " . . . make this vision a shared community vision," the teachers reluctantly conducted a telephone survey of their graduates, asking them why they had dropped out of college. Almost without exception, graduates said the following: "They made me write. I can't write!" Based on this fact-finding survey, the focus of the restructuring effort changed immediately and the school district began using data on an ongoing basis to provide a challenging curriculum that kept students engaged in learning, enjoying school—and writing!

One existing set of assessment criteria that meets the guidelines described above is the *Education for the Future Initiative* Continuous Improvement Continuums. The Continuous Improvement Continuums take the theory and spirit of continuous school improvement, interweave educational research, and offer practical meaning to the components that must change simultaneously and systemically.

The *Continuous Improvement* part of the title refers to the cycle of evaluating and improving this complex system on a continuous basis. *Continuum* is defined as "...a continuous extent, succession, or whole, no part of which can be distinguished from neighboring parts except by arbitrary division." (American Heritage Electronic Dictionary, 1995.)

Organization of the Continuums

The *Education for the Future Initiative* Continuous Improvement Continuums which appear individually at the end of chapters 4-10 and in total in Appendix A, are a type of rubric that represents the theoretical flow of systemic school improvement. The continuums are made up of seven key, interrelated, and overlapping components of systemic change: Information and Analysis; Student Achievement; Quality Planning; Professional Development; Leadership; Partnership Development; and, Continuous Improvement and Evaluation. It is important that all seven components are used simultaneously. A school can defeat the purpose of systemic improvement by adopting only one or two continuums.

These rubrics, extending horizontally from *1 to 5*, represent a continuum of expectations related to school improvement with respect to an *approach* to the continuum, *implementation* of the approach, and the *outcome* that results from the implementation. A rating of *one*, located at the left of each continuum, represents a school that has not yet begun to improve. A rating of *five*, located at the right of each continuum, represents a school that is one step removed from "world class quality." The elements between *one* and *five* describe how that continuum is hypothesized to evolve in a continuously improving school. The *five* in *outcome* in each continuum is the target.

Extending vertically, the *approach, implementation,* and *outcome* statements, for any number *one* through *five*, are hypotheses. In other words, the *implementation* statement describes how the *approach* might look when implemented, and the *outcome* is the "pay-off" for

The Education for the Future Initiative Continuous Improvement Continuums

implementing the *approach*. If the hypotheses are accurate, the *outcome* will not be realized until the *approach* is actually implemented. A brief description of each of the continuums follows:

Information and Analysis is a critical element in planning for change, and in supporting continual school improvement. Schools must analyze existing data and collect additional information to understand how to meet the needs of their clients in order to understand the root causes of problems, assess growth, and predict the types of educational programs that will be needed in the future. The intent of this continuum is to establish systematic and rigorous reliance on hard data for decision making in all parts of the organization. This continuum assists schools in thinking through appropriate information to gather on an ongoing basis and analyses to make that will prevent implementing changes on a piecemeal basis or in a manner that does not get to the root causes of the "problems" at hand.

Student Achievement describes processes for increasing student achievement—the school's "Constancy of Purpose." The intent of this component is to support schools in their efforts to move from a fire-fighting approach to one of systemic *prevention* of student failure; teachers from providers of information to researchers who understand and can predict the impact of their actions on student achievement; and, students from recipients of knowledge delivery to goal-setting self-assessors who produce independent, quality work. This continuum assists schools in thinking through who the students are, and understanding the *why* behind the curriculum, instruction, and assessment as opposed to describing and recommending approaches. Those critical processes have to be determined by staff and are beyond the scope of this book.

Quality Planning by schools must be strategic or change efforts will not be implemented. A well-defined and well-executed school improvement effort is based upon a strategic plan that provides a logical direction for change. This continuum assists schools in developing the elements of a strategic plan, including a mission that describes the purpose of the school; a vision that represents the long-range goals of the school; goals that promote the mission; and, an action plan—procedural steps needed to implement the goals, including timelines and accountability, outcome measures, and a plan for continuous improvement and evaluation.

Professional Development helps staff members, teachers, and principals change the manner in which they work; how they make decisions; how they gather, analyze, and utilize data; how they plan, teach, and monitor achievement; and how they evaluate personnel and assess the impact of new approaches to instruction and student assessment. Professional development provides individuals with opportunities to improve their personal performance on a continuous basis and to learn new skills for working with each other in reforming their culture and workplace. This continuum assists schools in thinking through and planning for appropriate professional development activities that will help them reach their school's vision.

Leadership focuses on creating a learning environment that encourages everyone to contribute to schools having a cumulative, purposeful effect on student learning. A quality leadership infrastructure emphasizes the prevention of problems, such as student failure, as opposed to short-term solving or covering up of problems, and makes the school change effort conceivable. This continuum assists schools in thinking through shared decision making and leadership structures that will work with their specific population, climate, and vision.

Partnership Development with the school's community must benefit all partners. This continuum assists schools in understanding the purposes of, approaches to, and plans for educational partnerships with business and community groups, parents, other educational professionals, and students.

Continuous Improvement and Evaluation of all operations of the school is essential to schools seeking systemic improvement in the manner in which they do business. This continuum assists schools in further understanding the interrelationships of the components of continuous improvement and in improving their processes and products on an ongoing basis.

The chapters that follow provide an overview of the research behind each *Education for the Future Initiative* Continuous Improvement Continuum, as well as the items that might appear in a school portfolio in support of each continuum. The actual continuum can be found at the end of each chapter with the same title, while the continuums, in total, appear in Appendix A, along with recommendations for their use.

Adopting the Continuous Improvement Continuums

The *Education for the Future Initiative* Continuous Improvement Continuums provide an outstanding outline for comprehensive school improvement. They are used in this book to illustrate how to make the school portfolio an effective assessment tool that can be used to assist schools with systemic school improvement. As you read this book, think about adopting these for use at your school, or putting your own criteria in their place.

Before adopting these criteria, staff should, at minimum, read the descriptions and the highest level of each continuum. If staff agree with and can commit to the outcome and the hypothesis represented in the highest category, they will probably agree with the hypotheses described between *one* and *five*.

Schools using the continuums have found them to be extremely effective in providing guidance and understanding of the principles and processes of systemic school improvement, and in ensuring that all components of the organization are being considered and are improving at the same time. School staff particularly find them to be useful in helping staff share a school vision, assess their efforts to achieve their vision, and for accountability.

Who Does the Assessment?

The *Education for the Future Initiative* Continuous Improvement Continuums are set up for self-assessment; therefore, it is school staff who do the actual assessment of where the school is on each continuum. The process of assessment is instructive and highly beneficial for everyone involved with the school's continuous improvement efforts.

Who specifically does the assessment varies by school. Some schools want the entire staff to make the assessments together. Larger schools may find the approach far too time consuming and difficult to manage. In those cases, a team of teachers might be asked to conduct the assessment on behalf of the teachers they represent and then bring those assessments to the whole staff for discussion. In most schools, each person makes an assessment of where he or she believes the school is at the given time, and then (as a group) staff discuss discrepancies in the ratings and come to consensus on an overall rating. The discussion is very informative for determining staff's understandings of the continuums, outcomes, progress, process, and next steps. Staff discuss causes of any variations in responses and then determine a collective response. In any case, it is preferred that everyone in the school be familiar with the assessment process, and know when the assessment is taking place so that every member of the school staff can contribute to the process.

Assessing Progress on the Continuums

Before making a determination of where the school is on each continuum, staff should become familiar with the principles and research behind each continuum.

The continuums are not steps. There may be wide gaps between levels, and the continuums may not fit a school exactly. In fact, it may be difficult at times to know when exactly the school can assess itself at the next level. It is easy on the other hand to know when the school is no longer at the former level. The idea is to find the statement that comes closest to describing the school's efforts.

To begin the assessment, choose a continuum and read all the statements listed in the column labeled *approach*. Determine the statement that best describes what the school is attempting to do with respect to that continuum and record the number that corresponds to that statement.

Next, review available information regarding what staff are implementing at the school and identify the statement in the *implementation* column that best describes the school's implementation efforts. Record the corresponding number.

Finally, review the evidence the school has collected (quantitative, qualitative, anecdotal) regarding the impact of the implementation, read and identify the statements in the *outcome* column, and then choose the one that best describes the results the school has produced. Record the corresponding number.

Eventually all the information that is taken into account to make the ratings, the ratings themselves, and their rationale will be summarized in the school portfolio.

How Often Should Progress Be Assessed?

With its open structure, assessment of a school's progress on these criteria may be performed at any time. The important thing is to establish definite times when everyone knows school progress will be assessed and documented. *Education for the Future Initiative* schools found it helpful to assess their progress three times during the first year they used the Continuous Improvement Continuums. With three assessment periods, a school is able to keep continuous improvement in the forefront, monitor processes and progress, and analyze, for future reference and planning, such things as which elements of the school process are easiest to change, which elements take extra effort, and which elements can leverage other elements. After the first year, two assessments should effectively monitor progress.

Chart the Progress

Each time an assessment is taken, display the results for each continuum in a bar chart or other type of graph. Document the discussion so everyone can see the progress over time. An example follows.

Figure 1

_VH_S————————————————————————— **VALLEY HIGH SCHOOL PORTFOLIO**

Continuous Improvement Assessment
Baseline Ratings

Valley High School staff met to conduct their baseline ratings on the *Education for the Future Initiative* Continuous Improvement Continuums. The ratings were reached by full staff consensus. The ratings and brief discussions follow.

Information and Analysis
Collectively, staff believe that Valley High School is a 3 in Approach, 2 in Implementation, and 2 in Outcome for Information and Analysis. They believe that schoolwide data are being collected on student performance, attendance, and achievement, and questionnaires are being administered. However, they feel the information has not been implemented in such a way that it is being used for planning purposes. These data are also limited to some areas of the school, depending upon the teachers' involvement.

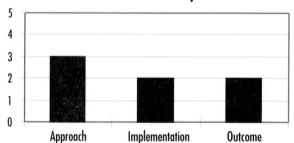

Next steps—
- We need to analyze and graph all existing data.
- We need to look at all data in a systematic way to help us plan strategically.
- We need to make sure that we get complete data.
- In October, we need to have a committee look at all the data that we have right now, begin to make some analyses based on what we have, and determine what additional information we need to gather.
- Following the meeting, the committee will bring back to the full staff this information, as well as the possibility of conducting a freshman survey that would ask such questions as: Why did you choose Valley? What are your goals for high school? What are your goals after high school? With these responses, we can begin to follow the students throughout their four years at Valley.
- The committee will also think about a questionnaire that will follow students who left Valley, for whatever reason, to find out why they left.
- Additionally, we need to think about asking questions in the spring: Did we meet your needs, goals, and expectations? How could we better meet your needs, goals, and expectations?
- We need to use these data to feed the systemic plan, to analyze information to get to the root cause of problems, and to track data for improvement.

Figure 1 (Continued)

---

^VH_S━━━━━━━━━━━━━━━━━━━━━━━━━━━━━━ **VALLEY HIGH SCHOOL PORTFOLIO**

Student Achievement

Valley staff rated themselves a 2 in Approach to Student Achievement, 2 in Implementation, and 3 in Outcome for Student Achievement. Staff felt that until more data are collected, tracked, and analyzed, they cannot get beyond the 2 stage in Approach and Implementation. There has been a lot of effort, however, to start working on tracking bits of data which has led to an increase in communication between students and teachers regarding teacher learning. Staff are quite happy with these beginnings.

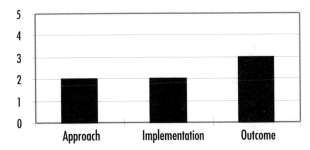

Next steps—
- We need to establish a schoolwide database that would allow a more systematic look at student achievement data and a closer look at the classroom data.
- We need to develop a comprehensive and consistent view of how students are evaluated at Valley.
- Schoolwide, we need to come to grips with the cross-curricular integration of the performing arts with core academics.
- We need to look back at the vision and mission and rethink the way courses are offered.

Quality Planning

Valley staff rated themselves a 2 in Approach, 2 in Implementation, and 3 in Outcome for Quality Planning. While staff realize the importance of a mission, vision, and comprehensive action plan, the current school plan is not a comprehensive representation of the vision for the school. Until it is, improvement cannot be systematic or schoolwide.

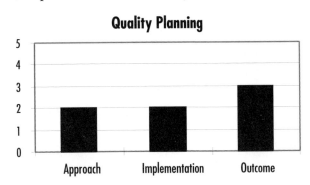

Next steps—
- We need to develop a systematic comprehensive schoolwide approach to planning that includes evaluation and continuous improvement.

Figure 1 (Continued)

^VH_S———————————————————————— **VALLEY HIGH SCHOOL PORTFOLIO**

Professional Development

Valley staff assessed themselves on Professional Development as 3 in Approach, Implementation and Outcome. Staff felt that the school plan and analysis of student needs have been used to target appropriate professional development for teachers. Inservice is helping them think through entire school processes and rethink the types of professional development in which the whole staff need to engage in order to get to the vision.

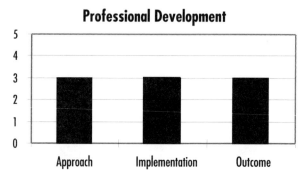

Next steps—
- We need the support to allocate more time for cross-curricular planning.
- We need to follow through on the departmental policy forms that were established last spring.
- We need to evaluate staff development activities to make sure they are getting us to our goals.

Leadership

Valley staff rated the school a 3 in Approach, 2 in Implementation, and 2 in Outcome with respect to Leadership. The rationale, folded into next steps, follows.

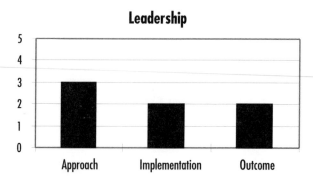

Next steps—
- We need to define a leadership structure for the school that is congruent with the school vision.
- We need to revisit the school vision to make sure it is congruent with staff's sense of where we want to go, especially as a performing arts school.

Figure 1 (Continued)

^VH_S — **VALLEY HIGH SCHOOL PORTFOLIO**

Partnership Development

Collectively, staff believe, with respect to Partnership Development that Valley High School currently is a 3 across the board in Approach, Implementation, and Outcome.

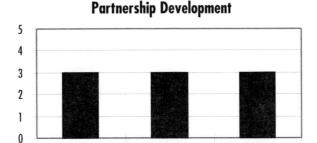

Next steps—
- There needs to be documentation of the comprehensive partnerships that exist throughout the school.
- This list of partnerships needs to be put out in a newsletter.
- We need to take a serious look at how all of our partnerships affect student achievement and the school vision.
- We need to plan how to establish partnerships with respect to our outcome.

Continuous Improvement and Evaluation

Valley staff rated the school a 3 in Approach, 2 in Implementation, and 2 in Outcome with respect to Continuous Improvement and Evaluation.

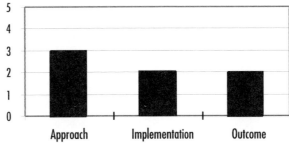

Next steps—
- Staff determined a need to research the impact of visual and performing arts on student achievement. This research will inform the vision for the school and how all the other pieces fit together.
- We need to clarify our vision for congruence throughout all aspects of the school, and make sure we are "walking our talk."

As in any self-assessment, it is important to encourage staff to describe honestly where they are on the continuums. Wherever the school is in the school improvement process is where it is. If any kind of negative consequences result (for example, dollars from the district are withheld because of poor results), the self-assessment process will become less than honest, staff may become adverse to risk, and the work related to improvement and the entire improvement effort will become obstructed. The beauty of the School Portfolio is that it will describe why progress was or was not made on any continuum. The description provides valuable information about the impact of external and/or internal influences on progress.

Chapter 4

INFORMATION AND ANALYSIS

Schools committed to improvement must collect and analyze data in order to understand:

- the current and future needs of the school, students, parents, teachers, and community
- how well the current processes meet the needs of these clients
- the ways in which the school and community are changing
- the root causes of problems
- the types of education programs and expertise that will be needed in the future

Schools that utilize and analyze information about the school community make better decisions about what to change and how to institutionalize systemic change. Research shows that schools that understand the needs of their clientele are more successful in implementing changes and remain more focused during implementation than those schools that do not identify specific needs. Information and analysis works hand in glove with comprehensive school improvement, and is a critical element in planning for and determining the effectiveness of change.

We live in a society that is data rich and information poor. While data are not information; translating fact to understanding means relating data to something you already know and can visualize.

Robert H. Waterman

Types of information and analyses that assist with planning for and sustaining systemic school improvement include demographics, assessment of current and desired practices, perceptions of the learning environment, student achievement data, and problem analysis, and are referred to below as multiple measures.

Figure 2

Multiple Measures

Allows the prediction of actions/processes/programs that best meet the needs of all students.

Tells us:
What processes/programs different groups of students like best.

Over time, interrelating data indicates changes in the context of the school.

Tells us:
If groups of students are "experiencing school" differently.

Tells us:
Student participation in different programs and processes.

Tells us:
The impact of demographic factors and attitudes about the learning environment on student learning.

Over time, shows how classrooms change.

DEMOGRAPHICS

Enrollment, Attendance, Drop-out Rate
Ethnicity, Gender, Grade Level
Language Proficiency

SCHOOL PROCESSES

Description of School Programs and Processes

Perceptions of Learning Environment
Values and Beliefs
Attitudes
Observations

PERCEPTIONS

Over time, interrelating data enables the assessment of impact.

Tells us:
What processes/programs work best for different groups of students with respect to student learning.

Standardized Tests
Norm/Criterion-Referenced Tests
Teacher Observations
Authentic Assessments

STUDENT LEARNING

Tells us:
The impact of student perceptions of the learning environment on student learning

Tells us:
If a program is making a difference in student learning results.

Over time, interrelated student learning data give information about student performance on different measures.

Tells us:
The impact of the program on student learning based upon perceptions of the program and on the processes used.

Figure 2 shows these multiple measures of data as overlapping circles (Bernhardt, V., *Data Analysis for Comprehensive Schoolwide Improvement*, 1998. p.15). When used together, these measures give schools the information they need to get different results. Each of these measures of data are valuable alone; however, together, they provide a powerful picture that can help us understand the school's impact on student achievement.

Demographics

Through the study of demographic information, such as population trends, we can predict with some accuracy the numbers of students and ethnic diversity with which the school can expect to work in the future. From an historical perspective, a school can analyze how well it has served its past and current population and can synthesize the demographic information and instructional approaches used to identify the changes needed to meet the needs of its future clients.

> *Because trends have clear direction, instead of causing turbulence, they actually help reduce it because they have a significant amount of predictability.*
>
> Joel Barker

Demographic information provides the context within which change is planned and takes place. While not all of these data will be readily available, the more information a school has to assist with decision making and planning, the better the plans and the decisions. It is worth spending extra time to gather as much of this information as possible to make accurate plans for the future. To help answer important questions that need to be asked, such as "can we expect our future student population to be the same size, from similar ethnicities, and have similar parental backgrounds?", some of the available data should be aggregated into charts and graphs that everyone can understand and use.

A list of possible demographics to gather and include in a school portfolio follows. Although the list looks intimidating, much of the data already exist in school and district offices and if they don't exist, they need to be gathered. Start with what is easily available. Gather additional information as time permits, and keep adding.

Table 1

Demographic Data

Possible Existing Data at School and District Levels

Student Demographics	School Level
Numbers of Students	History
Parent Income Levels	Funding
Parent Education Backgrounds	Safety
Parent Employment	Physical Plan
Families on Public Assistance	Uniqueness and Strengths
Free and Reduced Lunch (%)	Image in the Community
Drop-out Rates	Support Services for Students and Teachers
Graduation Rates	Number of Teachers and Administrators
Health Issues/Handicaps	Years of Teaching/Administering
Discipline Indicators (e.g., suspensions, referrals)	Ethnicity/Gender of Teachers and Administrators
Attendance Rates	Retirement Projections
Tardy Rates	Types of Certificates
Mobility	Student-Teacher Ratios
Number of Years at the School	Administrator-Teacher Ratios
Home Language	Turnover Rates
School Community	Teacher Salary Schedule
History	Support Staff
Location	**School District**
Population	Description of District
Race/Ethnicity	History
Socioeconomic Status	Number of Schools, Students, Teachers, and Administrators
Size	Support Services for Students and Teachers
Employment Status	Organizational Structure
Educational Backgrounds	
Housing Trends	
Health Issues	
Crime Rate	
Economic Base	

Perceptions

In addition to gathering demographic data, it is crucial to survey the clients of the school to understand what they think about current school processes and practices. Assessment of this information helps determine what the clients would prefer the school to be like for students and helps with the analyses of what the school needs to do to improve.

Most assessments of the current situation can be conducted through needs assessments, discrepancy analyses, or effectiveness questionnaires. Some can be made using group process techniques and/or interview techniques. Clients to survey may include the following:

Students	School and District Administrators
Former Students	School Board Members
Teachers	School Staff
Parents	School District Staff
Community Members	Local Business Owners

Reports that identify future trends, predictions, and skills needed for work in different industries can also assist schools in analyzing what curriculum will prepare students for the future world of work. Schools determining student learning standards must be knowledgeable of these kinds of reports as well as any federal, state, district, school, or local regulations that could have an impact on what is delivered and how it is to be delivered at the school.

> *Do not underestimate the importance of helping people recognize what they already know.*
>
> Michael Q. Patten

Analyzing current and desired practices helps determine discrepancies that exist between an observed state of affairs and a desired state of affairs. From these analyses, and the results of other analyses described in this section, priorities for change can be determined. Be sure to include questions about background and other relevant demographic information in questionnaires so appropriate subanalyses can be produced.

The wording of the questions will vary depending upon the client being surveyed. The type of question used will depend upon what information is needed, how the information will be used, and personal preference. Examples of three types of questions—open-ended, discrepancy, and multiple choice follow:

Open-ended

The individuals surveyed must supply their own responses, free from prompts.

Example:

What are the three most important skills you feel students must possess before they graduate from this high school?

What are the strengths of the school?

Of former students, one might ask —

Knowing what you know now, what do you wish you had learned in high school?

Discrepancy

An evaluation of current practices is paired with importance ratings.

Example:

For the questions that follow, please circle the number in the Effectiveness Column that best represents your evaluation of the effectiveness of Valley High School in developing the skills used in the column on the left. In the Importance Column, indicate how important you feel it is that these skills be developed at Valley High School.

	How *effective* is Valley High School in developing these skills?		How *important* is it that these skills be developed at Valley High School?	
	Not at all Effective	Extremely Effective	Not at all Effective	Extremely Effective
1. Word processing on the computer.	0 1 2 3 4 5		0 1 2 3 4 5	
2. Effective public speaking.	0 1 2 3 4 5		0 1 2 3 4 5	

Multiple-choice

Individuals select the response that best represents their thoughts from a list of possible responses.

Example:

Which of the following is the <u>most important skill</u> for students to have in mathematics when they graduate?

a. ability to perform mathematical functions in their heads

b. calculator proficiency

c. problem-solving abilities

d. calculus

An important analysis of current practice includes student and teacher perceptions of the learning environment and relationships within the school. In understanding student perceptions of the learning environment, one might design a questionnaire, or interview questions, around specific theories to which the school subscribes. For instance, a school may subscribe to the "quality schools" theory: all humans have five basic needs—survival (feel safe), freedom (choice), fun (enjoyment), power (significance), and belonging (caring)—that must be met before they can learn and produce quality products, (Glasser, W., *The Quality School*, 1990, 1992). Questions for students related to this theory may look similar to these basic needs statements. Related questions are appropriate to ask of teachers, administrators, parents, and community members. (Sample student, teacher, and parent questionnaires and are shown in Appendix D.)

Likewise, it is sometimes appropriate to ask teachers how they think students will respond to specific questions to get a sense of how "in-tune" the teachers are with the students. After all, the relationship between the teacher and student is highly correlated to how well student needs are being met, which has a direct correlation to student achievement.

Example:

Students from Beta Elementary School were asked to respond to a series of statements about their learning environment. Teachers were asked to respond to the same series of questions, but in terms of how they thought the students would respond. Student and teacher respondents indicated their responses by circling a number, 1 to 5, corresponding from strongly disagree to strongly agree. Charts were constructed to visually compare the differences in responses and to give an indication of how in touch Beta teachers were with their students. Figure 3 charts the percentage of students who strongly disagreed, disagreed, were neutral, agreed, or strongly agreed with six items, compared to teachers' predictions of how they thought students would respond to the same items. Figure 4 gives a visual image of the average differences of responses on all items of the same survey. From the charts, one can see that teachers in this school were very much in touch with their students, and that the student responses were extremely positive overall.

Figure 3

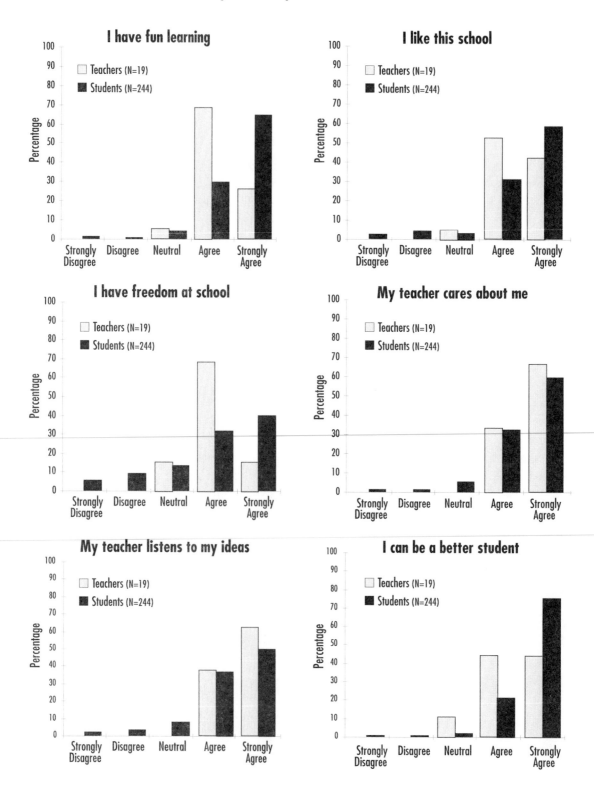

Student Responses Compared to Teacher Predictons

Figure 4

Student Responses Compared to Teacher Predicitions

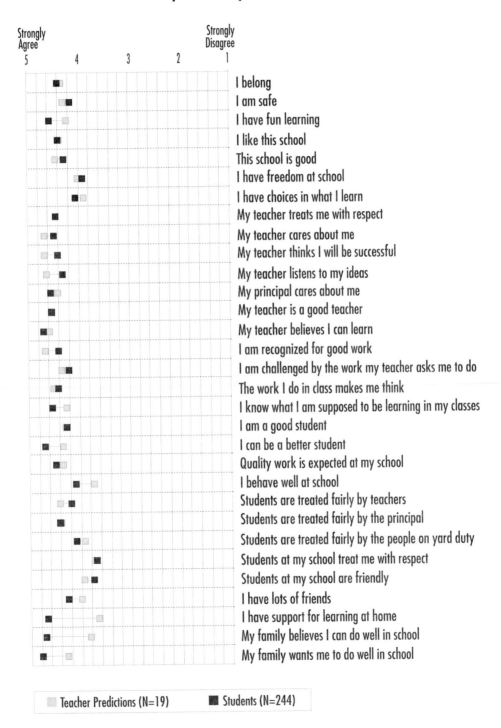

The student responses from Figure 4 were disaggregated by grade level and placed in a line chart (see Figure 5). Each icon joined by a line represents an ethnic group at the school. The heavy line that snakes through the icons and their connecting lines is the average student response on the items. The horizontal line that runs through the middle of the chart is the average of all student responses on each item which gives a general idea of the agreement of the student responses to the item. The heavy upper and lower horizontal lines in this example indicate one standard deviation above and below the overall average. The scores within these lines are "typical" responses to these types of questions for this group of students. The wider the gap between the deviation lines, the more variability exists within the groups of students. The narrower the gap, the more the group is similar in thought. The responses that fall outside either the upper or lower horizontal lines are attributed to special variation and usually represent issues to which the school needs to pay special attention. When one group's responses are considerably different from other groups' responses, this most often points to areas that need special attention.

Figure 5 indicates that the students, as a whole, are in strong agreement with this set of items. However, looking at the disaggregated lines, one can see that the third graders' responses were in more disagreement than the other students on several items.

Figure 5

Digging Deeper, by Grade

Average response of first graders to this Item. (First grade responses are also reflected in the overall average.)

The lowest average for sixth graders is neutral. How that came about needs to be looked at (i.e., were agree and disagree responses equally distributed? Or, were all sixth graders indifferent to the question?)

Line links first grade average item responses.

Item averages for the total group responding to the questionnaire.

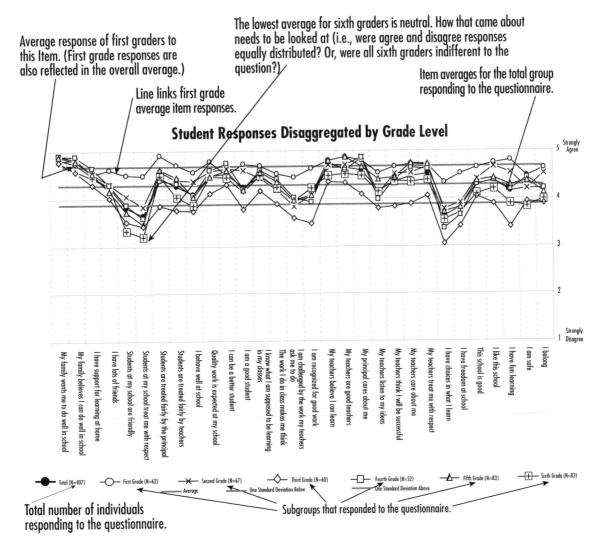

Student Responses Disaggregated by Grade Level

Total number of individuals responding to the questionnaire.

Subgroups that responded to the questionnaire.

Things to look for:

- Subgroups that "stick out" or look different from the others.
- Big gaps between one subgroup and the other subgroups.
- Differences in averages that result in opposite responses, such as agree-disagree.
- Subgroup trends that are unexpected.
- Size of subgroup that looks different from the other groups, although small numbers may still indicate issues that need to be addressed.
- Subgroups whose averages fall outside the standard deviation lines.
- Other analyses that would provide further understandings of the responses.

Things we found:

- There are some differences between group averages.
- First graders tend to be in strongest agreement with items on the questionnaire.
- Sixth graders tend to be in least agreement with questionnaire items.
- Third grade responses would be expected to consistently fall in the middle of all the subgroups.
- The third grade low scores appear as though they may be related.
- The lowest average for third grade is neutral. Might want to understand how that average came about (i.e., one-half of third graders agree and the other one-half disagree? Or, are all third graders indifferent to the question?) This issue, along with the possible relationship with the low scores, suggests we need to take a closer look at third grade.

To understand more about these third grade responses, the third grade averages were pulled out of the total group, disaggregated by ethnicity and charted (see Figure 6). This disaggregation indicates a potential problem that would need further consideration by teachers.

With the type of chart that Figure 6 illustrates, it is easy to detect if there are issues with a specific ethnicity—something teachers must consider as they gather data about what needs to change in the school for all students to succeed. These types of charts provide a wealth of information in an easy-to-read format.

Open-ended questions should not be overlooked when assessing students' perceptions of the learning environment. While open-ended responses to questions are very time consuming to compile, one can get a complete sense of the learning environment by asking children two questions—What do you like about this school? What do you wish were different?

"What I like most about this school are the teachers. I like the way they have fun making us learn."

"What I wish was different is, I wish we didn't ever have to leave this school."

It is also extremely important to get a sense of the degree to which the teaching staff think and feel as a unit. This can make a significant difference in the school's ability to implement change. The success a faculty has in implementing positive school change is highly correlated with the degree to which teachers share the mission and vision of the school and beliefs and values about teaching, learning, and children. If teachers are not able to share similar thoughts about teaching and learning, they are probably unable to share similar actions, and the school vision will most probably never be realized.

Figure 6

Digging Deeper, by Ethnicity

African-American third grade students disagree that:
• Students at my school treat me with respect.

Looking at the third grade responses by ethnicity, one can see that:
• Caucasian third grade students agree that students are treated fairly by the people on yard duty.
• African-American, Hispanic, and Asian students disagree with that statement.

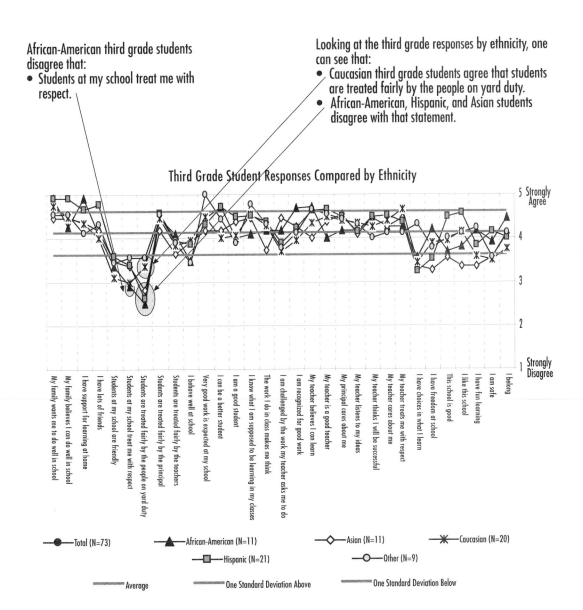

Third Grade Student Responses Compared by Ethnicity

Things to look for:
• Issues that surface needing further investigation to understand the issues behind the responses. In this example, there are issues surfacing related to ethnicity. Teachers might interview the third grade classes or disaggregate further to pinpoint an even more specific subgroup, such as African American males.

Figures 7 and 8, show average teacher responses for two schools charted for questionnaire items related to values and beliefs about students, teaching, learning, and increasing student achievement. These charts have three horizontal lines similar to those shown in previous examples—the overall average on all items for all teachers, one standard deviation above, and one standard deviation below the overall average. The width of the outer bands gives an indication of the cohesiveness of the groups of teachers in their thinking and how much they share the vision for the school.

Figure 7 illustrates a chart for an elementary school faculty who share values and beliefs. The response band is positive, in strong agreement, and its width relatively narrow, indicating a cohesiveness in thoughts with respect to these items. Figure 8 shows a school where teachers are all over the chart with these items. The chart could clue us in to some serious problems that need to be addressed before a shared vision is even a remote possibility.

Relationship of the Different Perceptions

How do these perceptions relate to student achievement or student perceptions? Think about this. Figure 7 is a school with staff who are committed to change. They have a shared vision and mission. They know what they are doing for children and why. What do students like most about the school? They love the way teachers help them learn. What do they wish were different? They wished they did not have to go to the middle school next year. They would love to stay at this school forever.

Figure 8 represents a middle school staff that is all over the board with their values and beliefs about school and children. There is not a single thing with which they agree. What do students say they like about the school? Most of them wrote, "nothing." Of course, taking into consideration their ages, that response is not so alarming. However, when asked about what they wished were different about their school, the students wrote, "we wish that if the teachers are going to assign homework, they would at least look at it before they throw it away." "We wish the teachers cared about who we are as people..." The comments go on and on. Is there a relationship between teacher attitudes, values and beliefs, and student perceptions of the learning environment? Do you think that relationship connects back to student performance? I think so.

Figure 7

Total Elementary School Teacher Responses

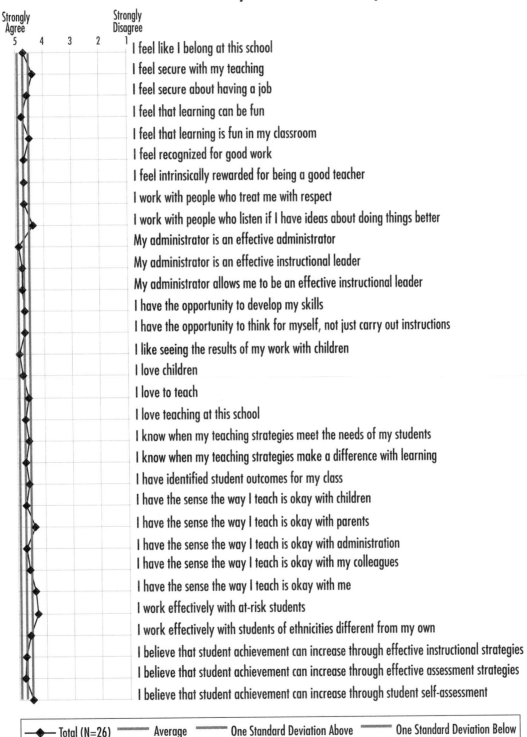

Figure 8

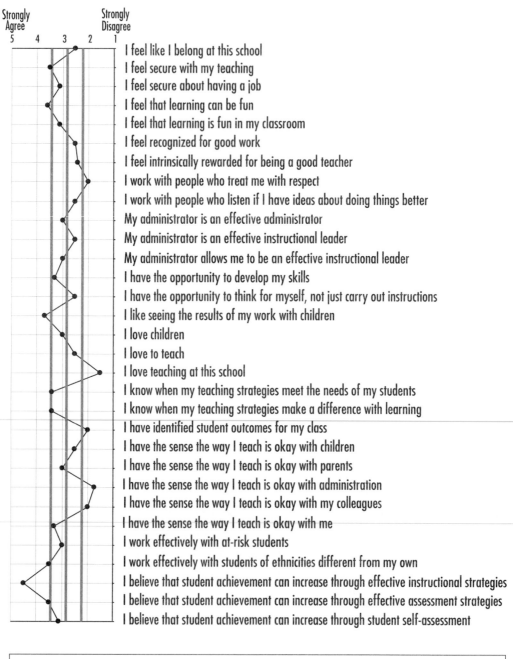

Total Middle School Teacher Responses

Student Learning

The focus of most comprehensive school improvement efforts is on what the school organization can do to ensure that every student achieves and to increase the achievement of all students. Assessing student learning has to be a teacher's hardest and most important job.

Typically, teachers' and school administrators' anxiety levels rise when standardized test scores are mentioned. School personnel are often criticized about low test scores even though the tests may not provide the best match between what is being taught and what is being tested. Unfortunately, until there are other measures developed that teachers can rely on to measure student achievement more accurately, we must glean as much information as possible from standardized test scores. It is important to understand how students perform on all available measures of achievement, which might include the following:

> *The way in which a local school assesses student outcomes accurately represents the educational outcomes that the school cares most about.*
>
> *Lawrence Lezotte and Beverly Bancroft*

Standardized Test Scores Over Time

Authentic Measures of Performance

Assessments of Student Learning Standards

Grade Point Averages

Letter Grade Distributions

Enrollment in College-bound Classes

Success Indicators of Graduates (e.g., numbers attending college, getting jobs)

Figure 9 shows Alma Elementary School Grade Four's Standardized Achievement Test results. Student results increased while the school district experienced decreases for the same two-year period. Generally, one would get the impression that Alma is doing a tremendous job in the area of increasing student achievement.

Figure 9

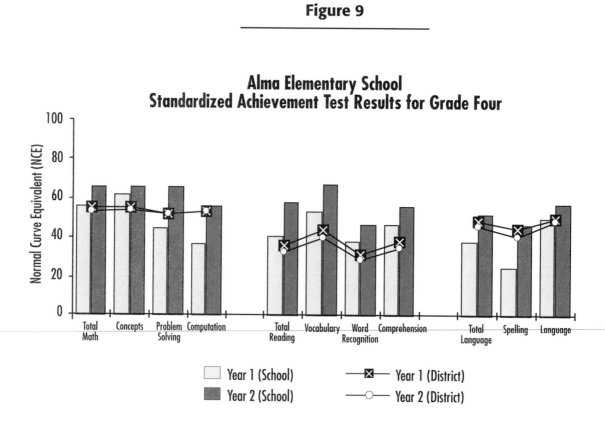

**Alma Elementary School
Standardized Achievement Test Results for Grade Four**

Disaggregating these data, however, revealed a different picture and a very real need at this school. Figure 10 shows how the major ethnic groups of the same school scored during the two years the school administered the Standardized Achievement Test. It is obvious that there were significant differences in the scores for the different population groups of the school (which are evenly distributed by members). Scores for two of the groups increased while two actually decreased in that second year. For faculty who believe all students can achieve, these data were disturbing. After reviewing the data, staff met to discuss how to increase the achievement of all ethnicities in the school. A task force of teachers was created to analyze the problem thoroughly. Their goal was to ensure a plan of action that would treat not the symptoms but the root causes of the problem. The example is continued in the problem analysis section later in this chapter.

Disaggregating student achievement data by student subgroupings, such as the Figure 10 example, can assist schools in evaluating current processes in relationship to the students they are serving and in identifying processes to be changed. Charts and graphs that visually tell the story are very important for these types of analyses.

Figure 10

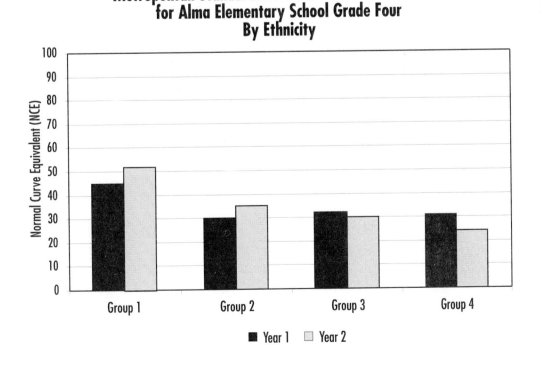

Admiralty High School used a six-point rubric to assess reading skills for their 10th graders. The bar charts show the percentages of students who met the standard of 4, exceeded the standard, and did not meet the standard.

Figure 11 reading scores were also disaggregated by gender for the Admirality High School 10th graders (see Figure 12).

Figure 11

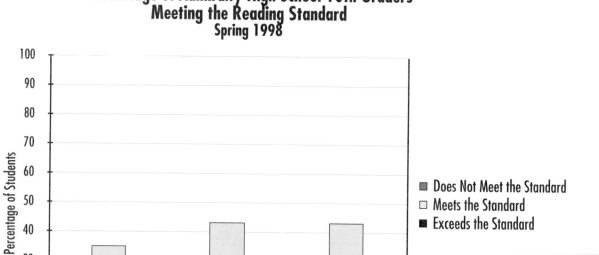

Percentage of Admiralty High School 10th Graders Meeting the Reading Standard
Spring 1998

Figure 12 shows quite a discrepancy in scoring for males and for females at the low and high ends. Twice as many females than males scored either a 4, 5, or 6 at the high end, and over twice as many males scored a 1 or 2 at the low end. Similar gender differences existed at the district and state levels, although not as pronounced.

Education for the Future Initiative schools routinely disaggregate data by ethnicity, gender, and other ways as needed to provide specific information about how their students are achieving. The disaggregation, in part, depends upon the makeup of the school and what staff want to know. For instance, in a school with a large migrant population, it makes sense to disaggregate historical student achievement data by students who regularly attend the school all year long, every year, compared to those who leave for a few months and then return to the school, and to those who leave and do not come back. This school might also follow the average length of time it takes to move non-English-speaking children to English-speaking classrooms, vary the length of English instruction, and monitor differences in achievement.

Figure 12

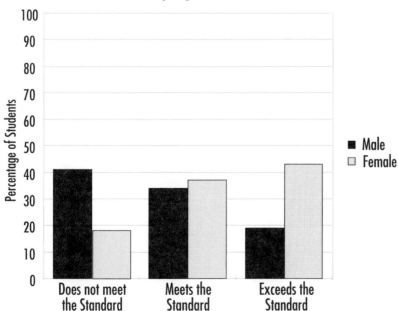

Admiralty High School 10th Graders by Gender
Meeting the Reading Standard
Spring 1998

School Processes

A description or flow chart of current school processes becomes an extremely valuable tool for understanding the schooling process, assisting with the standardization of treatment, and in understanding what needs to be improved, deleted, or revamped. Figure 13 is an example of a flowchart from Pacific High School's process for student work and assessment in a college-bound mathematics course. Basically, students are given an assignment. If they do the assignment, they receive a grade and get another assignment. The process repeats until the end of the unit or grading period, at which time students take a test and are given a grade. If, during this process, a student does not complete an assignment, he or she may or may not be given another chance to complete the assignment. At any point in the process, the student rejoins the other students in the flow. A student could be tested and never do an assignment to contribute to her or his overall grade. No matter what grade a student receives, the process starts over. The flowchart implies that it would be very easy for individual students to fall through the cracks.

> *Improvement is not achieved by focusing on results, but by focusing on improving the systems that create results.*
>
> National Leadership Network

Figure 13

Process Flowchart

Student Work and Assessment at Pacific High School

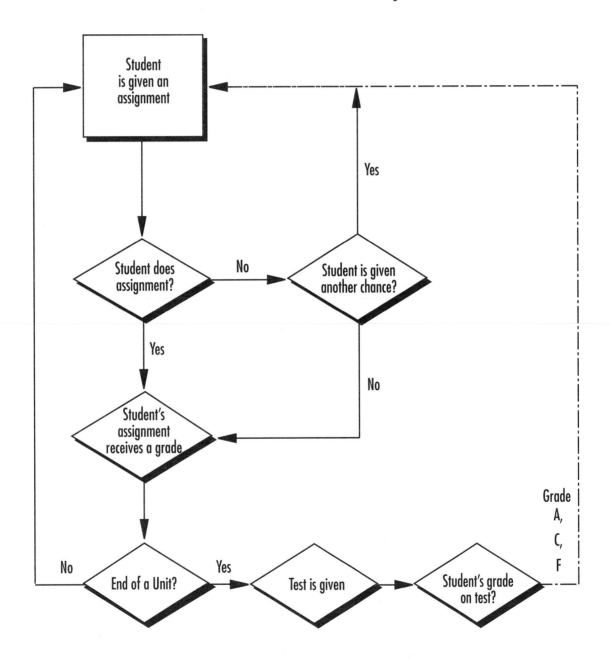

Problem Analysis

It is crucial to look beyond the obvious when reaching conclusions about solutions to school problems. It is also crucial to reflect upon the entire system and to understand how change in one part may affect many other parts. One of the purposes of gathering so many pieces of information is to understand completely all of the surrounding issues and find the root causes of problems.

> *Today's problems come from yesterday's solutions.*
>
> Peter Senge

Based upon the information gleaned from Figures 9 and 10, the teachers at Alma school could have determined that remedial classes for the low scoring ethnicities could be the answer to the problem of low test scores. Instead, they looked at all the data they had, talked with teachers and students, and made a completely different assessment of the changes needed.

When the task force reexamined the questionnaire results of student perceptions of their learning environment, they saw that the lowest scoring ethnicities on the achievement measures were the same as those who fell below the lowest standard deviation on crucial items assessed in the questionnaire. The items that fell below the lowest standard deviation were—

I feel that I belong at this school

I am challenged by the work I am asked to do

Teachers feel I am capable of learning

Teachers treat me with respect

I feel that I am treated fairly

I have choices in what I learn

The critical changes these teachers ultimately made had to do with their attitudes, their beliefs about, their treatment of, and processes used with all students. In the following year, these students' responses on the questionnaire were as high, or higher, than students of other ethnicities. Interestingly, their achievement scores for the next year also increased. The teachers' hypothesis about the source of the problem appears to have been correct.

The scenario above is a very simplistic example of problem analysis. A companion book, *Data Analysis for Comprehensive Schoolwide Improvement*, describes different process techniques and tools available to analyze problems and get to root causes. Select references from that book also appear in the reference section of this book.

After the comprehensive data about all aspects of the school are gathered, staff must synthesize all the data to determine the overall needs of students and the organization, and the overall changes that must be made. Evergreen Elementary School drafted a list of the most pressing issues that faced their school, and what they were going to do about it, synthesized from the data gathered as they began their school improvement efforts.

Synthesizing the Data

As the population in Evergreen Union School District continues to change and increase, teachers have become more and more concerned about how to deal with the implications of educating students whose backgrounds and home lives are very different from their own and different from students they taught in the past. Teachers can no longer expect students to speak the same language they do, or to come to school prepared, able to learn, with supportive parents at home. As we analyze our students' academic, social, and emotional needs, we know many issues need to be addressed in order to establish a quality educational system, including the following.

Through our questionnaires and analyses of data, we know we need to better meet the many emotional needs of all students. We especially need to work with and support social services organizations. We need to learn how to meet the needs of children who are victims of familial abuse and poor modeling. Our teachers need training and continual support in this area.

We are concerned about our at-risk students not making progress. At-risk students (i.e., Title 1, English Language Learners) are not addressed in a unified, systematic fashion. We need a comprehensive plan to meet the needs of these students, requiring much more flexibility with categorical, as well as regular education programs. We need to understand if the lack of progress with at-risk students is the label given to these students and its impact on their self-esteem, or if the lack of progress is because we are not meeting their needs. As we investigate this issue, we will need to make a decision—either we will discontinue using such terms and providing what we call "special" programs, or we will implement better strategies for serving these students within these programs.

As educators, we have not focused on continuous improvement and have conducted too few systematic analyses of what works, what doesn't work, and why. Staff need training in problem analysis and consensus building for solutions. A process and structure must be developed to ensure this vital element exists throughout the school.

We need to create a positive school environment that is noncoercive, cooperative, and focused on students performing quality, meaningful work—one in which faculty, staff, administration, and involved parents are committed to the implementation of a school vision that meets the needs of students and does not force students to conform to the needs of the school.

Evergreen wants to create a quality learning environment focused on the way students learn. In our efforts to develop a noncoercive, quality learning environment, we have focused on student learning styles. We know that students learn in different ways and that our curriculum needs to reflect these differences and harmonize with them. We are committed to restructuring the learning environment so that classrooms are organized and curriculum delivered in a manner that accommodates all students without extended pull-out programs or ability groupings.

Currently, our communication with parents and the community is unstructured and unfocused. Parents and the larger community have had little involvement in the structure and offerings of the school. We need to set goals together, and provide parents with clear messages about how to enhance their children's learning. We need to work with the business community in partnership to provide rich, real-world learning and internships for students.

Evergreen needs a system for the support and induction of new teachers. Our restructuring process has progressed enough that we cannot hire new teachers and hope they survive and do what we do. In order to sustain the progress we have made, we need to invest in and support our new hires and beginning teachers.

Evergreen faculty have determined that they must continue to be a cohesive group in order to make the necessary changes in the curriculum and school structure that will enhance every student's learning and enable faculty to model citizenship in the same fashion we expect students to practice citizenship.

Another approach to describing the data studied in this chapter is shown in the following narrative:

Paul Jones Elementary School located on the east side of the city of Jonesville is one of seven elementary schools in the Jonesville Union Elementary School District. Not long ago, Paul Jones was surrounded by open fields. Last year, four new housing developments sprung up all around the school. This construction will have an influence on Paul Jones' future enrollment and ethnic makeup. Currently, the older area around Paul Jones is laden with drugs, crime, and gangs.

In the past, very few Paul Jones students succeeded academically. This record of poor achievement was caused by several factors. Many students lack pre-literacy skills when they enter kindergarten; more than half of Paul Jones's 1st through 6th grade students arrive annually from Mexico with little or no formal education, immediately putting them at a disadvantage. In some cases, these families must deal with survival issues and have little time to devote to their children's education. Traditional school structures have not provided programs that support their special needs.

Kindergarten teachers report that 86 percent of incoming students do not have the skills that children need for early literacy development. As a result, the students' experiences with failure begin early. Retentions are common in the primary grades, and more than half of Paul Jones's 2nd graders cannot read. Only 25 percent of nonprimary English-speaking students have made the transition to English reading by the time they reach 6th grade. Their English-speaking classmates also fall behind in literacy development. About 80 percent of Paul Jones students fail to achieve grade-level standards and are not academically ready for middle school when they graduate.

This poor performance is even more evident on standardized tests. For example, in the last school year, 3rd graders scored in the 7th percentile in reading, the 12th percentile in written expression, and the 11th percentile in math. Students in the 6th grade scored in the 17th percentile in reading, the 28th percentile in written expression and the 47th percentile in math. The bottom line is that students are not developing the skills necessary to achieve in school.

What Paul Jones did to turn this situation around appears in Chapter 10.

If your school has not previously gathered any of the data described in this section, do not be intimidated. Start with what you have—basic demographics, historical achievement, and enrollment trends. As you begin your data collection effort, think in terms of what kind of information would help you accomplish whatever you plan to do first. Student and teacher questionnaires are probably the easiest place to begin. Construct questionnaires to understand the school from the perspective of the students and their families, and the collective thinking of teachers. Questionnaires can give you a comprehensive understanding of the learning organization from many different perspectives.

Table 2 is the Continuous Improvement Continuum for Information and Analysis. Using the sections in the continuum, as well as the paraphrased descriptions that follow, assess your school's *approach*, *implementation*, and *outcome* with respect to Information and Analysis.

Assessing Your School's Information and Analysis

Which statement below best describes your school's *approach* to Information and Analysis?

· ·

Approach

1. Basically no data is collected about teachers, students, or processes of the school.

2. Some student and teacher information are collected for special programs, projects, or whenever a problem needs to be solved.

3. Data on student and parent needs, perceptions, and expectations are gathered. Data are then analyzed in order to establish a quality plan for school improvement.

4. The school sees the benefit of collecting hard data for making decisions at the classroom and school levels. These data are disaggregated by subgroups, such as ethnicity, to understand more about how the students are performing with the current processes.

5. The school recognizes the value of continuous improvement analyses. Data are gathered about all aspects of the school. Teachers engage students in gathering information on their own performance.

    Your assessment _____   Date _____

Which statement below best describes your school's *implementation* of Information and Analysis?

. . . .

Implementation

1. Data are not used to make decisions about the school operation. Student or parent dissatisfaction is seen as an irritation as opposed to an indicator of needed improvement.

2. Only data that are commonly requested by the public or the district office are tracked, such as drop-out rates, student backgrounds. The information basically is not used.

3. Comprehensive data on current student needs and projections are collected and analyzed at the school level, in order to establish a quality strategic plan. Data are tracked in all areas considered for improvement. Attempts are made to understand what is really going on behind the numbers.

4. Teachers independently and collectively request evaluations from students throughout the year to understand how the instruction and curriculum are impacting student achievement. Student achievement data are disaggregated for diagnostic purposes and to understand the impact of teaching.

5. Teachers understand that problems can be prevented through the comprehensive use of data about students' perceptions and performances. Teaching processes are changed to meet the needs and structures of the students.

Your assessment _____   Date _____

Which statement below best describes your school's *outcome* with respect to Information and Analysis?

. . . .

Outcome

1. There are a high number of absences, drop outs, discipline problems, and vandalism which are blamed on the kids. Teachers and administrators hypothesize about why they have problems in these areas. Students are treated for behavior individually.

2. With very little information and analysis about the clients of the school, change is fairly isolated. Those areas of the school for which data are tracked do show some positive outcomes.

3. School staff believe that by analyzing the needs of students, parents, and teachers, and by looking at projections and evaluations of instruction, they can provide a relevant and exciting program of learning for students.

4. Because a comprehensive and systemic quality information system is put in place for performance feedback, positive trends begin to appear in many classrooms and across the school. The results are partially due to the fact that the data are documented on a systematic basis and teachers tend to think about what is documented.

5. With a comprehensive approach to collecting data, gains are experienced in all aspects of the school operation for all students. No student falls between the cracks. Students are excited about school and are proud of their own capabilities to learn and to assess their own growth.

Your assessment _____   Date _____

Table 2

Information and Analysis

	ONE	TWO	THREE	FOUR	FIVE
APPROACH	Data or information about student performance and needs are not gathered in any systematic way; there is no way to determine what needs to change at the school, based on data.	There is no systematic process, but some teacher and student information is collected and used to problem solve and establish essential student learnings.	School collects data on student performance (e.g., attendance, achievement) and conducts surveys on student, teacher, and parent needs. The information is used to drive the strategic quality plan for school change.	There is systematic reliance on hard data (including data for subgroups) as a basis for decision making at the classroom level as well as at the school level. Changes are based on the study of data to meet the needs of students and teachers.	Information is gathered in all areas of student interaction with the school. Teachers engage students in gathering information on their own performance. Accessible to all levels, data are comprehensive in scope and an accurate reflection of school quality.
IMPLEMENTATION	No information is gathered with which to make changes. Student dissatisfaction with the learning process is seen as an irritation, not a need for improvement.	Some data are tracked, such as dropout rates. Only a few individuals are asked for feedback about areas of schooling.	School collects information on students and graduates (e.g., student achievement and expectations), analyzes and uses it in conjunction with future trends for planning. Identified areas for improvement are tracked over time.	Data are used to improve the effectiveness of teaching strategies on all student learning. Students' historical performance are graphed and utilized for diagnostics. Student evaluations and performances are analyzed by teachers in all classrooms.	Innovative teaching processes that meet the needs of students are implemented to the delight of teachers, parents, and students. Information is analyzed and used to prevent student failure. Root causes are known through analyses. Problems are prevented through the use of data.
OUTCOME	Only anecdotal and hypothetical information is available about student performance, behavior, and satisfaction. Problems are solved individually with short-term results.	Little data are available. Change is limited to some areas of the school and dependent upon individual teachers and their efforts.	Information collected about student and parent needs, assessment, and instructional practices are shared with the school staff and used to plan for change. Information helps staff understand pressing issues, how to analyze information for "root causes," and how to track for improvement.	An information system is in place. Positive trends begin to appear in many classrooms and schoolwide. There is evidence that these results are caused by understanding and effectively using data collected.	Students are delighted with the school's instructional processes and proud of their own capabilities to learn and assess their own growth. Good to excellent achievement is the result for all students. No student falls through the cracks. Teachers use data to predict and prevent potential problems.

Items That Might Be Found In the
Information and Analysis Section of the School Portfolio

The following are appropriate items for inclusion in this section:

Student Demographics
- Parent income levels
- Parent education backgrounds
- Parent socioeconomic status
- Families on public assistance
- Free and Reduced Lunch
- Drop-out rates
- Graduation rates
- Retention rates
- Health issues/handicaps
- Discipline indicators
  (e.g., suspensions, referrals)
- Attendance
- Tardy
- Transiency rates
- Number of years at the school
- Home language

School Community
- History
- Location
- Population
- Race/ethnicity
- Socioeconomic status
- Size
- Employment status
- Housing trends
- Health issues
- Crime rate
- Economic base

School
- History
- Enrollment over time
- Safety
- Physical plant
- Uniqueness and strengths
- Image in the community

Staff
- Number of teachers and administrators
- Years of teaching/administering
- Ethnicity/gender of teachers and administrators
- Retirement projections
- Types of certificates
- Student-teacher ratios
- Administrator-teacher ratios
- Attendance rates of employees
- Turnover rates of employees
- Salary schedules
- Support staff

School District
- Description of district
- History
- Number of schools, students, teachers, and administrators
- Prediction of changes
- Support services for students and teachers
- Organizational structure

Other
- School's assessment on the information and analysis continuous improvement continuum
- Surveys to assess current and desired practices
- Perceptions of the learning environment
- Student achievement scores
- School processes
- Goals for improvement
- Analyses of root causes of problems
- Analysis of what needs to happen to move to the next steps in the continuum
- Photos

Information and Analysis Questions

The following questions are designed to help you think about what your school has in evidence of where you are with regard to Information and Analysis.

What data do you have (or would you like to get) that could build the context of your school, describe the students, their parents, your community, and their needs? (demographics, census, questionnaires, etc.)

What data do you have that can tell you about the results of your current processes with the students you have?

What additional data would you like to gather to inform your school about how your current processes are working with your students? (Include disaggregation information.)

What are your next steps with staff with regard to Information and Analysis?

The focus of school improvement is on creating a comprehensive learning organization that understands, cares about, and works for students. In a comprehensive learning organization focused on students, leadership works to prevent student failure as opposed to reactively implementing the latest innovations or taking a fire-fighting approach to making decisions that affect student learning. A focus on students causes leadership to move teachers from roles as providers of information to researchers who under-stand and can predict the impact of their actions on students and student achievement; and students from recipients of knowledge delivery to goal-setting, self-assessors who produce independent, quality products. In schools where students and student learning are clearly the focus, expected student outcomes are known, teachers collaborate and are skilled in action research, in knowing, predicting, and acting on the impact of their actions to increase student achievement.

Chapter 5

STUDENT ACHIEVEMENT

Until teachers are able to predict the impact of their actions on students, change their actions based on these predictions, corroborate the effect of their actions with students, and work with peers to build a comprehensive learning organization, any increase in student achievement and change in the classroom will be temporary.

It is often stated in the literature that it takes about five years from the time a school starts to rebuild for increased student achievement to the time it will see sustainable increases in student achievement directly attributable to school improvement efforts. This time may be decreased if the *entire school* is committed to the school improvement effort and understands the following at the school level and at the individual teacher level:

> To fully educate a student, teachers need to do their best during the temporary time together and to care just as much about the educational experiences that the student had before coming and experiences that the student will have after leaving. To believe that the job of a classroom teacher is to operate solely in the present with his or her immediate charge is to deny a school the opportunity to provide a cumulative, purposeful effect.
>
> Carl Glickman

- Who the school's clients are, and how they learn best
- The impact of current processes on all student learning
- What the school community expects students to know and be able to do

Understanding the Student

Every child has special needs and talents. It is the school's responsibility to discover what these are, to nurture the good, and to replace attitudes about failure with high expectations for success.

Every school has a unique student population. No two schools have identical populations. No one school has identical populations two years in a row. Students are very different; they have different learning styles, home lives, and personal needs.

> *The secret of education lies in respecting the pupil.*
> Ralph Waldo Emerson

A true learning organization will understand its student population. It will know who the students are—ethnically, socially, emotionally—what they value and believe, how they like school and learning, and what the impacts of current processes are on their learning. (This has been described in Chapter 4, Information and Analysis.)

Impact of Current Processes on Student Learning

More often than not, standardized achievement tests are administered in the spring and results are returned in the fall when students have moved on to different classrooms. This timing makes the scores for one teacher's class and for an entire school seem almost irrelevant.

These data, however, are a good source for understanding relative performance of subgroups of students and understanding the impact of current processes on a group of students. For example, these data, when disaggregated, can provide information that indicates where the increases or decreases occurred within the student population, performance differences for ethnicities, gender-related performance differences, or performance differences based upon the number of years of attendance at the school. Figure 6 in Chapter 4 shows data disaggregated by ethnicity at the school level.

> *We need to spend more time, energy, and attention on asking the question: Why are we assessing students— rather than how.*
> National Leadership Network

An example of how a school changed its processes and structure for the benefit of its school population follows:

Smith Elementary School knew it needed to understand its student population in any given year, but four years of changing populations was definitely testing their understanding and teaching repertoire. Every year, for four years, the student population changed due to boundary changes in the attendance area, the opening of a new school close by, a switch to year-round multi-track programs, and a new districtwide policy to provide students with the opportunity to attend the school of their choice. The latter change was a very important change. Not only did school personnel need to learn about the students in the neighborhood who were expected to come to Smith, they also needed to understand about those outside the neighborhood who were predicted to choose to attend the school. This information was crucial for understanding what programs and services to provide to meet student needs. Some data were estimated and then specific data were tracked when the attendance roster was known.

In studying the student population in the district, the surrounding neighborhood, and in easy commuting distance, it was estimated that 86 percent of the population would be Hispanic—about 40 percent with limited English-speaking skills.

Analyses were performed on the standardized achievement tests that had been administered by the district for the past five years. It was clear that the Hispanic students scored higher than the other populations of students in science and mathematics, while their reading and writing scores were much lower. With this and other information, the teaching staff researched strategies that could use this information to everyone's advantage.

The research resulted in Smith becoming a mathematics, science, and technology magnet school, utilizing hands-on activities in science, technology, and mathematics to build English language competence with the majority of their population, while increasing the science and mathematics knowledge of all students. Their school soon had a waiting list of students wanting to attend.

Student Learning Standards

Reaching consensus on what is most important for students to know and to be able to do has to be the most difficult piece of the entire school improvement effort. It takes time to identify what is most important for students to know and to be able to do, and then to represent it accurately in words. Considered the most important element in understanding and increasing student achievement, student standards (sometimes called essential student learnings or outcomes) are derived from the school mission and vision and include statements that determine curriculum and represent the goals of the school as it prepares students for lifelong learning and future work. Learning standards drive the purpose, the norms, and the culture of the school. They provide a ruler by which the school can gauge its success, statements of what the school wants its graduates to know and be able to do when they leave school. They are used to determine what will best prepare students for the future and to shape their future. Identifying learning standards is critical to building a continuum of learning that makes sense for preparing students for the world they will face when they are on their own. Student standards drive the assessment, curriculum, and instructional strategies down to the preschool level.

When standards are known, teachers can design a continuum of learning for students, articulate curriculum across grade levels and age groups, ensure basic skills attainment for all students, and ensure coverage of curriculum frameworks.

Student learning standards are derived from a future context, asking: What will these students face? What is the future going to be like when they get there? What must we make sure the students can do by the time they get there? All stakeholders must be involved in deriving the standards, which must reflect the shared mission, values, beliefs, and vision of the school.

Schools must identify what they want students to know and be able to do upon exiting the system, and work backward to translate the learnings into standards and action at all levels of the school. The most important words in these statements are the verbs. Results are defined by the verbs that are chosen. Verbs determine the nature and power of the competence students need to perform the work. Verbs must be powerful; students must do the verb, teachers must teach the verb, and assessment must perfectly embody the verb. Assessment must be a vehicle that allows the verb to be done! (The High Success Network, 1991.)

Using student standards, school staff must determine the processes which are critical to ensuring that all students at all levels leave the school having mastered these learnings. In order to meet the needs of specific groups of students, and to have them achieve student learning standards, the school must become aware of developments in assessment, instructional strategies, and technology. From the learnings, the curriculum and instructional and assessment strategies are formed. The learning standards and assessment should become one and the same and from these statements, the instructional strategies become apparent. Assessment must assess what is taught and what is taught must be what is assessed. Figure 14 is an example of essential learning goals, assessment, expectations, and instructional strategies from Los Naranjos Elementary School, Irvine, California.

Critical Processes for Increasing Student Achievement

If you know why you will figure out how.

W. Edwards Deming

As processes change, the impact can be understood by ongoing assessments. Teachers can see very clearly that the results they are getting are related to the processes used. If different results are desired, new processes must be implemented and measured on an ongoing basis to know the impact.

Figure 14

Example Essential Learnings

Essential Learning Goals, Assessment, Expectations, and Instructional Strategies

Kindergarten—Oral Language

Essential Learning Goals
- Student will use oral language for a variety of purposes
- Student will speak with clarity and confidence

Assessment
Student will make an oral presentation to the class such as:
- reciting a poem
- retelling a story
- explaining and showing how to do something (i.e., play a game)

Expectations
- Student will face the audience
- Student will speak with appropriate volume and clarity
- Student will relate ideas in sequence
- Student will use a minimum of five complete sentences

Instructional Strategies
- Teacher wil coach student on expectations privately and in small groups
- Teacher will videotape student and coach student on self-assessment of speaking with appropriate volume and clarity
- Teacher will give students numerous opportunities to practice presentation skills in class
- Teacher will conduct frequent informal assessments and occasional formal assessments during class
- Teacher will work with student to select appropriate material
- Teacher will work toward the same high standard with all students

It is very easy to *adopt* new strategies. It is very difficult to *implement* them, especially consistently and congruently throughout the entire school.

Effective leadership teams make the actual implementation of new strategies throughout the school a priority. Leadership teams ensure that professional development activities are structured to lead to actual implementation using components like peer coaching and collaborative action research. (More discussion of these concepts are found in the chapters on Leadership and Professional Development.) While some schools use a combination of teacher portfolios, peer coaching, and teacher action research to support the implementation of new strategies, others have gone one step beyond to monitor implementation with the use of staff-developed rubrics.

Based on the same philosophy as the *Education for the Future Initiative* Continuous Improvement Continuums, staff-developed rubrics can monitor, guide, and assess the implementation of new strategies both at the classroom level and collectively at the school level. At the top of the scale, these rubrics describe how classrooms will look, with respect to instruction, assessment, curriculum, and outcomes when the vision is implemented. The other points on the scale represent the continuum of implementation.

An example of rubrics developed by staff to assist the implementation of new classroom strategies appears in Appendix B. The story of their origin follows.

Frank Paul Elementary in Salinas, California was grateful for the Education for the Future Initiative Continuous Improvement Continuums (CIC) approach which helped the school accomplish its goals and promote a shared vision. The continuums helped clarify for everyone at the school what they wanted to accomplish in the different categories. After one year of continuum ratings, Frank Paul staff knew there was one category in which the school had not progressed as planned—the implementation of the vision. Frank Paul leaders were concerned that this might be an indication that their entire reform effort was for naught—although the staff had adopted new classroom strategies, there was not enough solid evidence that the strategies were being implemented. Staff determined that a process comparable to the CIC's at the classroom level would help teachers implement the same school vision.

Frank Paul teachers were committed to the total rethinking of the classroom environment, instructional strategies, and assessment. The rubrics define the typical progression of implementation, based upon the research. The vision for full implementation is described at level 5.

Frank Paul teachers conduct self-assessments on the rubrics, and utilize them in conjunction with teacher portfolios and collaborative action research to plan and monitor change. They feel this combination has led to real classroom change. The teachers feel that the combination has helped them become all-around more effective teachers, which is why it has replaced Frank Paul's traditional teacher evaluation process, and why the district has supported this new approach to teacher evaluation.

The benefits of utilizing implementation rubrics are four-fold—

1. Rubrics require teachers to describe in writing the way the classrooms will look when the strategy is implemented. This requires a shared understanding of the vision and seriously thinking through strategies for implementation.

2. Teachers assess where they are on the continuums three or more times a year. This self-assessment approach is extremely powerful for reflecting on the critical processes that are being implemented and for establishing plans for improvement. The assessment also adds an element of accountability to the implementation efforts.

3. The rubric approach effectively communicates to the school community that implementing a new strategy is comprehensive, complex, and takes time. One cannot go from low implementation of a particular strategy to full implementation in a very short period of time.

4. Rubrics make it very clear to the school community where they are headed and to what they have committed.

Teacher Action Research

Teacher action research is an effective approach to ensuring that every student will learn. Using this research, teachers analyze the achievement patterns of individual students on many measures, learn what motivates the learner, and come to understand the students' values and beliefs.

The action research example, Figure 15, shows three measures of reading ability charted for 35 students in one 6th grade classroom graphed at the beginning of the school year. The charts show Comprehensive Tests of Basic Skills (CTBS) reading scores, Informal Reading Inventory (IRI) scores, and student scores on an exhibition composite with a possibility of 16. The major questions in establishing these charts were centered around exhibition scores. The teacher wanted to know how these compare to more traditional measures

Figure 15

Teacher Action Research

Multiple Measures of Student Learning

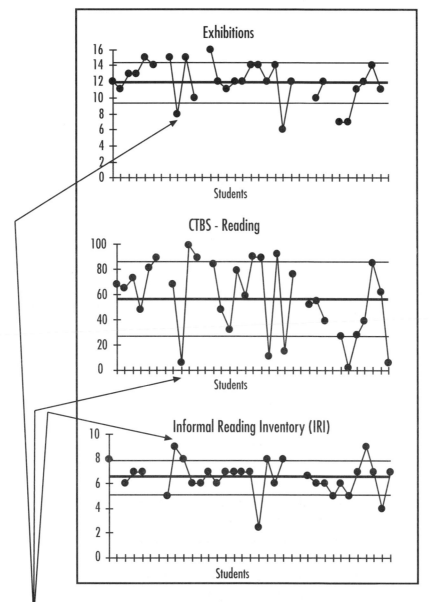

Teachers could ask the following questions:

- Of all the sixth graders having difficulty reading, how did they perform on each of these measures?

- Are there characteristics of non-readers that we can identify at the sixth grade level?

- Can we identify similar characteristics at the 5th, 4th, 3rd, 2nd, and 1st grade levels?

- Are there interventions we can use with these identified characteristics to prevent non-reading?

Looking at individual student measures gives teachers valuable information about how the different measures perform, learning styles and motivation of individual students, and begins to build a continuum of learning for students.

of student achievement and if they provide information that can help the teacher and the student understand what they need to do to increase the students' achievement in real-world skills of reading, researching, writing, and presenting information. She also wanted to know if exhibition scores were reliable indicators of student achievement.

> *Since we cannot change reality, let us change the eyes which see reality.*
>
> Nikos Kazantzakis

When studying the charts, the teacher was initially surprised at the variation in CTBS scores. She was also surprised to realize that the exhibitions the teachers had been using for four years and the IRI scores did not vary much. She was also amazed at how each 5th grade teacher interpreted the exhibition rubrics so differently. The previous year's exhibition scores did not give her as much helpful information as she would have liked.

The patterns on the three measures for individual students were quite different. The teacher interviewed students to see if they could help her understand the discrepancies. The responses she got from the students made her next steps crystal clear. For instance, student 9 scored a 3 on CTBS, an 8 on exhibitions—very low scores. However, this same student was assessed on the Informal Reading Inventory (IRI) as the best reader in the class—reading at the 9th grade level. When the student was asked how this could be, he said that CTBS was not important. He had heard teachers talking about CTBS being meaningless to them, so why should it have meaning to him? Regarding his performance on exhibitions he said, "Why should I put out for exhibitions when they don't matter? They're not graded, they're not anything." About the IRI, the student described the quiet room he went into with just the reading specialist, about how he really liked the short story he picked to read, and how neat it was to talk with the specialist about what he read. He said, "I could do this all day!"

After interviewing all their students, the 6th grade teachers got together and held a discussion centered around the following. We can see that the patterns on these three measures are very different. They are measuring different things. The real question is: of the students having difficulty with reading in 6th grade, how did they score on each of these measures, and what does that mean? Of the students who are having difficulty reading at the 6th grade level, are there common characteristics? If so, what are they, and what do we do about them?

In discussions with the rest of the staff, the 6th grade teachers asked, what were these students' characteristics in 5th grade, 4th grade, third grade, second grade, first grade, kindergarten? Reflecting upon these questions and their own findings, teachers in the other grades discussed which students in current classes have similar characteristics, and what they need to do at each of these levels to prevent reading difficulty in later grades?

Teachers had much to discuss at their next faculty meeting. In addition to the obvious discussions about where and when adult-level conversations need to take place at school, the teachers decided to have students work with them to revise their exhibition rubrics and to advise them on how to make them "count." Changes were made in the exhibitions immediately.

The action research approach has also led to increased staff collaboration and constructive conversations centered on students and focused on a comprehensive continuum of learning for all students. These conversations are leading to systemic change. They are so inspiring that the conversations and the analyses have become institutionalized for these teachers. Action research has become a way of doing business on an ongoing basis. These teachers are now working to prevent student failure as opposed to reacting to student failure. Teachers are thrilled to see a real continuum of learning evolve for students, and to see student learning increases that are a result of their analytical efforts.

The efforts described here to determine appropriate teaching and assessment strategies sound immense. However, if this kind of attention is not taken to determine how to meet the needs of the students through these or similar strategies, teachers will find themselves exactly where they are now—wondering why these students are not learning! It is crucial to throw away all preconceived notions of the school's students, their backgrounds, and how the current processes impact their learning, and replace those notions with facts. Data analyses just might show a different student than what was assumed. The school's population may have changed enough that it is time to reanalyze who is enrolled. Start with existing information and work to add more over time. The more facts that are utilized, the easier the process of implementing new strategies will become—the rewards will be there.

Table 3 is the Continuous Improvement Continuum for Student Achievement. Using the sections outlined in the continuum, as well as the paraphrased descriptions that follow, assess your school's *approach*, *implementation*, and *outcome* with respect to Student Achievement.

Which statement below best describes your school's *approach* to Student Achievement?

· ·

Approach

1. There is little interest in a concerted plan to increase student achievement. The school feels that whatever results from whatever they do is what happens. Teachers believe in the normal curve—some kids will always fail, most will score about average, and some kids will do better than most.

2. Teachers want to improve student achievement and begin analyzing some student achievement data to understand the impact of current and past processes.

3. Essential student learnings are identified and are articulated across student groupings. Current processes for instruction and assessment are compared with these learnings.

4. Teachers, believing that all kids can learn and wanting to understand how they can make this happen, are committed to improving student achievement. They utilize every kind of data they have to decide appropriate instructional strategies and assessments to reach all students.

5. The school is committed to increasing student achievement. Teachers conduct action research to study student performance in their classrooms. They are able to diagnose student needs and accurately predict instructional strategies that will help each student.

Your assessment _____ Date _____

Which statement below best describes your school's *implementation* of Student Achievement?

. . . .

Implementation

1. Teachers tend to teach in the way that they were taught. There is no individualization of instruction, and no communication with students to understand school from their perspective.

2. There is some effort to understand the impact of current instructional strategies on student learning. This includes looking at achievement data and questionnaire results.

3. Teachers work together and understand that analyzing all types of achievement data is very instructive in understanding the impact of instruction and assessment on students. Teachers ask students for feedback to help them understand achievement results.

4. There is strong reliance on data and student feedback, leading to the implementation of effective instruction and assessment strategies in all classrooms. A continuum of learning for students results. Teachers support each other with peer coaching and/or action research focused on student achievement.

5. Teachers utilize data and effectively collaborate with one another to ensure that their instructional and assessment strategies are leading to the achievement of all student learning standards, for all students.

Your assessment _____ Date _____

Which statement below best describes your school's *outcomes* with respect to Student Achievement?

· ·

Outcome

1. Students feel there is little they can do to improve their performance—they're either smart or they aren't. They report that school is boring and that they are not challenged. Teachers blame students' backgrounds for low student achievement and the high number of absences each day.

2. A few isolated areas show student achievement increases.

3. Student feedback on the instructional and assessment strategies of the school are taken into consideration. Through their studies and data analyses, teachers come up with effective approaches to increasing student achievement.

4. Increases in student achievement is evident throughout the school because teachers are meeting the needs of the students and providing instruction that students want and care about.

5. Both students and teachers conduct self-assessments to continually improve their own performances. Teacher and student satisfaction is evident. Achievement is high and clearly linked to instruction. No student falls between the cracks.

Your assessment _____   Date _____

Table 3

Student Achievement

	ONE	TWO	THREE	FOUR	FIVE
APPROACH	Instructional and organizational processes critical to student success are not identified. Little distinction of student learning differences is made. Some teachers believe that not all students can achieve.	Some data are collected on student background or performance trends. Learning gaps are noted to direct improvement of instruction. Student essential learnings are identified.	Essential student learnings and a continuum of learning throughout the school are identified and set up as standards. Student performance data are collected and compared to these standards in order to analyze how to improve learning for all students.	Data on student achievement are used throughout the school to pursue the improvement of student learning. Teachers collaborate to implement appropriate instruction and assessment strategies for meeting essential student learnings articulated across grade levels. All teachers believe that all students can learn.	School makes an effort to exceed student achievement expectations. Innovative instructional changes are made to anticipate learning needs and improve student achievement. Teachers are able to predict characteristics impacting student achievement and to know how to perform from a small set of internal quality measures.
IMPLEMENTATION	All students are taught the same way. There is no communication with students about their academic needs or learning styles. There are no analyses of how to improve instruction.	Some effort is made to track and analyze student achievement trends on a schoolwide basis. Teachers begin to understand the needs and learning gaps of students.	Teachers study effective instruction and assessment strategies to increase their students' learning. Student feedback and analysis of achievement data are used in conjunction with implementation support strategies.	There is a systematic focus on the improvement of student learning schoolwide. Effective instruction and assessment strategies are implemented in each classroom. Teachers support one another with peer coaching and/or action research focused on implementing strategies that lead to increased achievement.	All teachers correlate critical instructional and assessment strategies with objective indicators of quality student achievement. A comparative analysis of actual individual student performance to essential student learnings is utilized to adjust teaching strategies to ensure a progression of learning for all students.
OUTCOME	There are wide student variations in attitudes and achievement with undesirable results. There is high dissatisfaction among students with learning. Student background is used as an excuse for low student achievement.	There is some evidence that student achievement trends are available to teachers and are being used. There is much effort, but minimal observable results in improving student achievement.	There is an increase in communication between students and teachers regarding student learnings. Teachers learn about effective instructional strategies that will meet the needs of their students. They make some gains.	Increased student achievement is evident schoolwide. Student morale, attendance, and behavior are good. Teachers converse often with each other about preventing student failure. Areas for further attention are clear.	Students and teachers conduct self-assessments to continuously improve performance. Improvements in student achievement are evident and clearly caused by teachers' and students' understandings of individual student learning, linked to appropriate and effective instructional and assessment strategies. A continuum of learning results. No students fall through the cracks.

Items That Might Be Found In the
Student Achievement Section of the School Portfolio

The following are appropriate items for inclusion in this section:

- School's assessments on the Student Achievement Continuous Improvement Continuum
- Description of current instructional and assessment strategies
- Standardized test scores, over time, by subgroup (i.e., ethnic, sex, language proficiency, socioeconomic status, how long they have been at the school, comparisons to the district, state, other schools, if appropriate) [Might also appear in Information and Analysis]
- Other measures of student learning, over time, by subgroup (e.g., authentic assessment scores, other tests)
- Analyses of the results of different assessment strategies
- Instructional implications for the student population
- Gaps in learning/analysis of student learning needs
- Essential student learning standards and how they were determined
- Description of instructional and assessment strategies desired to implement to meet student learning needs
- Reasons teachers know these strategies will meet the needs of the students and prevent student failure
- Plan for implementation
- Description of strategy to support implementation (e.g., action research, rubrics, peer coaching) [Might also appear in Professional Development]
- Evaluation of implementation and impact of strategies
- Exhibits of quality student work
- Goals for improvement
- Analysis of what needs to happen to move to the next steps in the continuum

Student Achievement Questions

The following questions are designed to help you think about what your school has in evidence of where you are with regard to Student Achievement.

What do you have for documentation for the Student Achievement section of your school portfolio?

What other things do you need to gather and document in the Student Achievement section?

What are your next steps with staff with respect to Student Achievement?

Chapter 6

QUALITY PLANNING

All organizations need a *vision*. All organizations must *plan* for the vision or the vision will never be realized.

A well-defined and well-executed school improvement effort begins with a comprehensive schoolwide strategic plan that provides a logical framework for clarifying and achieving the vision. The school plan includes: an *assessment* of where the school is today and what factors can be expected to influence it in the future; a *mission statement* describing the school's purpose and function; a *vision* that reflects the *values* and *beliefs* of the individuals who make up the organization; *long-range goals* that make the intents of the mission and vision tangible; an identification of *outcomes*; a plan for evaluation and continuous improvement; an *action plan* that identifies the procedural steps needed to implement the goals, including timelines, responsibility, accountability; and, an estimation of *budget needs* based on the action plan.

> *Vision without action is merely a dream. Action without vision just passes the time. Vision with action can change the world.*
>
> Joel A. Barker

Strategic Planning

Strategic planning is the process of answering the following questions:

- Where are we?
- Where do we want to go?
- How do we get there?
- Are these processes getting us to where we want to go?
- How will we know when we are where we want to be?

The data gathered in Chapter 4, Information and Analysis, answer the question, "Where are we?" The school mission, vision, and goals, along with the values and beliefs of the school community are elements that, in conjunction with the data, will help answer the question of where we want to go. How we get there is determined through the identification of procedural steps which could include instructional assessment strategies discussed in Chapter 5, and the development of a comprehensive action plan. The school's plan for continuous improvement and evaluation addresses whether the processes are getting us where we want to go and ensuring how we will know when we are where we want to be. The first step in strategic planning is to determine the guiding philosophy of the school—its values and beliefs, purpose, mission, and vision.

> *Strategic planning is the process of determining the long-term vision and goals of an enterprise and how to fulfill them.*
>
> William C. Bean

Values and Beliefs

Values and beliefs are at the core of who we are, what we do, and how we think and feel. Values and beliefs reflect what is important to us—in work and in life. They describe not only how we think about work, society, and how the world operates, but also how we think they "should" operate.

Values and beliefs influence how teachers teach and their expectations and feelings for children. Basically, humans will not act in ways different from their values and beliefs. They are the shaping force behind the vision.

The first step in establishing a mission and shared vision is to determine who the people of the school community are, what they believe about school, teaching, learning, and children, and what they value. From individual values and beliefs, collective values and beliefs can, and need to, emerge.

> *Man is not the creature of circumstances; circumstances are the creatures of men.*
>
> Benjamin Disraeli

Example of a teacher's personal values and beliefs:

I value—

- *honesty, respect, and responsibility*
- *the individual differences of all students*

I believe—

- *all students are capable of learning. It is the teacher's job to figure out how to meet the needs of each student to help her/him get to the point of self-motivation*
- *the culture of the individual child must be nurtured in the learning environment*

Example of collective values and beliefs established by school staff:

We value—

- *the human values of respect, honesty, trustworthiness, altruism, compromise, humility, personal responsibility, and social responsibility*
- *social, emotional, cultural, and intellectual similarities and differences in all individuals*

We believe—

- *teachers, administrators, "schools," home, and community must model the human values of respect, honesty, trustworthiness, altruism, compromise, humility, personal responsibility, and social responsibility*
- *every individual is unique socially, emotionally, culturally, and intellectually and must be respected and valued for her/his uniqueness*

Example of why it is important to clarify values and beliefs:

A court school is made up of students who have been expelled from public school, taken from their family homes, and placed in group homes. Court school teachers are often disturbed that these students appear in their school again after they "serve their time" and are sent back to public school. They want to know why they are having no impact on these students.

The first question we ask the teachers is, "What is the purpose of your school?" It never fails that half the teachers say, "The purpose of this school is to punish the students. If they had not done something wrong, they wouldn't be here." The other half say,

"The purpose of this school is to give kids a second chance. We should be providing them with the nurturing they never received before. That is why they get into the trouble they do."

It is clear that these values and beliefs translate into two very different sets of actions on the part of the teachers. Without an agreed upon approach, these two sets of values and beliefs translate into actions that equal no impact on the students!

Mission

An effective mission must stretch and challenge the organization, yet be achievable. It is proactive, concrete, value-driven, energizing, and moves the organization forward. It is crisp, clear, engaging—it reaches out and grabs people in the gut. People "get it" right away; it requires little or no explanation . . . A mission should walk the boundary between the possible and impossible; setting a mission requires an intuitive sense for that boundary.

Collins and Porras

An organization's *mission* statement is a brief, clear, and compelling goal that describes its purpose and function. The prerequisite to establishing a mission statement is to determine the general purpose of the organization. A statement of purpose comes from the values and beliefs of the individuals in the organization and should not just reflect what the organization is doing now. It needs to be broad, inspirational, enduring, and grab the "soul" of each member of the organization.

Example: *The purpose of school is to help children acquire the knowledge and skills they need for lifelong learning and to empower them to become capable and responsible citizens.*

Once the purpose of the organization is determined, the mission of the specific organization is fairly easy to generate.

Example: *The mission of Los Naranjos Elementary School is to enable all students to become contributing members in a global society, empowered with the skills, knowledge, and values necessary to meet the challenges of a changing world.*

School mission statements need to focus on preparing students to be successful in the future, as opposed to preparing them to be successful students.

Representatives from all factions of the school community need to be involved in the development of a mission statement, as the discussions held during the process are crucial. In fact, the discussions may be more important than the actual statement, as they empower and motivate those participating to assume responsibility for the school's ultimate direction.

It takes a long time to create a statement that describes the mission in a manner that everyone in the school community can understand in the same way. However, the work is not done on the mission when the statement is written. As more is learned about the school improvement process, and as more information about the clients of the school is collected and analyzed, the mission will need to be revisited and revised. Additionally, the mission will need to be revisited as individuals within the school organization change, since the mission is determined through the values and beliefs of the individuals participating in the school community.

Shared Vision

Peter Senge advises organizations wanting to establish a shared vision to encourage individuals within the organization to develop their own personal vision first. This is because the only vision that really motivates individuals is their own, and the best shared vision for a group must be representative of the group's individual visions. A clearly stated shared vision that everyone can understand and commit to is one of the most important elements of a quality school plan because it helps determine "where we are going." A vision is based upon information and analysis, and the mission, values, and beliefs of the school community. It is a visual image of the mission. It defines what the school wants to become, is written in practical, concrete terms and is clear enough that everyone can see the same vision. A vision describes what the school will look like in the future, is stated in the present tense, and communicates a clear image of the future. A vision is a specific description of what the school will be like when the mission is accomplished. It transforms the mission from words into pictures and brings it to life. On the following page is a part of Evergreen Middle School's vision for the future.

> *Shared visions emerge from personal visions. This is how they derive their energy and how they foster commitment.... If people don't have their own vision, all they can do is "sign up" for someone else's. The result is compliance, never commitment.*
>
> Peter Senge

83

When this plan is implemented, the following scenario will be true:

Jill, Romero, Seth, and Maria discuss the most efficient garden crops to grow as a food supply as Seth downloads from the Internet the latest germination data received from the space lab. These data are combined with the soil reports secured by Jill and Romero from the County Department of Agriculture. Comparisons are made between the results of the shady and sunny gardens, and are shared along with the information described above, via hand-held computers. In the afternoon, the development of the presentation continues. Ms. Soares helps Susie and David with graphics for the presentation, while Ms. Pell helps each group finalize their written reports. Some art students prepare the pictorial component and develop their color photographs in Mr. Mitchell's darkroom. The video component of the multimedia documentary of the entire 12-week project is under development by another group of students. The group from the sunny garden reanalyze and chart the results of their fertilization and pollination experiments. The students are excited about the one comprehensive multimedia report they will produce from the integration of their many subreports.

Initially a school can expect enthusiasm for the vision. However, as people's realization of the gap that exists between the vision and reality becomes pronounced, there is a dramatic decrease in enthusiasm. The lack of enthusiasm is often replaced by cynicism. While teachers need the opportunity to be cathartic, leadership needs to keep staff positive, perhaps by celebrating how far they have come already. In a positive, non-judgmental environment, the vision will take hold again. Similar to the mission statement, as more possibilities for improvement are learned and the community changes, the vision will need to be updated and refined.

School Goals

School goals clearly and practically define what needs to happen to accomplish the vision. They are the answers to the question, "How will we get there?" School goals work backward from the vision to outline the major steps required. They grow out of the pressing issues of the school. Evergreen Elementary School described very clearly their school continuous improvement goals and intent in terms of a Plan-Do-Check-Act cycle, as follows:

. . . .

PLAN

Student Learning Standards

Student learning standards focus the curriculum on what students need to know and be able to do, what teachers need to teach, and how performance will be assessed. Student learning standards reflect what the school community and greater society consider to be important, and are known by all. Current Evergreen student learning standards need to be reviewed and articulated across grade levels during the next school year. The articulation of student learning standards with the feeder high school is a priority for the following year.

Basic Needs

Evergreen advocates Glasser's theories that all humans have five basic needs: survival, fun (enjoyment), freedom (choice), power (significance) and belonging (caring). We know that teachers must manage the learning environment to ensure that these needs are met before students can learn and produce quality products.

We also know that adults have these same basic needs. The major role of the school is to manage the system to ensure that teachers' needs are being met and supported—to allow them to produce quality work. Teachers will continue training in Reality Therapy starting in August, and will be supported throughout the year in implementing this philosophy. Ongoing assessments will ensure that both student and teacher needs are being met.

Pre-assessment

Evergreen students will be assessed using the Curriculum Based Measurement System (CBM) to ensure attainment of student learning standards and to understand how to meet the needs of all students. This information will be used to plan the curriculum. CBM will be administered on an ongoing basis for diagnostic information for those students experiencing difficulties in learning. Special Education resources will be used to augment and support mainstreaming in the regular education program.

. . . .

DO

Curriculum

Beginning in the fall, Evergreen's curriculum will be integrated to an even greater degree than it is presently. The goal is to have all subjects become transdisciplinary, with meaningful, real-world applications. The curriculum will be challenging and focused on depth versus breadth. Teachers will support each other through team teaching and peer coaching. Teachers will be trained in a technological approach to classroom observations. Feedback from this approach provides teachers with objective data to analyze how to improve what they do in the classroom. This process will replace the administrator's evaluation of the teacher. In August, beginning and new teachers will be provided with training by current staff in all aspects of this plan and Evergreen expectations.

Behavior

A major goal of the school community is to produce a learning environment that is noncoercive, provides a direct link to meeting the needs of students, and produces capable, self-reliant citizens. We believe that when students' five basic needs are met, behavior is not a issue. School rules will be replaced by students' rights and responsibilities. Teachers' understanding and implementation of Control Theory (Glasser), Natural Helpers (Roberts, Fitzmahan & Associates), Raising Self-reliant Children in a Self-indulgent World (Glen & Nelsen), and Class Meetings (Nelsen) will support them in creating a rich learning environment for all students. Teachers will participate in training in this area throughout the year.

Student Activities and Instruction

To actively engage all students in learning, the curriculum must become active and meaningful. To this end, students will engage in problem-solving and hands-on activities, with community partnerships supporting the special needs of each student. Students will have access to all school/community resources and will have a choice of meaningful, long-term projects and approaches to learning. Community service will become an element of student activities that will support the teaching and modeling of values. Community partners will help establish contact with businesses and parents.

Technology

Technology will become a powerful resource for learning and instruction. Technology will allow students to access and to create products that are meaningful. Computers will provide a means of communication, through a networked system and a means of record-keeping, that will reduce the time teachers spend on paperwork and increase the time they spend with students. Performance-based assessments will utilize all forms of technology. Evergreen teachers understand technology to be more than computers. They know the positive impact of videotaping student presentations as a means of continuous improvement, for instance. In order to increase and support teachers' uses of technology, an instructional technology support specialist has been hired.

. . . .

CHECK

Student Assessment

At all levels of the school, students will be expected to exhibit their mastery of student learning standards. The distinction between outcomes and assessment will become blurred as student performance and products are linked directly to outcomes. Several methods of assessment will be utilized in an ongoing manner. CBM will be administered at least twice each year for all students, or as many times as needed for students who are at risk for diagnostic purposes and evaluation of the instructional process. Teacher observations will focus on meeting social, emotional, and academic needs of the student. Performance-based assessments such as student portfolios, exhibitions, projects/products will be utilized to assess knowledge and growth. As much as possible, assessments will be computerized. Special Education and Social Service resources will be utilized to augment and support the regular education program. Student performance progress will be communicated to parents through student portfolios and narrative report cards. Letter grades will no longer be used. Teachers will be supported in becoming teachers as researchers.

Systemic Assessment

Assessments will be conducted throughout the year to analyze achievement results, assess the impact of system processes, and to ensure a systemic focus on continuous improvement. Assessments will guide the next years' implementation efforts.

· ·

ACT

Act to Improve

Many aspects of the continuous improvement process can be improved on an ongoing basis. Comprehensive analyses will be made each year to establish goals and plans for the next year based upon assessments and Total Quality Management analyses.

Action Plan

A comprehensive action plan defines the specific actions needed to implement the vision, sets forth when the actions will take place, and designates who is responsible for the action being accomplished.

> *. . . people overestimate what they can accomplish in a year— and underestimate what they can achieve in a decade!*
>
> Anthony Robbins

A comprehensive action plan outlines all activities the school must engage in during a specified period of time, including those related to required programs and program reviews. The action plan is the key to the accountability of the actual implementation of the school's goals. It is important to build one comprehensive action plan related to the school vision. It is important to also visit it annually and build a comprehensive action plan for the year that clearly identifies who does what by when. Figure 16 is a version of a school's action plan developed out of their school goals.

There are many different approaches to building an action plan which often require several drafts as elements are shuffled around to leverage work, time, and people. In most cases, the first draft will demand more "action" days than there are days in the calendar year. Priorities must be set and adjustments made until there is a flow of activities in congruence with the school vision and goals.

Figure 16

_____

Action Plan

ACTION	Responsible Person	Due Date	SEPT	OCT	NOV	DEC	JAN	FEB	MAR	APR	MAY	JUN	JUL	AUG
Develop Standards														
Create task forces in each subject area	Cindy Lam	1/15					X							
Task forces meet	Task Force	Ongoing						X··········	··········	·········X				
Task forces report to each other	Cindy Lam					X		X						
Report results	Cindy Lam	6/1										X		
Conference for Revisiting Student Learning Standards														
Plan the conference	Sarah Ball	1/31					X							
Hold the conference	Principal Skinner	4/15								X				
Writing Assessments														
Locate appropriate assessment	Sandra Cooke	3/31							X					
Plan for implementation of assessment	Sandra Cooke	3/31							X					
Pilot the assessment	Sandra Cooke	5/1									X			
Report on the results of the pilot	Sandra Cooke	5/30									X			
Study current processes	Wendy Kim	3/31							X····	····X				
Recommend new processes for teaching writing	Wendy Kim	5/30									X			
Administer new assessment	Sandra Cooke	9/1,12/1	X			X								
Report on results	Sandra Cooke	9/15,12/15	X			X								
Implement new processes	Every teacher	Ongoing				X··········								
Reading Assessments for Freshmen														
Locate appropriate assessment	Jamie Garcia	3/31							X					
Plan for implementation	Jamie Garcia	3/31							X					
Pilot the assessment	Jamie Garcia	5/1									X			
Report on the results of the pilot	Jamie Garcia	5/30									X			
Study current processes for teaching reading	Phil Jones	3/31							X····	····X				
Recommend new processes for teaching reading	Phil Jones	5/30									X			
Administer new assessment	Jamie Garcia	9/1, 12/1	X			X								
Report on results	Jamie Garcia	9/15,12/15	X			X								
Implement new processes	Every teacher	Ongoing				X··········								
Improve Class Structures														
Study current approaches	Nicholas Shelton	4/1								X··········	·········X			
Study new approaches	Nikko Nguen	4/1								X··········	·········X			
Report on implementation plan	Nikko Nguen	4/15								X				
Establish Database for Data Analysis	George McBonner	2/15						X						
Get classroom level data to teachers	George McBonner	4/15 & ongoing								X··········				
Review where we are as a school	George McBonner	5/15									X			
Celebrate Our Successes	Everyone		Last Day of School											

The creation of an action plan is invaluable for thinking through all the elements required to accomplish a goal and for understanding the interrelationships of all parts of the organization. The steps in developing the comprehensive action plan are shown as Figure 17.

When thinking through the elements required for each goal, it is best not to get bogged down by the order of events. If a special computer program for action planning is not being used, writing one element on a note pad or piece of paper will allow you to go back after all the elements are defined and place them in order with ease.

Think through the interrelationships of the elements and subelements and which action must precede what activity. Creatively think about subelements that could work together as one to achieve both, and identify elements that can leverage the implementation of other elements.

Figure 17

Steps in Action Planning

① List the school goals and any other required program goals (e.g., implement integrated instruction).

② Below each goal, list the elements that need to be accomplished to implement the goal (i.e., derive student learning standards, provide teachers with professional development training in integrated instruction).

③ Identify any subelements that need to be accomplished within the context of each element (for example, professional development training might require "identify trainer" or "reserve meeting room").

④ Begin to arrange the elements and subelements required by each goal in chronological order. (Keep this version for later reference.)

⑤ Using the goals, elements, and subelements, begin fine-tuning the plan in chronological summary form, starting with the action to be taken first.

⑥ In a planning form, label columns—Action, Person Responsible, Due Date, and Timeline. Place the reorganized elements and subelements in the action column in a manner that is easiest for staff to utilize later. In the column next to each action, identify the person ultimately responsible for the action. Try not to use team names in the "person responsible" column. Accountability is most effective if the responsibility is delegated to an individual. Responsible persons determine how accountability reviews are conducted.

⑦ In the column next to Person Responsible, determine the Due Date. For each subelement or element (depends on the topic and structure for implementation) determine when the activity absolutely must be completed.

⑧ In the columns that represent months, weeks, and sometimes days, make notations that will indicate when the activity will begin, its duration, and when it will be completed.

⑨ Determine how activities will be evaluated.

Budget Plan

Using the action plan shown in Figure 16, determine the costs associated with each action. This budget, developed in conjunction with the action plan, will determine what can be done during a year. A working budget plan for the example action plan is shown as Figure 18. Note that the budget plan is an extension of the action plan and that all school funds are used with the one resulting school plan. Everything in the school should be working toward that one plan—the school vision. Therefore, all school money is a part of this plan.

The budget is usually developed after the action plan has been *drafted*, then the plans are used together to determine what realistically can be done during any given year. Alterations are made simultaneously and balanced back and forth, while looking for items that can leverage other items. Dollars sometimes limit activities. School staff are often surprised, however, to discover that many times what they have to spend is equivalent to what they can do in a year's time. If the latter does not hold true, the school has important and specific information (i.e., the action plan and budget plan) to utilize in seeking additional support for their efforts.

Figure 18

Example Budget Plan

ACTION	Consultants Needed	Resources Needed	Existing Resources	Costs	Comments
Develop Standards Create task forces in each subject area Task forces meet Task forces report to each other Report results	Math consultant Language arts consultant	2 release days	Staff	$4,000 plus release days	Need staff work
Conference for Revisiting Student Learning Standards Plan the conference Hold the conference	Inspirational speaker $2,000	Refreshments $200	Staff	$2,200	Will be held on student-free days
Writing Assessments Locate appropriate assessment Plan for implementation of assessment Pilot the assessment Report on the results of the pilot Study current processes Recommend new processes for teaching writing Administer new assessment Report on results Implement new processes	Might want an assessment expert for 2 days @ $1,000 day	Site visits 2 release days for 4 teachers	Staff	$2,000 plus release days	Most of this requires staff commitment and work release days will be helpful
Reading Assessments for Freshmen Locate appropriate assessment Plan for implementation Pilot the assessment Report on the results of the pilot Study current processes for teaching reading Recommend new processes for teaching reading Administer new assessment Report on results Implement new processes	Might want an assessment expert for 2 days @ $1,000 day	Site visits 2 release days for 4 teachers	Staff	$2,000 plus release days	Most of this requires staff commitment and work release days will be helpful
Improve Class Structures Study current approaches Study new approaches Report on implementation plan	Might want an assessment expert for 2 days @ $1,000 day	Site visits	Staff	$2,000	We can benefit from an outsider's view
Establish Database for Data Analysis Get classroom level data to teachers Review where we are as a school	5 days @ $1,000 day	Technical help	Staff	$5,000	Completing the database will be helpful
Celebrate Our Successes		Refreshments	Staff	$500	

Putting the Planning Pieces Together

The following example shows an elementary school's mission, vision, plan, and goals budget.

Figure 19

MISSION

The school community provides students the opportunity to learn in a developmentally appropriate environment.

VISION

The school will establish and implement a framework for school change that incorporates—

- site-based management
- shared decision making driven by information and analysis of school processes
- strategic quality planning
- utilization of quality analytical tools
- professional development and support for continuous learning
- parent, business, and community involvement
- comprehensive, ongoing evaluation that assures continuous improvement in becoming World Class Quality and meeting the academic and personal needs of students preparing for work in the 21st Century

Figure 20

Example Elementary School Plan: Curriculum

Area	Professional Development/ Resources	Who	Cost	Source
• Continue to align primary curriculum with developmentally appropriate practices	Ongoing dialogue and peer support	• RC • Primary Staff • RSP/Psych.	$680	District Developmental Education
• Adapt Mathlands to multi-age level	Planning time and peer support • Mentors	• Staff	$680	District Developmental Education
• Extend developmentally appropriate practices to the Intermediate Academy levels, continue support at the primary level	Professional Development	• CURAT • Consultant	$8,000	• H-A Grant • Developmental Education
• Increase student competency in use of technology for multimedia presentations	• Presentation software • Professional Development (extended year)	• RC • SP	$2,000 1,750	• H-A Grant • SBCP
• Continue diversity awareness	Time on extended year	Principal		
• Expand on current plans to promote a safe environment (cross-age buddies; life skills; Challenge Day; ITI Thoughtful Education	• ITI Summer Institute • Professional Development • Planning time	• CURAT • RC	$12,000	• SBCP • H-A Grant • Mentor • PTA
• Expand cross-age buddy program		CURAT		
• Begin developing resource bank at each grade level aligned with units of study • Purchase instructional materials	Time on extended year	• Staff • Volunteers • RC	$5,000	• H-A Grant • Developmental Education • SBCP
• Expand arts program	• District music teacher • MOCHA Art Program	• CURAT • Principal	$9,000	• SBCP • H-A Grant • PTA
• Use Learner Profile for Mathland assessment	Peer coaching	• RC • SP		
• Plan/Implement Family Math/Science Festival		Teacher reps. at each level	$100	SBCP
• Explore developmental programs for outdoor education • Continue Academy Science week		• RC • CURAT	$3,000	• PTA • H-A Grant
• Implement year two of Technology Plan		RC	$24,000	• PTA • H-A Grant • SBCP
		Total Curriculum Cost	$66,210	

AAT	=	Assessment Action Team
CAT	=	Community Action Team
CURAT	=	Curriculum Action Team
H-A	=	Hewlett-Annenberg

RC	=	Reform Coordinator
SBCP	=	School Base Coordinated Program
SP	=	Support Provider

Figure 21

Example Elementary School Plan: Assessment

Area	Professional Development/ Resources	Who	Cost	Source
• Complete intermediate continuums	• Consultants • Time	• RC • Intermediate • Teachers	$755	H-A Grant
• Evaluate portfolio design and content	Grade and cross-grade levels meet once a trimester	AAT	$2,655 subs	H-A Grant
• Measure student progress in reading, writing, math, and science	Grade, cross-grade level, and support staff meet at least once a report card period and extended year	• Staff • CAT • RC	$3,000	• SBCP • H-A Grant
• Administer continuous improvement continuum	Annual activity—January faculty meeting	SP		
• Revise developmental report card	Grade level meeting	• Primary • Teachers		
• Align assessment with AUSD benchmarks and reporting method at intermediate level	Consultant, meeting time (extended year)	• AAT • RC	$1,700	• H-A Grant • Developmental Education • District
• Introduce and pilot Newtons as an assessment tool at upper level	Workshop with mentor and follow-up coaching	• AAT • Mentor • RC	$680	SBCP
• Continue to address parent communication education for development assessment		• AAT • SP • RC		
• Evaluate Newton's effectiveness in lower levels	Meeting with mentor	• AAT • Primary • Teachers		
		Total Assessment Cost	$8,790	

AAT	= Assessment Action Team	RC	=	Reform Coordinator
CAT	= Community Action Team	SBCP	=	School Base Coordinated Program
CURAT	= Curriculum Action Team	SP	=	Support Provider
H-A	= Hewlett-Annenberg			

Figure 22

Example Elementary School Plan: Community

Area	Professional Development/ Resources	Who	Cost	Source
• Administer teacher, parent, and student surveys		• CAT • SP	$100	Site
• Identify parent/community needs for support	Study data	• CAT • RC		
• Continue to search for new partnership developments because of Navy base closure		• CAT • RC		
• Define and outline roles and responsibilities of new partners	Time	• CAT • RC	$510	SBCP
• Improve school environments, physical/emotional/social (i.e., end of trimester celebrations)		• CAT • RC	$5,000	• Site • H-A Grant
• Complete development and continue implementation of landscape plans		• Principal • CAT • RC • Academy	$12,000	• SBCP • PTA • H-A Grant • Grants
• Plan all school events		• Principal • PTA • Staff	$1,200	• District • PTA
		Total Community Cost	$18,810	
OVERALL TOTAL COST $93,810				

AAT	= Assessment Action Team	RC	= Reform Coordinator
CAT	= Community Action Team	SBCP	= School Base Coordinated Program
CURAT	= Curriculum Action Team	SP	= Support Provider
H-A	= Hewlett-Annenberg		

Values and beliefs, purpose, mission, and vision are extremely important to establish as the school improvement process begins. They are the core of the school and are critical throughout the process. Behind these guiding principles is the compelling why of school improvement. The principles must be kept in the forefront throughout the improvement process and throughout every aspect of school operations. Leadership must reinforce and model their use. Planning is very important for schools whether they want to undergo drastic change or not. Too many schools attempt to balance multiple school plans, unsuccessfully. With one comprehensive school plan, priorities can be determined, elements can be leveraged, and a vision can be accomplished.

Table 4 is the Continuous Improvement Continuum for Quality Planning. Using the sections in the continuum, as well as the paraphrased descriptions that follow, assess your school's *approach*, *implementation*, and *outcome* with respect to Quality Planning.

Assessing Your School's Quality Planning

Which statement below best describes your school's *approach* to Quality Planning?

. . . .

Approach

1. The school operates the way it always has operated. Teachers feel there is no need for improvement and no need to utilize data to make any changes.

2. An overall direction has been determined. The school understands the importance of planning and has allocated dollars for that purpose.

3. A shared decision-making structure has been put in place congruent with the mission and vision of the school. The leadership team guides staff toward a comprehensive plan for implementing the school vision. The plan includes evaluation and continuous improvement assessments.

4. A comprehensive strategic plan has been developed for the continuous improvement of the school. Everyone knows the importance of the school plan and her or his own role in its implementation. All school efforts are a part of this plan.

5. The leadership of the school ensures that the comprehensive plan for school improvement and student achievement is implemented throughout the school.

Your assessment _____   Date _____

Which statement below best describes your school's *implementation* of Quality Planning?

. . . .

Implementation

1. With no overall guiding plan, dollars are allocated on an as-needed basis, and individuals in the school determine what work they will perform, independently of others.

2. School personnel begin planning for change by defining the mission, vision, beliefs, and values of the school and the essential student learnings.

3. The comprehensive quality plan for school improvement is in place, complete with its goals, responsibilities, due dates, and timelines. Support structures are set in place to reinforce and enable implementation of the plan.

4. The quality strategic management plan is implemented throughout every element of the school. Everyone knows what to do and why they are doing it. All actions are driven by the school's guiding principles.

5. The mission, vision, and essential student learnings are articulated throughout the school and with feeder schools for the benefit of the students. The attainment of expected student learning standards is linked to the comprehensive effort to plan and improve the quality of instruction for every student.

Your assessment _____   Date _____

Which statement below best describes your school's *outcome* of Quality Planning?

. . . .

Outcome

1. With no plan, and no budget, only crisis items receive attention. Staff members feel that there is an inequality in the way the dollars are allocated.

2. The school community is focused on improving the quality of the school and works on developing a continuous improvement plan.

3. Individual classrooms are clearly implementing the elements of the school's comprehensive plan. However, they are not yet well-linked and improvements are neither systematic nor systemic.

4. It is evident that a schoolwide plan exists and that quality improvement is resulting from this comprehensive plan. Staff are committed to the implementation of the mission and vision of the school. Personnel, monetary, and time resources are allocated in congruence with the plan.

5. With the total commitment to the mission and vision, plans for achieving both are effectively put into place throughout the school. It is evident that teachers are focused on students and on implementing exciting instruction and assessment in the classroom.

Your assessment _____   Date _____

Table 4

Quality Planning

	ONE	TWO	THREE	FOUR	FIVE
APPROACH	No quality plan or process exists. Data are neither used nor considered important in planning.	The staff realizes the importance of a mission, vision, and one comprehensive action plan. Teams develop goals and timelines, and dollars are allocated to begin the process.	A comprehensive school plan to achieve the vision is developed. Plan includes evaluation and continuous improvement.	One focused and integrated schoolwide plan for implementing a continuous improvement process is put into action. All school efforts are focused on the implementation of this plan that represents the achievement of the vision.	A plan for the continuous improvement of the school, with a focus on students, is put into place. There is excellent articulation and integration of all elements in the school due to quality planning. Leadership team ensures all elements are implemented by all appropriate parties.
IMPLEMENTATION	There is no knowledge of or direction for quality planning. Budget is allocated on an as-needed basis. Many plans exist.	School community begins continuous improvement planning efforts by laying out major steps to a shared vision, by identifying values and beliefs, the purpose of school, a mission, vision, and essential student learnings.	Implementation goals, responsibilities, due dates, and timelines are spelled out. Support structures for implementing the plan are set in place.	The quality management plan is implemented through effective procedures in all areas of the school. Everyone knows what she/he needs to do, and when it needs to be done to accomplish the school goals.	Schoolwide goals, mission, vision, and essential student learnings are shared and articulated throughout the school and with feeder schools. The attainment of identified essential student learnings is linked to planning and implementation of effective instruction that meets students' needs.
OUTCOME	There is no evidence of comprehensive planning. Staff work is carried out in isolation. A continuum of learning for students is absent.	The school community understands the benefits of working together to implement a comprehensive continuous improvement plan.	There is evidence that the school plan is being implemented in some areas of the school. Improvements are neither systematic nor integrated schoolwide.	A schoolwide plan is known to all. Results from working toward the quality improvement goals are evident throughout the school.	Evidence of effective teaching and learning results in significant improvement of student achievement attributed to quality planning at all levels of the school organization. Teachers understand and share the school mission and vision, the impact and importance of quality planning, and accountability.

Items That Might Be Found In the
Quality Planning Section of the School Portfolio

The following are appropriate items for inclusion in this section:

- School's assessments on the Quality Planning Continuous Improvement Continuum
- Descriptions of the school's—
  - analysis of what needs to change, unless it can be found in another section
  - purpose, mission, vision, values, and beliefs,
  - description of how this vision will meet the needs of students
  - goals
  - improvement plan
  - other plans or requirements of regulatory organizations
  - action plan
  - budget plan
- How the school plan was developed, how it was able to get the commitment of staff, and how it was used
- Evidence of use of the overall school plan (implementation) and effectiveness
- Goals for next year in the area of planning
- Analysis of what needs to happen to move to the next steps in the continuum

Quality Planning Questions

The following questions are designed to help you thing about what your school has in evidence of where you are with regard to Quality Planning.

What do you have for documentation for the Quality Planning section of your school portfolio?

What other things do you need to gather and document in the Quality Planning section?

What are your next steps with staff with respect to Quality Planning?

Schools committed to improvement must reculture themselves for change. They must establish new systems for teamwork, communication, and collaboration. These schools must create new norms of behavior, and must develop leadership and continuous improvement skills in all employees. This process of creating a new school culture requires that teachers, principals, and staff be able to work well together—to communicate clearly and effectively with each other, and to trust and respect each other.

Chapter 7

PROFESSIONAL DEVELOPMENT

In effect, most schools working to improve are asking staff to change significantly the manner in which they work—how they make decisions; analyze and use data; plan for change; teach; monitor student achievement; evaluate and train personnel; and, assess the impact of new approaches to instruction and student assessment.

Improving schools also ask staff to change significantly the manner in which they *think* about work—to replace assumptions and hunches, especially about students and their learning, with facts; to open up their classroom doors and work with colleagues in teams; and, to consider their every action in terms of its impact on others and the learning organization.

Ongoing professional development activities that are planned in congruence with the school goals and calendar provide school staff with opportunities both to improve personal performance and to learn the new skills they need to reform the school culture and support the development of a true learning organization.

> *The greatest waste in America is failure to use the abilities of people. Training is essential to an employee carrying out his work with satisfaction. There should be a continual education and improvement of everyone on the job—self-improvement.*
>
> W. Edwards Deming

There are two major categories of professional development training discussed in this chapter that are crucial to the success of the school improvement process.

Training that—

+ provides staff with the skills needed to reculture the school
+ helps staff transform curriculum and instructional approaches in the classroom related to the shared vision

The former is the glue that keeps the school improvement process going—systems thinking, communication, teamwork, and collaboration. The latter, supported by the implementation and evaluation components identified in this chapter, ensures implementation of new teaching strategies in the classroom.

Professional Development for School Improvement

Systems Thinking

School is a complex, interdependent, interrelated, and interactive system made up of parts. These parts must be congruent and work together effectively in order for a school to become a true learning organization. Teachers and other school employees need to understand and appreciate systems thinking, the complexities of the school system, and how their individual efforts have an effect—good or bad—on other people's efforts. Professional development, as it relates to systems thinking, centers around—

> *A system is an interconnected complex of functionally related components that work together to try to accomplish the aim of the system.*
>
> W. Edwards Deming

+ understanding the purpose and processes of the school
+ understanding the current and projected customers of the school and their needs
+ establishing school community values and beliefs
+ creating a mission and vision with all members of the school community that are shared collectively and continually
+ planning together to create a congruent comprehensive quality organization that has taken all processes of the organization into account
+ understanding the areas of greatest leverage for overall change related to the vision
+ skill building for performing in a new organization

Without a focus on systems thinking, changes frequently are implemented in a piecemeal fashion, sometimes with unintended consequences. The example that follows illustrates the point.

Ideal High School increased its mathematics graduation requirements in response to criticism that students were graduating without being able to think or perform mathematically. Because appropriate changes in instruction and assessment were not also made, this change led to a dramatic increase in students failing mathematics, and an increase in the number of students dropping out of school—not what the teachers intended.

If Ideal High School staff had evaluated the problem from a systems thinking perspective, they would have, at minimum, determined why students were graduating without necessary mathematical skills. Next, they would have reviewed current processes and practices and analyzed how and what students had learned in the past. They would have then worked with the school community to derive student learning standards for mathematics and determine what resources they needed for students to achieve them. Then the teachers would have received appropriate training and used their new skills to coach students in achieving the standards, and to analyze the impact of the changes on the overall learning organization. However, before systems thinking can take hold and before the individuals within the school can share its vision, a positive culture that supports collaboration and teamwork must be established.

Reculturing the School for Change

Reculturing means changing the culture of the school (traditions, behavior patterns, beliefs, and communication structures) so that the culture is conducive to and supportive of change. Neither the use of shared decision making nor professional development alone will automatically establish a culture conducive to change. A school culture ready for improvement consists of colleagues able to share their personal values, beliefs, and visions; able to communicate and collaborate with one another to build and implement a shared vision and mission; and, able to trust each other enough to behave in a manner consistent with a new school mission and vision.

> *You cannot continuously improve interdependent systems and processes until you progressively perfect interdependent, interpersonal relationships.*
>
> Stephen Covey

Building the capacity of individuals in an organization to share a vision and collaborate with each other requires that four basic human needs be met—the need for human growth and development, the need to be treated well, the need to contribute and have meaning, and the need to be treated fairly (Covey, 1989, 1992, 1994).

These needs must be met in professional development training in just the same way that students' basic needs have to be met before they can learn. School staff must know that training will lead to personal growth and that they will be treated well in win-win relationships with colleagues and leaders. They must be able to attach personal meaning to the school's vision. They must believe that the investment in learning new skills will contribute to the school's vision and to the good of the cause.

If the needs of the individuals who make up the school are not met, the culture will never be conducive to change. Consequently, the school vision will never be realized. After all, it is the unmet needs that motivate individuals—not the satisfied needs.

Communication and Collaboration

Teachers in traditional schools are typically isolated, autonomous, and concerned primarily with their own classrooms. Shared decision making, school improvement efforts, and systems thinking make the improvement of the system and the continuum of student learning every school employee's concern, requiring strong communication and collaboration skills from each individual involved and an end to the isolation and autonomy that teachers have grown used to.

> *The key to effective communication is trust. The key to trust is trustworthiness.*
>
> Stephen Covey

The success of any shared decision-making and school improvement process is dependent upon staff understanding both the system and their roles in that system. Success also depends upon effective communication practices that connect the parts of the system. Professional development that promotes effective communication and collaboration is necessary to maximize the interconnectedness of the system and to enable colleagues to work together to understand what and how to change.

The ultimate goal of effective communication is to help teachers and staff develop a collegial organization characterized by purposeful, adult-level interactions focused on the teaching and learning of students. Staff must know how to communicate before they can solve problems together and create a comprehensive learning environment.

Teachers will collaborate when they understand that they are a part of a larger system, that their individual actions impact the system, and that collaboration is necessary to create and implement a shared vision. However, teachers will not collaborate if they do not feel respected.

Skills related to communication, collaboration, and leadership include effective listening, positive interpersonal communication, win-win negotiating, team building, problem solving, decision making, consensus building, conducting effective meetings, delegating, and representing others.

Norms of Behavior for Collegiality

A culture of strong communication, collaboration, and risk-taking can lead to true systemic change. School organizations, working to have employees communicate and collaborate in ways that are unfamiliar to them, are wise to establish norms of behavior congruent with the mission, vision, values, and beliefs of the organization.

Norms establish guidelines that encourage and reinforce the new desired behaviors. Norms need to focus on win-win strategies to establish adult-level interactions about students. Accountability and consequences must also be established and agreed upon by staff to reinforce new behavior.

> *When placed in the same system, people, however different, tend to produce similar results.*
>
> Peter Senge

An example follows.

Figure 23

Example: Norms of Behavior

- Each member of this school will strive to understand the other person before trying to be understood.
- We will not make assumptions. We will ask for clarification.
- We will not talk behind each other's backs.
- There will be no cross-talk in open meetings.
- Feelings will be expressed openly, without judgment.
- We want to be respected.
- There is no such thing as failure; there are only results.
- There are win-win solutions to every problem. We will find them.
- Our commitment is to help every student succeed. All of our actions are focused on this commitment.
- We value trust and will act with trustworthiness.

We are each accountable to the other to uphold the intent of these guidelines. When we all work together to behave in a manner that will increase our abilities to meet the needs of students, our reward will be the achievement of our outcomes—increased student achievement.

Team Building

Did you ever wonder what it would take to capture the team spirit in a school staff in the same way that an athletic coach captures the team spirit in a baseball team? What does a successful baseball team have that some school teams do not have?

Successful teams have the following eight characteristics in common (Larson and LaFasto, 1989):

- A clear, elevating goal
- A results-driven structure
- Competent members
- A unified commitment
- A collaborative climate
- Standards of excellence
- External support and recognition
- Principled leadership

It is true that successful baseball teams know why they are doing what they are doing, what it takes to win, including how to work together, how to utilize team members' strengths to win, and what the rewards are. Successful baseball teams have strong coaches who set the standards and create the climate to win. Neither incompetent individuals nor those uncommitted to winning are allowed to play.

> *It's easy to get the players. Getting 'em to play together, that's the hard part.*
>
> — Casey Stengel

Team building is a process of aligning and developing the capacity of the team (team learning) to attain the results its members truly desire. With school improvement, the result desired is the achievement of a shared vision. Team learning builds on personal mastery. "Personal mastery is the discipline of continually clarifying and deepening our personal vision, of focusing our energies, of developing patience, and of seeing reality objectively...it is an essential cornerstone of the learning organization" (Senge, P. 1994).

Team building can lead a school staff to a cohesive team spirit stimulated by a common vision and sense of bonding, provided two major elements exist: a collaborative climate and a trustworthy leader capable of moving the team to the vision. It can increase morale, trust, cohesiveness, communication, commitment, productivity, and can ensure staff that they are not in it alone. Team building is necessary if a school wants to establish an atmosphere characterized by continuous discussions of substantial educational concerns.

In many schools it takes a two- to four-day retreat, away from the school, to establish a team focused on a shared vision, to lay a foundation for team communication, and to begin staff bonding. This first stage in team building is largely spent learning about colleagues' strengths, learning to appreciate them for who they are, and learning process skills that enable staff to interact with a constructive and productive focus on the ultimate outcome.

Team building is accomplished not just during professional development training or staff retreats. Team leaders must understand and reinforce the steps in building and maintaining strong, effective teams on an ongoing basis.

Professional Development for New Teaching Strategies

A continuously improving school links new approaches to assessment, curriculum, instruction, professional development, and teacher evaluation together with collective values and beliefs and the school mission and vision, to positively impact student learnings. New skills and understandings are necessary for teachers to successfully make these linkages and to implement these new approaches fully and confidently.

> *In a perfectly rational society the best of us would be teachers and the rest of us would have to settle for something less.*
>
> Lee Iacocca

In order for professional development training to increase the skills and knowledge of teachers in a manner that leads to *classroom implementation* of these new skills and knowledge, the training must be ongoing, planned well in advance, be congruent with the overall school plan and vision, and have an implementation component (such as peer coaching or collaborative teacher action research) that works in conjunction with a support/accountability component (such as staff-developed rubrics).

One-shot staff development days and the "cafeteria approach" to professional development (whereby individual teachers choose a workshop to attend on the new concepts they want to learn more about) do not result in classroom change. Planned, ongoing training with an implementation component and accountability does. It will also lead to *schoolwide implementation* where the school culture is conducive to change, and when changes in the organization are congruent and work in conjunction with individual improvement.

Professional development activities must be a key part of the school's improvement goals and plans, congruent with the school mission, vision, values, and beliefs, and planned in advance as a priority on the school calendar.

111

Districts can have a great impact on a school's successful professional development practices by supporting and encouraging a comprehensive school plan based upon the school's vision, and by not interfering with planned professional development days. An example of a professional development plan is shown as Figure 24.

Implementation Components

Professional development training, used in conjunction with an implementation component such as peer coaching and/or collaborative action research, supports the attainment of new skills as it helps to build a collaborative school environment—provided there exists a school culture conducive to change.

Peer coaching, combined with the acquisition of new teaching skills, is an expedient, positive, and supportive way for teachers to implement new strategies in the classroom. Peer coaching consists of teachers establishing teams. Working together at the classroom level, these teams meet to establish individual goals that are congruent with the overall school goals. They also plan for the implementation of these goals, observe each other's classrooms, and meet in postobservation conferences to provide *positive* feedback and support for each other's implementation efforts. The use of peer coaching requires a solid action plan, effective communication skills, incentive, and some means of accountability.

Collaborative action research focuses on preventing student failure through identifying and understanding the impact of the teacher's actions and activities on individual student learning, and by making changes to these actions and activities based upon research findings. This requires analyzing diagnostic information on each child, including historical performance measures, root causes of problems, and learning how to reduce special cause variations.

Collaborative action research can focus on hypotheses, specific questions, implementing new strategies, or general impact. Used throughout a school, collaborative action research can bring staff together to discuss positive approaches to articulating learning across grade levels, or other student groupings, content areas or developmental levels. Working with colleagues, individual teachers determine how to continually improve their teaching. A teacher action research example was described in Chapter 5, page 71.

Figure 24

One Year Professional Development Plan

	SEPT	OCT	NOV	DEC	JAN	FEB	MAR	APR	MAY	JUN	JUL	AUG
Full staff retreat with facilitator • Team building: communication skills • Revisit mission, values, beliefs • Establish shared decision-making structure • Leadership training: effective meetings • Coming to consensus										3 days		
Small groups meet to— • Refine new shared decision-making structure • Write strategic school plan											✓	✓
Individuals plan for the personal implementation of school plan and vision Individuals study approaches and read research											✓	✓
Full staff retreat with facilitator Review, refine, and come to consensus on summer teamwork: • Agree on implementation procedures and professional development for the year • Continue to clarify roles and responsibilities • Continue leadership training												2 days
Action teams meet to study and discuss approaches to the implementation of the school plan and goals • Team leaders keep leadership team informed of team progress	✓ ✓	✓ ✓	✓ ✓	✓ ✓	✓ ✓	✓ ✓	✓ ✓	✓ ✓				✓ ✓
Action teams make recommendation presentations to leadership team					✓							
Leadership team integrates the action team recommendations into a strategic plan for implementation					✓	✓	✓					
Present plan to full staff for review and approval						✓	✓					
New action team structure is developed for implementation							✓					
Implementation teams develop plan for implementing school plan							✓	✓				
Present plan to leadership team and revise							✓					
Present plan for approval to full staff								✓				

A *teacher portfolio* can be an extremely effective vehicle for assisting with the implementation of new strategies and concurrently monitoring the impact of those strategies on student achievement. Staff who adopt a teacher portfolio approach should determine the content of a portfolio together so that the content supports the school goals as well as the goals of individual teachers. When determining the content for teachers' portfolios, consider using teacher evaluation criteria and focus on the changes that need to be made in order to implement the school vision.

Teacher portfolios can be a compilation of professional effort that focuses on the teacher's role within the context of a larger learning organization. A portfolio is also an excellent storage place for professional analyses that lead to the continuous improvement of the teacher and her/his students. Sections of a teacher portfolio might include the following:

About Being a Teacher

Establishes the background of the teacher, the context for the portfolio, and reflections of the individual as a teacher. Includes elements that are important to the learning organization, for instance, values and beliefs and personal vision for the school.

Information and Analysis

Describes the students, their past and current assessment results, their needs, and establishes critical focus areas.

Classroom Environment

Helps determine the congruence of the setting for the goals attempted.

Student Achievement

Describes effectiveness of current processes and establishes plans for improvement based upon data. Should include student work, including examples of quality work.

Professional Development

Describes and reflects on past professional development and establishes plans for effective future professional development.

<u>Parent, Business, and Community Involvement</u>

Describes past partnerships, and reasons, desires, and plans for effective partnerships in the classroom.

<u>Continuous Improvement</u>

Includes a description of what is, plans for improvement, and how these plans relate to the larger learning organization.

Teacher Evaluation

To reinforce the importance of the impact a teacher's actions can have upon school improvement, the evaluation or appraisal of personnel must be considered within the goals of the larger learning organization. Teacher evaluation can be designed so that it leads to real classroom improvement while reinforcing the implementation of school goals. It must measure what is important to the overall learning organization. If team work is an important attribute to the role of the teacher in the new organization, a teacher's ability to function as a contributing team member is something that needs to be evaluated or measured. If the improvement of teaching strategies is important, the plan for improvement needs to be clearly defined and its implementation measured.

Traditional teacher evaluations neither assess teamwork nor the context of the school in determining how well the individual has performed. They seldom ask the teacher to reflect on her or his performance in a meaningful way or to be analytical about student performance. As a consequence, traditional teacher evaluations often foster mediocrity, destroy motivation and self-esteem, and do not lead to improved personal performance.

Through professional development structured to support school improvement, teachers learn about the current organization and about the organization they want to create. They also learn that their actions and knowledge have an impact upon the larger learning organization—extremely important information for teachers to use effectively.

Teacher portfolios, peer coaching, and collaborative action research combined with self-assessment strategies provide extremely positive tools for non-traditional teacher evaluations. The goal is to strategize for a win-win-win across the board—meet the requirements for teacher evaluation and support teacher improvement, student achievement increases, collegial conversations, action research, performance reflection, collaboration, teamwork, and the implementation of new school goals.

Professional Development for Non-teaching Staff

What about professional development for staff members other than teachers? Should they attend professional development activities? Should they have their own training? The answer to both is a resounding *absolutely*.

All persons within an organization need to understand their role and how their performance impacts the total organization. Classified staff need to understand what their positions should look like, sound like, and feel like in order for them to perform the best job imaginable in the new organization. Professional development for classified staff can help them understand how to perform their roles in the most professional manner. Attending professional development training for the teaching staff helps classified staff understand teachers' goals, to understand what they can do to support the teachers' goals, and to ensure the congruence of all parts of the system. To illustrate this point, an example follows:

> *An organization's commitment to and capacity for learning can be no greater than that of its members.*
>
> Peter Senge

Eastwood school is located in a high crime area with little support for student learning in the home. Many of the students who go to Eastwood do not have fathers living at home.

The first person to arrive at the school each morning is John, the custodian. He arrives around 5:30 a.m. to make sure the school is ready for the day. Within 15 minutes, as many as ten little boys appear at the school to "hang around" John. They follow him, sometimes help him, many times ask his advice on their personal problems. Mostly they just want to be with him. John asked if he could attend the professional development training that teachers had at the school. He was concerned that he did not know what he should be saying to the students when they asked his advice. Also, he knew the teachers' goals were to treat children with respect and fairness. He wanted to know what they did, so he could act consistently and support their efforts.

The teachers were delighted to have John join them. It hadn't occurred to them that the classified staff needed the same kinds of information that they did. It also did not occur to them how little training classified staff get once they are on the job. John not only learned much about how to treat and motivate children within the context of the new school goals, he brought with him a perspective that helped the teachers understand the students better.

The keys to professional development training that will lead to successful school improvement and real change in the classroom are to—

- *make sure the content, approach, and efficacy of the training will help the school reach its vision*
- *make sure everyone shares the same vision, and knows what she or he is expected to implement*
- *plan and schedule the training well in advance*
- *add a support and implementation component that has an element of accountability, and provides the time to use it effectively*
- *determine incentives for committing staff to ongoing, long-term professional development (e.g., the implementation process combined with self-assessment and planning will replace the current evaluation process)*
- *make sure all staff are involved in appropriate professional development*

Assessing Your School's Professional Development

Table 5 is the Continuous Improvement Continuum for Professional Development. Using the sections in the continuum, as well as the paraphrased descriptions that follow, assess your school's *approach*, *implementation*, and *outcome* with respect to Professional Development.

Which statement below best describes your school's *approach* to Professional Development?

. . . .

Approach

1. Leadership sees no reason to provide training. Somebody else can do the job. In other words, if someone is considered incompetent, the prevailing thought is to get rid of the person.

2. A school beginning a shared decision-making structure understands the need to receive training in leadership, because this is something nobody at the school has done before. The school also understands that teachers must do things differently in their classrooms. Independently, teachers are allowed to choose the professional development activities they want to take. Leadership might also bring in many different professional development experts to present one-day workshops on specific content areas. However, the school must rely on the school improvement days allocated to them by the district.

3. Everybody in the school recognizes the need for quality professional development training. This need and a plan for its implementation are spelled out in the school plan. The training is ongoing throughout the school year and combines theory and peer collaboration with practice.

4. The entire staff at the school is committed to continuous improvement. Teams of teachers continue to study and disseminate the research to understand how they can better meet the needs of all students in their classes. The principal as a team member works with teachers to analyze and implement classroom improvement strategies that replace traditional teacher evaluation. Quality professional development training related to the school mission and vision drives the plan.

5. Staff members passionately embrace the concept of continuous personal and professional improvement as a means of ensuring that they are doing everything humanly possible for every student to succeed. Teachers use collaborative action research in specific areas to improve their performance.

    Your assessment _____   Date _____

Which statement below best describes your school's *implementation* with respect to Professional Development?

· ·

Implementation

1. There is no professional development. Staff evaluations are inspections for error; performance evaluations often lead to firing if there are too many mistakes.

2. Without a plan for professional development, teachers are trained in a variety of new instructional strategies, in a manner that does not lead to long-term, or even short-term changes in the classroom. All staff, or maybe just the members of the leadership team, receive training in shared decision making to learn how to make and share decisions at the school level.

3. The entire school community is provided with quality training in shared decision making, including such skills as conducting effective meetings, team-building, communications, and utilizing continuous improvement tools for decision making. Teachers begin to organize into teams to receive training.

4. Teachers receive training in new skills and how to collaborate in teams to implement the new skills. Teacher teams analyze classroom results, hypothesize about how to make improvements in the results, discuss teaching research, and support each other in making appropriate changes. Time is provided for teachers to hold collaborative discussions about improving student achievement and developing a comprehensive learning experience for every student.

5. Teachers synthesize information they have about specific aspects of the instructional strategies they are using to continuously improve their teaching. Information includes student and parent feedback on the instructional program; student assessments and self-assessments; analyses of assessment and instructional strategies; progress toward the achievement of student learning standards; and collaboration.

Which statement below best describes your school's *outcome* with respect to Professional Development?

. . . .

Outcome

1. Without any kind of professional training for individuals, there is no increase in their ability to do the job, except for what experience might bring. There is little ownership for doing a good job, resulting in very low staff morale which is detected by the students. This approach by administrators impacts the manner in which teachers relate to students—mistakes are audited and individuals are allowed to fail.

2. Overall, nothing much is changing at the classroom level to support a new approach to teaching and learning. Teachers are frustrated because they want to implement things they enjoyed learning about in professional development classes, but they do not seem to have much information to rely on once they are back in their classrooms attempting to make the changes. Those who received the leadership training have a difficult time applying the shared decision-making skills.

3. Teachers feel supported in making difficult changes in their classrooms. Due to the training, the school is beginning to take on a new culture, one where staff can communicate effectively with one another and one that provides consistency in dealing with students. Staff are pleased and feel their input about the way the school is organized is being heard through the shared decision-making process. Meetings are effective and efficient.

4. Evidence supports the fact that a true collaborative school has been formed. Teachers feel they can have meaningful discussions with each other on any educational issue, even if they do not agree with each other. The curriculum is articulated across student groupings and subject areas. Increases are noticeable in student achievement.

5. Teachers take pride in the fact that students are receiving a strong continuum of learning throughout the school due to effective training, implementation, and collaboration. Teachers are aware that they are able to adjust instructional approaches as needed to meet the needs of every student in their classroom. They understand the impact of each strategy on students with varying achievement characteristics.

Your assessment _____ Date _____

Table 5

Professional Development

	ONE	TWO	THREE	FOUR	FIVE
APPROACH	There is no professional development. Teachers, principals, and staff are seen as interchangeable parts that can be replaced.	The "cafeteria" approach to professional development is used, whereby individual teachers choose what they want to take, without regard to an overall school plan.	The school plan and student needs are used to target appropriate professional development for all employees. Staff is inserviced in relevant instructional and leadership strategies.	Professional development and data-gathering methods are used by all teachers and are directed toward the goals of continuous improvement. Teachers have ongoing conversations about student achievement research. Other staff members receive training in their roles.	Leadership and staff continuously improve all aspects of the school structure through an innovative and comprehensive continuous improvement process that prevents student failures. Professional development is appropriate, supportive, collegial, effective, systemic, and ongoing. Traditional teacher evaluations are replaced by collegial coaching and action research focused on essential student learnings.
IMPLEMENTATION	Teacher, principal, and staff performance is controlled and inspected. Performance evaluations are used to detect mistakes.	Teacher professional development is sporadic and unfocused, lacking an approach for implementing new procedures and processes. Some leadership training begins to take place.	Teachers are involved in year-round quality professional development. The school community is trained in shared decision making, team building concepts, and effective communication strategies.	Teachers, in teams, continuously set and implement student achievement goals. Leadership considers these goals and ensures appropriateness of professional development. Teachers utilize effective support approaches as they implement new instruction and assessment strategies.	Teams passionately support each other in the pursuit of quality improvement at all levels. Teachers make bold changes in instruction and assessment strategies focused on essential student learnings and student learning styles. A teacher as action researcher model is implemented. Staffwide conversations focus on systemic reflection and improvement.
OUTCOME	No professional growth and no performance improvement. There exists a high turnover rate of employees. Attitudes and approach filter down to students.	The effectiveness of professional development is not known or analyzed. Teachers feel helpless about making schoolwide changes.	Teachers, working in teams, feel supported and begin to feel they can make changes. Evidence shows that shared decision making works.	A collegial school is evident. Effective classroom strategies are practiced, articulated schoolwide, and are reflective of professional development aimed at ensuring student achievement.	True systemic change and improved student achievement result because teachers are knowledgeable of and implement effective teaching strategies for individual student learning styles, abilities, and situations. Teachers are sensitive to and apply approaches that work best for each student.

Items That Might Be Found In the
Professional Development Section of the School Portfolio

The following are appropriate items for inclusion in this section:

- School's assessment on the Professional Development Continuous Improvement Continuum
- Description of the current approach to professional development, including implementation components
- Plan for professional development, including teacher outcomes
- How the plan was determined and how it will assist with school change
- Types of professional development needed to implement the school improvement plan, tied to the mission and vision, and taking into account teachers' individual goals
- Incentives for teachers to want to change current practices
- Professional development calendar for the year, with evidence that time is allotted for professional development
- Structure for communication in the school
- Norms of behavior
- Evaluation of effectiveness of professional development training and implementation
- Evidence that new skills are being implemented
- Budget reflecting professional development needs (might also appear in Quality Planning)
- Teacher and staff performance evaluation processes
- Plans for improvement
- Analysis of what needs to happen to move to the next steps in the continuum
- Photos of staff supporting each other in implementing new ways of doing business

Professional Development Questions

The following questions are designed to help you think about what your school has in evidence of where you are with regard to Professional Development.

What do you have for documentation for the Professional Development section of your school portfolio?

What other things do you need to gather and document in the Professional Development section?

What are your next steps with staff with respect to Professional Development?

In order for schools to become true learning organizations, they must put into place a formal leadership infrastructure that allows necessary improvements—from within the organization and supported outside of the organization. A quality leadership infrastructure emphasizes the prevention of problems (such as student failure) as opposed to short-term fixes or the covering up of problems, and focuses on the creation of a learning organization that encourages everyone to contribute to making school have a cumulative, purposeful effect on student learning.

Chapter 8

LEADERSHIP

Before a meaningful and useful leadership infrastructure can be put into place, there must be an agreed upon purpose for the school; an understanding of the values and beliefs about teaching and learning held by the individuals who make up the school; a mission; and, there must be a clearly defined vision *shared* by these individuals.

Systemic school improvement requires understanding and implementing many new and interrelated components at the same time. Shared decision making and site-based management are structural approaches to school leadership that, when used in conjunction with each other, allow individuals within the organization to create and maintain an effective learning organization.

An essential factor in leadership is the capacity to influence and organize meaning for the members of the organization.

Tom Peters

The evolving roles of the school leaders and teams are extremely important in developing and maintaining a leadership infrastructure that will ensure the comprehensive implementation of the school vision. The school leadership structure must look like the school vision.

Shared Decision Making

Typically in the past, the school principal made all major school decisions. When teacher input was considered, the principal still made the decision, and teachers taught whatever they thought was important for students to know in the isolation of their own classrooms.

In any organization, top-down decision making neither evokes a vision shared by all its workers nor fosters a commitment to that vision. Shared decision making is a school leadership structure determined by those people closest to the "action" which allows them to recommend and make appropriate changes and to take responsibility for these changes. To be effective, shared decision making requires a shared vision, staff commitment, and collaboration. At the same time, shared decision making helps develop that shared vision, that staff commitment, and collaboration. It also tends to improve staff leadership and communication skills.

> *If a school is to foster educated citizenry for a democracy, then the school itself must be an example of a democracy ...*
> *The substance of a school democracy are the decisions that improve the education of students, both collectively and individually, and the quality of educational life for the entire school community.*
>
> Carl Glickman

Shared decision making requires teachers and community members to take on new roles as active decision makers and leaders who keep improvement, the mission, and the vision alive throughout the school community.

Shared decision making by no means implies that the principal no longer makes any of the decisions or that she or he no longer has a role in decision making. The role that each principal assumes in shared decision making varies by school, but most principals ensure staff commitment by becoming facilitators of the improvement process, coaches, cheerleaders, resource and information brokers, team members, and keepers of the vision.

The *benefits of shared decision making* are many—having input into decisions empowers staff, gives shared meaning to the effort, provides motivation to get involved, gives staff an increased sense of commitment, ownership, and professionalism, and develops potential leaders. Schools find that decisions are better and more well-rounded because the people who are the most knowledgeable and who need to implement the decisions are involved in making the decisions. Shared decision making also typically improves communication, accountability, and staff morale in the school.

The *downside of shared decision making* is that full staff input into decisions takes time (to hold meetings and to come to consensus) and occasionally some staff members refuse to be involved. Shared decision making is more work, and teachers and principals often lack skills in facilitating effective meetings and reaching consensus. If a principal is uncomfortable or not knowledgeable about her or his role in shared decision making, there typically is no real shared decision making implemented at that school. An overly controlling or weak principal can keep shared decision making from working, although a strong coordinator, or leadership team leader, can sometimes compensate for the lack of a principal's leadership skills. Similarly, a district's lack of support for shared decision making or its assertion of too much control can squelch any school's efforts. Sometimes it is the district that presents the largest stumbling block to implementing shared decision making at the school level.

Shared Decision-making Structures

Developing a shared decision-making structure responsive to the needs of an individual school takes time. In the beginning, teachers, principals, and staff members experience confusion about their respective roles in shared decision making, largely because each individual has a unique idea of what the process and structure look like. As these individuals work with and through the process, and begin to build a structure using staff ideas, a shared vision for the structure will evolve. This shared vision is necessary for the evolution of a shared decision-making structure that will work best for implementing the school vision.

The intent is to have staff determine the structure—not the principal in isolation of staff. It is also intended that the shared decision-making structure will comprehensively replace old structures—not merely be an addition.

Many different structures can work to involve principals, teachers, staff, and students in shared decision making. The *action team* approach is commonly utilized as the shared decision-making structure of choice when there are changes to be made throughout the school. Action teams are established to—

- study new approaches to improving the school process for meeting students needs
- implement the recommended changes
- lead the improvement process and day-to-day school events
- perform specific work details on an ad hoc basis

Study Teams

Most shared decision-making schools use a system of action *study teams* or committees that take responsibility for researching and making recommendations about specific approaches to achieving the school vision and goals. Study teams conduct vital research activities, such as—

*   investigating new instructional strategies or programs for potential implementation
*   visiting schools that have implemented new strategies and programs
*   analyzing costs and efficacy of implementation at the school
*   evaluating the abilities of the new strategies to meet the needs of the school population
*   determining what it would take to implement
*   formulating an overall timeline for implementation

Ideas for study can come from any direction. They can come from the teams themselves, from principals, district staff, or from teachers on other teams. It is very important that all teachers feel that the input process is open and that everyone's opinion is helpful and appreciated. Study teams usually include representatives of every function that exists in the school community, such as grade level teachers, subject matter teachers, classified staff, school and district administrators, students, parents, and community members.

Implementation Teams

Study teams are often disbanded when their recommendations have been approved for implementation. After a comprehensive school-level action plan is developed from the study team's recommendations, *implementation teams* are formed to give the recommendations meaning and to guide implementation within their jurisdiction, i.e., subject area and student groupings. Implementation teams monitor the timelines and quality of implementation in a supportive fashion.

The structure that implementation teams take is very important for realizing the vision and the school goals. For example, if the vision for a high school is to integrate subject matter with team teaching across the disciplines, the implementation teams should consist of integrated team members and not be set up by subject matter areas. Having the interdisciplinary team plan together, and coach and monitor each other, will greatly assist the implementation of the new strategy throughout the school.

Having a *leadership team* integrate recommendations from the action study teams helps ensure congruence with the school mission, vision, beliefs, and values. The leadership team, most often made up of team leaders from the action teams, administrators, and school community representatives, ensures that the implementation of the new strategies flows in an articulated fashion.

The leadership team is responsible to the full staff. The amount of decision-making power granted to the team by the staff varies from school to school. At the point when final decisions need to be made, some schools rely on whole staff meetings, others use town-hall-style meetings, and still others give authority to the leadership team to make the final decisions. In the former case, the leadership team works as a liaison between the study and implementation teams and the full staff, with final decision-making power held by the full staff. In the latter case, the leadership team takes the recommendations of the action teams, integrates the input, makes the decisions, and then communicates those decisions to the staff.

Example of how action teams evolved at Pelican High School:

After thoroughly analyzing student achievement results over time, students' evaluations of school processes, and the newly developed school vision, Pelican High School teaching staff felt they could better meet the needs of their students if they could decrease the number of students teachers saw every day. They also knew they could provide instruction in an integrated fashion with more "real-world" applications. Staff determined that they needed to look into a school-within-a-school approach; they needed to understand more about the behavior and developmental issues of high-school-age students, as well as new approaches to instruction and assessment, including utilizing technology. The staff divided into teams (Figure 25) to study these issues with respect to the school's vision and mission. Each study team was structured to have representation of each grade level and subject area in the school. Additionally, a leadership team (made up of the leaders of each study team and of school administrators) was developed to monitor and encourage the study teams.

Figure 25

Pelican High School
Study Team Structure

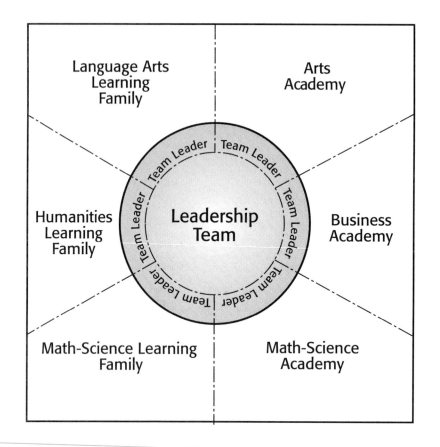

As they worked, study teams reported progress regularly to the leadership team who listened carefully to ensure congruence of each team's focus with the school mission and vision; to make sure the teams were not overlapping efforts when inappropriate and that they were overlapping efforts when appropriate; to gently redirect the teams in meaningful ways when necessary. When the study teams finished their research, they made recommendations to the leadership team and then to full staff. The leadership team was given the charge by the full staff to synthesize the study teams' recommendations and make a comprehensive overall recommendation with an action plan. After the overall recommendation and action plan were approved through total staff consensus, a comprehensive strategic plan was developed by the leadership team which was then reviewed, revised, and *approved by the full staff for implementation. A new shared decision-making structure with implementation action teams (Figure 26) was established, congruent with the strategic plan and the new school structure described in the school vision.*

Figure 26

Pelican High School
Implementation Team Structure

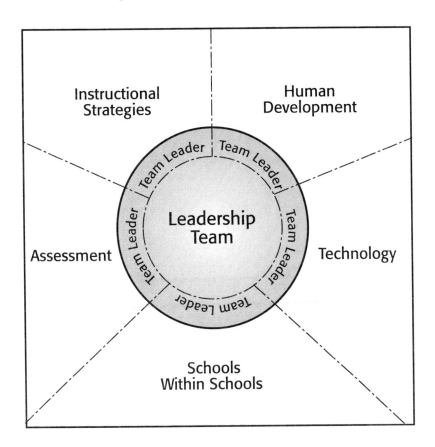

Each implementation team established its own mission and vision with the context of the overall school vision. With respect to shared decision making, the teams determined which decisions would be appropriate for each team to make, which decisions needed full staff consensus, and which decisions could and should be made by the leadership team or the principal alone. Times for meeting were established around the timelines for implementation, and accountability spelled out in the strategic plan.

Ad Hoc Teams

As shared decision making becomes institutionalized, more sophisticated forms of teamwork will evolve for making decisions on specific items or perform specific regular school tasks and then disband. There are specific tasks that schools do every year which can be delegated to ad hoc teams—items that do not require full staff approval and do not directly impact the school improvement efforts, such as staff holiday parties, regulatory program renewals, sports supervision, and parents' night. Ad hoc teams are great for helping to organize the year in advance and to enable staff to plan and perform their work in a proactive manner throughout the year.

There are many *benefits of the action team approach*, as described above. Action teams help schools "divide and conquer" the work by creating a system for dialogue, planning, and research in which everyone can take part and contribute based upon the abilities and interests of each. They create ownership of the process because everyone is involved. Action teams provide a system for sharing the research work so that individual teachers do not need to become "experts" on everything. They provide leadership opportunities and provide individuals with the opportunity to express opinions in small groups rather than in front of the entire school community so more opinions are heard. Action teams provide a forum for staff members who may have particular concerns but are afraid to address them to school administrators. They give teachers of different student groupings and subject areas opportunities to work together, ending years of relative isolation, and reinforce the fact that everyone is committed to doing something different in the classroom. Action teams help schools focus on purpose, student learning standards, student achievement, achievable goals, articulation across student groupings, and establish a new culture of collaboration for the school.

There are *downsides to the action team approach*, including the amount of time required to hold meetings, to research issues, to share information, and to reach consensus. There may be scheduling conflicts until the team structure is institutionalized, and a lack of participation by some staff members. Sometimes, there is a lack of support by the district. The logistical difficulty in communicating effectively with everybody in the school may be a problem at schools with year-round and multiple-track schedules.

Leader of the Leadership Team

Because of the enormity of the task of establishing a shared decision-making structure, and of implementing school improvement, things will run much smoother if someone is assigned, or elected by staff, to coordinate the efforts. This leader or coordinator is usually not the principal, although, in some situations, the principal may be the most appropriate person. This person also plays a key leadership role as a keeper of the school vision and mission, ensuring that everyone stays involved, on track, and committed to improvement. Overall, leaders must be well-organized, capable of visualizing the big picture, dedicated to improvement, thick-skinned, and approachable. The leader's responsibilities might include the following tasks:

- Serve as primary communication contact within the school and outside of the school, including serve as public and community relations officer for the improvement effort.

- Keep the "big picture"—school vision, mission, values, and beliefs—in the forefront.

- Monitor the shared decision-making structure, develop agendas, and facilitate leadership team meetings.

- Supervise and coach action teams.

- Coordinate the budget.

- Attend district meetings to keep the two-way communication flowing.

- Plan retreats.

- Schedule and monitor staff development activities.

- Assist with the recruiting of partnerships with business and community groups.

- Delegate tasks to share the work that staff and leadership determine is needed.

- Downplay personal viewpoints and agendas, and work to consolidate ideas.

- Be a good listener and sounding board for ideas.

The role of leader requires tremendous time and energy, although, as the school community becomes more familiar with the principles of shared decision making, the leader's role becomes less strenuous. Some schools use co-leaders to ease the time constraints for individuals who may also have classroom teaching duties. Other schools have restructured their staff workload to have at least one teacher on special assignment who can lead their school improvement efforts. The shared decision-making leader is such an important person for school improvement that revamping the school budget to institutionalize the position would be smart for schools that plan to improve continuously.

Site-based Management

Site-based or school-based management allows important decisions about learning activities and student achievement to take place at the school site, with all stakeholders involved in that decision. Site-based management is neither about having the school secede from the district nor is it about no longer having district participation and oversight. Once a school has established its mission and goals within the context of the district's mission and goals, site-based management leaves it to the school to achieve its goals in its own way. It gives schools the ability to make decisions about budget, curriculum, and personnel—independently of the district.

This process of decentralizing decision making has encountered as much resistance from district level administrators as shared decision making has from principals at some school sites. In many cases, district staff agree with the notion of site-based management in principle, but feel the schools do not know enough to merit autonomy.

Similar to the role of the principal in shared decision making, the role of the school district's staff in site-based management needs to evolve so that district staff provides needed support and cooperation, but does not impose final decisions about how a school should operate. Ultimately, the district should become the deliverer of services and support to their customers—the schools.

Superintendents claim minor roles in school improvement in their district, but in reality their policies at the district level have a huge impact on the success of improvement at the individual school level. In general, the role of superintendent needs to evolve along with that of the district staff to support the schools when they begin to take on new roles. After all, what is the purpose of a school district if it is not to support its schools in providing the best education possible for the students?

Some districts are unprepared for the change of pace and the innovations adopted by their schools. The best way to keep the district supportive of school improvement efforts is to give them a role, keep them informed at all times, work with them to help them understand the compelling *why* of the school's approaches to change, and help them understand what it will look like when it is implemented to alleviate any concerns about accountability. Eventually a supportive relationship will evolve that allows the school to make the improvements it feels and knows is necessary. In a matter of time, the school's innovations will be shared throughout the entire district.

One of the major *benefits of site-based management* is that it gives school staff more responsibility and ownership of the process of school improvement. Positive improvements made at one school will begin to spread to other schools throughout the district as teachers and principals share their experiences. At some point the district will see the need to evolve its own processes and procedures to serve the schools within a new vision for the district.

On the downside, district involvement, bureaucratic red tape, and antiquated district policies and procedures can slow the pace of school change. Obtaining waivers is a difficult, time-consuming process that many schools must continue to endure until site-based management matures.

Keys to Effecting Shared Decision Making and Site-based Management

Shared decision making works when there is *commitment* of team members to attend meetings, and to share ideas, opinions, and the work; *trust* in fellow teachers and in the process of improvement itself; constant *communication* between leaders and their team members, with other leaders and other teams; a *mixture* of team members who are detailists and visionaries, and somebody to bring it all together gracefully; support and *leadership* of the principal; and, *support* and leadership of school district administration. Team building, communication training, commitment, collaboration, leadership training, and experience are necessary ingredients to move from a traditional structure to an effective shared decision-making structure. Action teams and/or a shared decision-making structure must be site specific, determined by staff, not the principal, designed to ensure implementation of school goals, flexible enough to accommodate change, and congruent with the school goals and tasks that need to be performed.

Shared decision making will not work until regular meeting times for action and leadership teams are built into the school week, preferably by rearranging the work week to create the time. Meetings must be effective, efficient, and professional to keep people focused and working on the vision, and to keep them coming to meetings. This includes setting and distributing the agenda before meetings, sticking to agenda times, allowing everyone to speak, delegating tasks, and distributing minutes to all staff members after the meeting. It also means letting go of the old structures/committees/meetings that are no longer congruent with the new school vision (e.g., department meetings).

Consensus is an extremely important element of the shared decision-making process. Consensus makes the difference between all staff implementing a vision and only some staff implementing the vision. Consensus is not a vote, not majority rule. It is coming to a decision that everyone can live with and will implement. Voting leaves some people who will not get their way, leading to their lack of implementation.

The decision to use shared decision making and site-based management should be made by the school staff. Staff will know if these approaches are appropriate for their vision, and they should determine whether they are capable of implementing either approach. These innovative structures should never be mandated.

The important piece is for the leadership structure to resemble the vision.

Leaders are keepers of the vision. In a continuously improving school, the job of leadership is to help those in the organization understand their individual role in implementing the vision.

The keys to effective shared decision making include: designing a leadership structure that looks like the vision; ensuring that everyone in the organization knows their role; and, clearly defining who makes what decisions, when.

Table 6 is the Continuous Improvement Continuum for Leadership. Using the sections outlined in the continuum, as well as the paraphrased descriptions that follow, assess your school's *approach, implementation,* and *outcome* with respect to Leadership.

Which statement below best describes your school's *approach* to Leadership?

. . . .

Approach

1. No structure exists to solicit or obtain staff input on how the school operates. Decisions are reactive to state and district mandates, and the principal is the top-down leader.

2. Staff get school community commitment to develop a new leadership structure, mission, and vision for the school which they believe will improve student achievement. Most decisions are reactive and are focused on solving immediate problems.

3. Commitment to the school vision solidifies. Members of the leadership team begin to understand their roles and the role of staff in relation to the mission of the school. Leadership works to keep staff involved, committed to, and working toward the vision. Leadership establishes study teams and provides time to gather and analyze information and to study different approaches to reaching the school vision.

4. The leadership team makes comprehensive management decisions based on study team recommendations. Roles are clear and known by all: which decisions are made by whom; how decisions receive staff input and are communicated to the staff. The focus is on students and the vision.

5. Information-based, shared decision making with a focus on students is the culture of the school. The vision for the school is implemented and continuously evaluated for improvement across the grade levels (or student groupings) and into the next level of schooling. Community members are involved in meaningful and active ways in the operations of the school. The district is confident that the school is operating in an efficient and effective manner.

Your assessment _____   Date _____

Which statement below best describes your school's *implementation* with respect to Leadership?

. . . .

Implementation

1. Teachers work in isolation of each other and, for the most part, feel they have no voice in decision making.

2. A shared decision-making structure for school improvement is formed and teaching teams are designated. All begin to focus on the school plan and student learning standards.

3. The school community volunteers to serve on study teams consisting of representatives of all the grade levels, or other student grouping structures, staff, and community. Time is restructured to enable the study teams to meet during the week. The teams focus their recommendations on improving student learning. A structure for communicating, discussing, and integrating team recommendations is effectively utilized by the leadership team.

4. Teachers and school community feel they have a voice in decision making since the leadership team acts on their study team recommendations in implementing the school vision. There is a culture of collegiality at the school.

5. The shared decision-making structure is institutionalized in the school and is congruent with district structures. Meetings are effective and efficient, and communication is excellent. Students are the focus of school decision making and professional conversations. Teachers continue to implement, evaluate, and improve on the new strategies they are implementing in their classrooms.

Your assessment _____   Date _____

Which statement below best describes your school's *outcome* with respect to Leadership?

. . . .

Outcome

1. There is little staff buy-in to leadership decisions and/or little staff interest in the overall operations of the school. School does not have a cumulative effect for students.

2. Making the transition to shared decision making results in frustration at times; however, the school community is excited about gaining the opportunity to shape the future for their students. The leadership team struggles with who makes what decisions and how to use the mission effectively in decision making.

3. An effective shared decision-making structure begins to emerge. The entire school community feels involved in the possibilities for an exciting, improved school. There might still be occasional problems in implementation, such as the dissemination of information.

4. All teachers are planning together and supporting each other's implementation of new strategies. Teachers feel excited about learning new skills and know that the new approaches will have a positive impact on student learning. They see the challenge and student rewards in working toward continuous improvement.

5. Teachers know they operate the school with students as the focus. Their communications with each other are professional and often center on student learning. Through their study and discussion they are learning how to prevent student failures. The improvements in the classroom are making a difference in student achievement. Teachers know that school improvement has no end.

Your assessment _____   Date _____

Table 6

Leadership

		ONE	TWO	THREE	FOUR	FIVE
APPROACH		Principal as decision maker. Decisions are reactive to state, district, and federal mandates. There is no knowledge of continuous improvement.	A shared decision making structure is put into place and discussions begin on how to achieve a school vision. Most decisions are focused on solving problems and are reactive.	Leadership team is committed to continuous improvement. Leadership seeks inclusion of all school sectors and supports study teams by making time provisions for their work.	Leadership team represents a true shared decision making structure. Study teams are reconstructed for the implementation of a comprehensive continuous improvement plan.	A strong continuous improvement structure is set into place that allows for input from all sectors of the school, district, and community, ensuring strong communication, flexibility, and refinement of approach and beliefs. The school vision is student focused, based on data and appropriate for school/community values, and meeting student needs.
IMPLEMENTATION		Principal makes all decisions, with little or no input from teachers, the community, or students. Inspect for mistakes is the leadership approach.	School values and beliefs are identified; the purpose of school is defined; a school mission and student essential learnings are developed with representative input. A structure for studying approaches to achieving essential student learnings is established.	Leadership team is active on study teams and integrates recommendations from the team's research and analyses to form a comprehensive plan for continuous improvement within the context of the school mission. Everyone is kept informed.	Decisions about budget and implementation of the vision are made within teams, by the principal, by the leadership team, and by the full staff as appropriate. All decisions are communicated to the leadership team and the full staff.	The vision is implemented and articulated across all grade levels and into feeder schools. Quality standards are reinforced throughout the school. All members of the school community understand and apply the quality standards. Leadership team has systematic interactions and involvement with district administrators, teachers, parents, community, and students about the school's direction.
OUTCOME		Decisions lack focus and consistency. There is little staff buy-in. Students and parents do not feel that they are being heard. Decision making process is clear and known.	The mission provides a focus for all school improvement and guides the action to the vision. Teachers and community are committed to continuous improvement. Quality leadership techniques are used sporadically.	Leaders are seen as committed to planning and quality improvement. Critical areas for improvement are identified. All faculty feel included in shared decision making.	There is evidence that the leadership team listens to all levels of the organization. Implementation of the continuous improvement plan is linked to essential student learnings and the guiding principles of the school. Teachers are empowered.	Site-based management and shared decision making truly exists. Teachers understand and display an intimate knowledge of how the school operates. Teachers support and communicate with each other in the implementation of quality strategies. Teachers implement the vision in their classrooms and can determine how their new approach meets student needs and leads to the attainment of essential student learnings.

Items That Might Be Found In the Leadership Section of the School Portfolio

The following are appropriate items for inclusion in this section:

- School's assessment on the Leadership Continuous Improvement Continuum
- Shared decision-making structure and process—picture and description
- Types of decisions made at the school and analysis of who makes what decisions
- Roles and responsibilities of—
  - action teams
  - staff
  - principal
  - leader/coordinator
  - superintendent
  - district office
- Approach to consensus building
- Meeting structure/calendar/minutes
- Site-based management and relationship with the district office
- Outcomes/benefits/strengths of approach
- Goals for improvement
- Analysis of what needs to happen to move to the next steps in the continuum

Leadership Questions

The following questions are designed to help you think about what your school has in evidence of where you are with regard to Leadership.

What do you have for documentation for the Leadership section of your school portfolio?

What other things do you need to gather and document in the Leadership section?

What are your next steps with staff with respect to Leadership?

Chapter 9

PARTNERSHIP DEVELOPMENT

Schools that seek to prepare students to live and work in the communication age would do well to establish partnerships with businesses, the community, and parents. These partnerships can make instructional programs exciting and relevant to the purpose of developing all students into successful citizens and quality workers. Partner-ships help to reinforce learning at home and may provide solutions to some of the problems teachers face when trying to teach children who are not prepared to learn.

Partnerships can provide schools with information to guide curriculum and instruction, and can help schools to set priorities and achieve goals. Businesses, community groups, and parents are all clients of the school. Involving clients in the continuous improvement of the product—the students—enables schools to make use of talents, resources, and advice from people who have a vested interest.

When establishing a partnership agreement, the organizations lay out goals, and identify desired outcomes and approaches to measuring the success of the partnership. With a comprehensive and detailed strategic plan and the school portfolio, prospective partners can see how they can contribute to the school's larger vision. The key is to let all partners benefit and contribute meaningfully—and celebrate successes, together.

> *The key to effective partnerships—both partners must contribute and both partners must benefit.*
>
> Jere Jacobs

Establishing a Partnership Plan

Successful, appropriate partnerships do not just happen. They must be researched and organized to be beneficial to the school, to partners, and especially to students. Successful partnerships often are those that are specific in nature, narrowly defined, and clearly stated so that both parties know the aim of the partnership. In this arena, it is best to start small and to continually reinforce the reasons for the partnership. In any partnership, large or small, partners must agree first on the specific goals of the partnership, and on what constitutes progress and reasonable evidence of success. Figure 27 shows steps in developing a partnership plan in a shared decision-making school.

> *Power in organizations is the capacity generated by relationships.*
>
> Margaret Wheatley

Most schools serious about partnerships create a team to coordinate partnerships. With the overall school plan in hand, this team conducts research on how partnerships will help the school achieve its goals, and benefit student achievement. Initially, the team learns about effective partnerships in other schools, and they think about creative ways in which partners could work with their school. From their research, the team creates a plan for partnerships that is submitted to staff for input and approval. Although it is important to have a comprehensive plan, it is also important to keep the plan flexible enough to accommodate input from the partners after they are identified.

Once staff give input and approve the plan, the partnership team interviews, meets with, telephones, or sends surveys with letters to potential partners. The team learns about the prospective partners' interests and capabilities, informs the partners about the kinds of partnerships in which the school is interested and why, and arranges for a face-to-face meeting and on-site visit.

Whether the prospective partners come to the school for a site visit, or host a meeting at their offices, the school portfolio can quickly orient them to the school—its mission, values, beliefs, vision, student learning standards, goals, current operations, the improvement process, and the school culture. It can help the school team present a clear message about the school in order to make it easy for

Figure 27

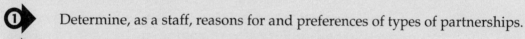

Steps to Establishing a Partnership Plan in a Shared Decision-making School

① Determine, as a staff, reasons for and preferences of types of partnerships.

② Create a team to coordinate and plan for partnerships.

③ Team investigates how partnerships can help the school staff achieve student learning standards and their school improvement goals.
- Visit other schools with successful partnerships
- Read research
- Brainstorm areas in which partnerships will benefit students

④ Partnership team creates plan for partnerships at the school and submits plan and rationale to staff for discussion.

⑤ Staff adds to and approves partnership plan.

⑥ Partnership team contacts prospective partners to determine interest.

⑦ Interested prospective partners meet with partnership team to exchange information about interests, and to learn about each other's organizations.
- Prospective partners describe why they want a partnership with the school and how they would like to continue
- Partnership team utilizes school portfolio to describe the school's mission, vision, values and beliefs, student learning standards, and current operations and processes

⑧ Partners prepare an agreement, establish outcomes, and determine how the partnership will be monitored and improved on a continuous basis.
- Regular meeting times are established
- Cost and personnel requirements for the partnership are identified
- Celebrate and thank the partners for their contributions.

prospective partners to see where their contributions might benefit students. In negotiating creative partnership possibilities, the partnership team must be as oriented to the partners' needs and goals for a partnership as they are to their own.

When establishing a partnership agreement, the organizations lay out goals, and identify desired outcomes and approaches to measuring the success of the partnership. All partnerships must be evaluated on an ongoing basis to ensure the attainment of the overall objectives and to ensure that both parties are getting what they need out of the partnership. Additionally, schools should always encourage, acknowledge, and thank the partners for their contributions, and, together, celebrate accomplishments.

Business Partnerships

School partnerships with business typically range from businesses giving products and services to schools to businesses providing students, teachers, and administrators with skill-building experiences at the business site. Although schools too often look at business partnerships as an easy way to get money, supplies, and equipment, and businesses too often believe that they have the answers to school problems, there are many ways in which school-business partnerships can be established to benefit both parties. For example, school communities identify "job-related" skills as student learning standards for all students. Business-high school partnerships can help students achieve these standards in a manner similar to the example below.

Admiralty High School established a Business Academy to serve the needs of their 11th and 12th grade students who might otherwise have dropped out, as well as their career-oriented students. The mission of the Business Academy is to provide students with practical technical training, integrated with academic skills, that will lead them to better than minimum-wage jobs or to community college programs. The Business Academy sought partners from their business community to mentor these students. In the mornings, students receive academic training. In the afternoons, they report to a job site to work with their mentors. The results: these students who typically were absent or late for school a great deal of the time are now found outside the school in the mornings waiting for the doors to be unlocked, and frequently return

> *Partnerships between education and business are key to reaching the shared goals of finding new ways to prepare a work force for the twenty-first century and encouraging lifelong learners.*
>
> Apple Computer Company

to the school after their work session to continue to work on projects long after the school day is over. The drop-out rate was cut in half and the employment rate after graduation increased significantly. The school is proud to offer a program that students are excited about, that appropriately prepares and motivates them to be good citizens. The business mentors and their companies are happy to have input into the upcoming work force, the exposure to future customers, and the positive public image that results from the partnership.

Businesses can help students understand why they need to know the information they are learning in school, and how the knowledge is applied in a real job situation. For example:

A teacher at Alvarado Elementary School invites a variety of professionals into his class and visits other professionals to illustrate classroom lessons. When students are learning about precision in measurement, the teacher walks his 4th graders two blocks from the school to talk with and watch a neighborhood sheet metal cutter. The sheet metal cutter very clearly and quickly can explain and show why it is important to know how to make precise measurements and the consequences of inaccurate measurements. Students dislike the thought of materials being wasted. The image is clearly in their minds as they return to their classroom to practice making accurate measurements. To reinforce the lesson, a local surgeon is also invited to demonstrate how measurement is used in medicine, i.e., temperatures, blood pressure, blood cell counts, blood types, even precision cutting during surgery. The students do not need additional coaching to understand the impact of inaccurate measurements in this career field! The main benefits of these partnerships are fairly obvious, and with this type of learning the students are also receiving exposure to different types of careers.

Another example:

Introducing its female students to a variety of career choices, especially those in the math and science fields, was the goal the Los Molinos High School set out to accomplish when it began its "Speaker of the Month" program. This high school, located in rural northern California, wanted to increase the number of female students choosing math and science careers. As part of their school's partnership plan, they established partnerships with local businesswomen to help achieve this goal. Each month a different professional businesswoman comes to the high school and talks to the students about what she does for a living. The students accompany the speaker to her place of work or to a job site to experience what the job entails.

In testimony to the success of this partnership, the number of female students going on to college from Los Molinos High School has increased, and the numbers choosing math or science as a career has also increased.

By becoming involved with schools, business people can make personal contributions and become good corporate citizens for their community, which ultimately enhances their public image. The partnership also gives business the opportunity to influence curriculum and attract employees to an area that has quality schools in which business is actively involved.

Business partnerships can benefit students indirectly by increasing specific skills of teachers. In ongoing partnerships with businesses, teachers can learn about specific subject areas such as information management, data-based decision making, conducting research, team-building, collaboration, shared decision making, public relations, marketing, and technology. Business partners can also supply expertise by helping teachers with classroom research and by helping leadership and shared decision-making teams with organizational development, strategic planning, and managerial skills.

Many times, large corporations have undergone rigorous restructuring (or downsizing) and have skills schools can use for building a vision, establishing a mission, facilitating meetings, preparing presentations and proposals, developing strategies for problem solving and goal setting, identifying and finding resources, and establishing procedures for evaluation and accountability. As an example, Arthur Andersen & Co., San Francisco, has contributed its expertise in the area of Total Quality Management techniques to help the Alameda Unified School District analyze needs, create a vision, plan and implement changes, and evaluate their overall continuous improvement efforts.

Many schools establish partnerships with their city, as shown in the example below:

The city of San Carlos, California, and the San Carlos Elementary School District formed a partnership with the goal of maintaining high-quality services in spite of shrinking resources. Over a two-year period, this partnership has expanded the number of recreation programs and courses offered by the city through the use of school buildings and facilities after hours, relieving pressure on overused city parks, providing additional revenue to both the city and the school. After-school enrichment classes for latchkey kids were created and are taught by city recreation department instructors. Also added was a new children's theater program, sports camps, classes, and "drop-in" basketball games for teens and adults. This successful partnership is now pursuing the sharing of equipment, working to solve traffic safety and maintenance problems, and increasing the use of technology by both organizations. The partnership offers new and enhanced services to the citizens of San Carlos, and has enriched school and recreational activities available to the city's school children.

Partnerships with Parents

Probably the most common type of school partnership is with parents. In spite of this, the two greatest teacher complaints about teaching continue to be—

- children do not come to school ready to learn
- there is not enough parent involvement in children's learning

There is evidence that parent involvement leads to increased student achievement. The key to increasing the amount and quality of parent involvement and to establishing ongoing partnerships with parents is to help parents understand what they can do to make a difference and to allow them to contribute in meaningful ways. Teachers must take an active role to encourage and motivate parents to get involved in educating their children. Often parents do not feel they are knowledgeable enough to assist at the school or even in the education of their children. Many parents also feel that their participation would be of little value to the teachers.

> *Parents play one of the most essential roles in the educational process. They provide the environment in which students learn, the discipline and the dedication needed to be successful, not only in school but also in life. Parents must instill in their children a deep respect for hard work, achievement, and learning.*
>
> Therese Knecht Dozier

Teachers and other school staff members must communicate often and regularly with parents. Teachers may choose to increase communication with parents through notes, newsletters, narratives, telephone calls, and parent conferences. Many teachers believe that narrative report cards might encourage parent involvement in their children's learning at home—teachers say parents become more supportive and involved. When using narrative report cards it is important for teachers to objectively describe the student's work as well as the expectations for the work. Narrative reports can benefit teacher-parent relationships—parents know what to do and can help to support their children's learning. Too often, however, the narratives are not used to their fullest potential.

149

A very effective approach to a win-win strategy that lets everybody of all ages know the expectations for the week is an easy-to-read teacher-constructed newspaper-style page that goes home with the students each week. If possible, it should be in the language spoken in the home. It should describe the curriculum for the week, the homework for each day, the intent of the work assigned, extra credit projects for students to tackle at home, teacher's philosophy of grading, tips for working with the student on assignments, and tips for praising and correcting student mistakes. Both parents and students see in writing what will be covered during the week as well as what will be expected of students. Parents also see what they can do to help as teachers masterfully guide parent involvement with homework and special projects. Many schools include the newsletter in an envelope that goes home each week and is signed and returned with space for parent comments. Other items that are included in the envelope are notices, student work, test results, and art work.

To some teachers and parents, parent involvement means coming to school and assisting in the classroom. Many teachers feel that the learning environment is better with more adults in the classroom. To encourage this involvement, teachers need to prepare parents for helping in the classroom and offer them meaningful jobs. Parents who have time during the day can often help students read or work on mathematics problems in small groups or one-on-one. Some parents might also be able to deliver a lesson or example to the entire class. It takes getting to know parents and their capacities and interests for this level of involvement to be effective.

In working to increase parent involvement and participation, schools must acknowledge the fact that many parents work or have small children at home. They cannot always be at the school during normal school hours. Many schools have voice-mail telephone systems used to communicate with parents who are not able to come to school during the day. For instance, teachers leave brief messages each day that parents can access anytime after 4:00 p.m. Messages usually describe the work done in the classroom that day, and offer suggestions reinforcing students' understanding of the concepts at home.

Parent-student conferences are a good way to begin developing relationships with parents. During conferences, schools establish lists of parents' interests, abilities, and desires to work and/or perform volunteer work in the school. Teachers then use these lists to identify parents to contact for special projects or curriculum units in their classrooms.

To increase parent participation, many schools encourage parents to visit the school. Some schools even provide a special room for parents and their families—a place where parents know they are always welcome. One school established a "family" room to provide a safe, quiet place for parents and families after school hours in response to frequent complaints by students that their neighborhood is so noisy that it is very difficult for them to read or do homework at home. The parents are pleased to have a place for their children and family to go to be safe. Teachers report that students are completing their homework when they use the family room. Parent volunteers often use the family rooms during the day and at night to meet with children who need someone to read with them or help them with homework and for helping teachers with clerical tasks. The family rooms are places where parents know they are always welcome.

Parent input is extremely valuable and communication crucial as schools engage in extensive school improvement efforts. Parents are stakeholders who represent different points of view than those held by the typical educator. Their opinions about how to "educate" students need to be heard and they need to be kept informed along the way as changes are made.

Some parents will emerge as leaders who can help the school improvement cause. They can add to the process by serving on a committee, action team, or shared decision-making council. Many teachers notice that the presence of parents on committees and teams helps to create a true adult atmosphere, where individuals on the team tend to listen to each other carefully and to ask for clarification rather than jump to conclusions. When parents become involved, they become community advocates for activities the school wishes to pursue. Parent advocacy is extremely important and helpful. One example, described here, illustrates this point.

Evergreen School District enjoys a positive public image. Its students tend to score highly on standardized tests of achievement, and the public is very confident that the schools in the district are doing what they need to be doing to help their students continuously improve. After Evergreen had been restructuring for a number of years, the faculty determined that if they really wanted to move on to the next step of their continuous improvement effort they needed eight kid-free days during the next year for training. The staff committed to the eight days of training, and a master calendar was constructed. Parents protested. Their main concern was child care. What do we do about our kids on those eight days? Is the school going to provide child care? That's eight more days that we have to pay for, because you're not holding school. Teachers and administrators used a variety of techniques to describe to parents the benefits that they would ultimately see from the training, but to no avail. The school faculty was distraught. That's when the parents who had been serving on the school's decision-making committee kicked into action. The parents sold the idea to the community and the staff got their eight days.

Community Partnerships

Partnerships with community service organizations can help schools project a positive public image and can give students experience providing service to the community. Schools must not wait to be invited to be a part of the service community; they need to approach potential community partners with positive win-win propositions.

Many schools have created successful partnerships with community clinics and mental health organizations which provide access to health and social service professionals at school. By integrating these services at the school site, students get needed services that schools normally cannot provide, and service agencies get access to their clients during school hours.

One high school funds a half-time health services coordinator through grant funds. This person connects students and their families who have no health insurance to health care agencies and support systems.

Schools can interest community organizations (e.g., Rotary, Lions, Soroptimists) to become partners by first offering to provide services to the organizations that, at the same time, support the attainment of student learning standards. They might start by having students present speeches or entertainment and then expand student participation to assist with service delivery. In return, many of these organizations will "adopt" schools and support the school's improvement efforts.

Many schools are partners with local recycling companies to encourage students to recycle newspapers, cans, and bottles and contribute to the environment in a meaningful way. Other schools have established partnerships with local nursing homes, senior citizens groups, and special education program facilities as a means of attaining student learning standards such as presentation skills, performance skills, letter writing, and citizenship.

At the beginning of the year, a teacher at Alvarado Elementary School in Signal Hill, California requires his students to volunteer to provide some sort of service one hour a week. Service might include cleaning up litter on the school grounds or around the city;

recycling; or, helping senior citizens, special education or handicapped students write letters—all for the purpose of becoming good citizens. By the end of the year, anyone visiting the school campus could see evidence of the impact of the volunteering efforts of these students. Typically, one will see students scurrying around picking up litter, helping handicapped children carry their lunch trays and move around the campus, writing letters to senior citizen pen-pals, or making plans for some of their next events. If one asks students why they are performing these duties, the most common response is "because it makes me feel good."

School and Higher Education Partnerships

Colleges or universities physically close to schools are often overlooked as school partners, but these institutions are a source of rich and diverse skills that are useful to most K-12 schools. There are usually faculty members interested in and willing to help schools in a variety of ways. University and college personnel can become partners in the school's improvement efforts by helping them develop and achieve a vision, mission, and plan, and possibly perform in the role of external change agent or school coach. Like other prospective partners, universities and colleges need to know that a partnership with them is desired and how they can help.

Teachers in schools engaging in systemic school improvement need skills beyond what most teacher preparation programs offer. When new teachers join these schools, the schools must be able to orient the new teachers to the school's practices and procedures quickly. A partnership with teacher training institutions helps with this transition. One of the benefits is that the partnership gives the teacher training institutions an opportunity to create model teacher education and administrative education programs that reflect new developments in changing schools. Partnerships with teacher training institutions and schools can also take the form of teacher development centers and internships, whereby university teacher candidates and interns work with teachers in the school improvement school as a part of their training. In return for their mentoring efforts, teachers are able to occasionally leave the classroom to the student teacher or novice and work on their school improvement efforts. An example of an elementary school-university partnership follows.

Los Naranjos Elementary School established a partnership with the University of California, Irvine, Teacher Training Program when staff discovered how difficult it was to integrate new teachers into an otherwise stable teaching force—one that had worked very closely together on systemic school improvement for approximately five years. A committee of teachers from Los Naranjos and a committee of professors from UC worked together to determine the outcomes for the partnership and outlined a win-win strategy for the partnership. The partnership evolved into an Internship Teacher Development Center whereby two teacher interns were hired to work with Los Naranjos teachers each year. The interns' salaries provide a financial savings to the school that help support the release time for an experienced teacher-leader to work on special assignment. Interns have a coach available to assist them with their teaching duties. The teacher on special assignment can also supervise several student teachers placed at the school during the year as well as take the classes of other teachers at Los Naranjos to free them up for peer coaching activities with colleagues. Interns become participants in a very special program that allows them to be paid while learning on the job, and UC receives committed support for a training program that incorporates the latest innovations and instructional strategies and assessment.

At the high school level, partnerships with higher education institutions allow high school students to take courses for college credit. High schools are able to provide students with the opportunity to take courses that they could not offer otherwise. Colleges and universities benefit by recruiting future students who have a successful academic track record.

For the most part most people want to work with schools. Many people do not know how to get involved with schools and what they might suggest or offer as a partnership. A school plan and vision can clarify for all exactly how prospective partners can assist the school in meeting its goals. Partners like to know how their talents can be utilized and that they will make a difference in the overall effort to improve the school. With a comprehensive and detailed strategic plan and the school portfolio, prospective partners can see how they can contribute to the school's larger vision. The key is to let all partners benefit and contribute meaningfully—and celebrate successes, together.

Table 7 is the Continuous Improvement Continuum for Partnership Development. Using the sections outlined in the continuum, as well as the paraphrased descriptions that follow, assess your school's *approach, implementation,* and *outcome* with respect to Partnership Development.

Assessing Your School's Partnerships

Which statement below best describes your school's *approach* to Partnership Development?

· ·

Approach

1. The school prefers to operate without outside input.

2. The school begins to investigate different approaches for, and the benefits of, including businesses, the community, and parents in the school improvement process.

3. The school understands why partnerships with businesses, the community, and parents increase student achievement. The school concentrates on establishing win-win partnerships.

4. Partnerships with businesses, the community, and parents are strategically planned and operate within and across all student groupings to the benefit of all parties.

5. The benefits of partnerships are evident both within the school and in the wider community which sponsors learning opportunities beyond the school's walls.

     Your assessment _____   Date _____

Which statement below best describes your school's *implementation* of Partnership Development?

. . . .

Implementation

1. The school discourages involvement of outsiders. The school continues to operate as it always has.

2. A team of school staff members are assigned to establish goals and plans for receiving and involving input from businesess, the community, and parents.

3. Partnerships with businesses, the community, and parents are implemented throughout the school. The partners are clear on how they can and do support learning at home and through their businesses.

4. Staff strategically integrate partnerships with businesses, the community, and parents throughout the school and community, continually evaluating their effectiveness.

5. Partnerships are implemented across and within every student grouping and are evaluated for continuous improvement. Student learning regularly takes place beyond the school walls.

Your assessment _____   Date _____

Which statement below best describes your school's *outcome* with respect to Partnership Development?

· ·

Outcome

1. Little or no involvement of the larger community and ultimately very little support.

2. Staff begin to see the benefits of partnerships. Community members and parents are regularly invited and are visible all over campus.

3. Student achievement increases in those areas where business and the community have participated in providing real-world curriculum to the students.

4. Students display characteristics of responsibility, respect, and increased achievement as a result of partnerships. Absences, tardiness, and drop-out rates decrease significantly and student achievement increases. There is effective communication and mutual benefits between partners.

5. Previously non-achieving students show great gains in achievement. The real-world opportunities provided by the partnerships makes a great difference for these students. Parents see school as a center of learning for themselves as well as their children and enthusiastically support school programs.

Your assessment _____   Date _____

Table 7

Partnership Development

	ONE	TWO	THREE	FOUR	FIVE
APPROACH	There is no system for input from parents, business, or community. Status quo is desired for managing the school.	Partnerships are sought, but mostly for money and things.	School has knowledge of why partnerships are important and seeks to include businesses and parents in a strategic fashion related to essential student learnings for increased student achievement.	School seeks effective win-win business and community partnerships and parent involvement to implement throughout the school and community. Desired outcomes are clearly identified. A solid plan for partnership development is known.	Community, parent, and business partnerships become integrated across all student groupings. The benefits of outside involvement are known by all. Parent and business involvement in student learning is refined. Student learning regularly takes place beyond the school walls.
IMPLEMENTATION	Barriers are erected to close out involvement of outsiders. Outsiders are managed for least impact on status quo.	A team is assigned to get partners and to receive input from parents, the community, and business in the school.	Involvement of business, community, and parents begins to take place in some classrooms and after school hours. All begin to realize how they can support each other in achieving school goals. School staff understand what partners need out of the partnership.	There is a systematic utilization of parents, community, and businesses schoolwide. Areas in which the active use of these partnerships benefits student learning are clear.	Partnership development is articulated across all student groupings. Parents, community, business, and educators work together in an innovative fashion to increase student learning and to prepare students for the 21st Century. Partnerships are evaluated for continuous improvement.
OUTCOME	Little or no involvement of parents, business, or community at large. School is a closed, isolated system.	Much effort is given to establishing partnerships. Some spotty trends emerge, such as equipment donations.	Some substantial gains are achieved in implementing partnerships. Some student achievement increases can be attributed to this involvement.	Gains in student satisfaction with learning and school are clearly related to partnerships. All partners benefit.	Previously non-achieving students enjoy learning, with excellent achievement. Community, business, and home become common places for student learning, while school becomes a place where parents come for further education. Partnerships enhance what we do for students.

Items That Might Be Found In the
Partnership Development Section of the School Portfolio

The following are appropriate items for inclusion in this section:

- School's assessment on the Partnership Development Continuous Improvement Continuum
- Description of why the school wants partnerships and what all partners will get out of the relationship
- Matrix of student learning standards and how business, parents, and community can help the school and students meet these standards
- School partnership plan
- Descriptions of current parent, community, and business involvement with the school
- Descriptions of desired parent, community, and business involvement with the school
- Evidence of all partnerships' impact on increasing student learning, e.g., attendance, dropout rates
- Photographs of partners working together or celebrating
- Newspaper clippings
- Evaluation of the impact of the partnerships on the school and the partners
- Description of what the partners get out of the partnership
- How the partnerships can be improved
- Analysis of what needs to happen to move to the next steps in the continuum

Partnership Development Questions

The following questions are designed to help you think about what your school has in evidence of where you are with regard to Partnership Development.

What do you have for documentation for the Partnership Development section of your school portfolio?

What other things do you need to gather and document in the Partnership Development section?

What are your next steps with staff with respect to Partnership Development?

Chapter 10

CONTINUOUS IMPROVEMENT AND EVALUATION

Continuous improvement and evaluation is the process of assessing plans, implementation, processes, and progress to determine what needs to improve and how to make those improvements. The assessment and improvement steps are then repeated on an ongoing basis. These principles have been used successfully in the corporate world for many years and can be used successfully in the school improvement process as well.

The key to the successful application of continuous improvement concepts to the school improvement process is the active use of data. Measuring the school's progress against identified criteria—such as the *Education for the Future Initiative* Continuous Improvement Continuums—provides a benchmark that schools can use to see if their actions have created the results they intended. These measures are supported by analyzing data gathered through interviews with clients of the school, questionnaires, and observations of the learning environment. When these measurements are taken on a regular basis, the data clearly document trends and provide information that assist schools in deciding what steps for improvement to take next. Again, the school's guiding principles must be kept in mind to understand the true impact of the data.

> *Continuous improvement causes us to think about upstream process improvement not downstream damage control.*
>
> Continuous Improvement: Teams & Tools

Continuous Improvement Process

One cannot read about continuous improvement without being introduced to the PDCA (plan, do, check, act) cycle, the framework for the continuous improvement process conceptualized along with theories of statistical quality control by Walter A. Shewart during the 1920s and 1930s. His former student, Dr. W. Edwards Deming, later altered the cycle to PDSA—plan, do, study, act. Even though today one can see a variety of versions of the cycle, the intent is that every task or job in an organization is part of a process that consists (or should consist) of planning, doing the plan, studying the implementation of the plan, and then improving the plan.

> *It is the job of management to improve constantly and forever the system of production and service.*
>
> W. Edwards Deming

Figure 28, the Continuous School Improvement Cycle, depicts continuous improvement philosophies applied to the school improvement process. At the core of the cycle are the guiding principles of the school—its mission, vision, values, beliefs, purpose, and the academic learnings that the school community feels are essential for all students. At all points in the school improvement process, these guiding principles are the compelling *why* any of the change is taking place. All elements of the plan and all components being implemented and improved at the school must be congruent with the school's guiding principles. If they are not, there will not be a strong base for the improvement process. A lack of congruence also indicates that the school does not yet have a strong shared vision which will make improvements throughout the school possible. Appendix B shows a detailed flow chart of the school improvement process. The discussion that follows refers to how the two work together.

Figure 28

Continuous School Improvement Cycle

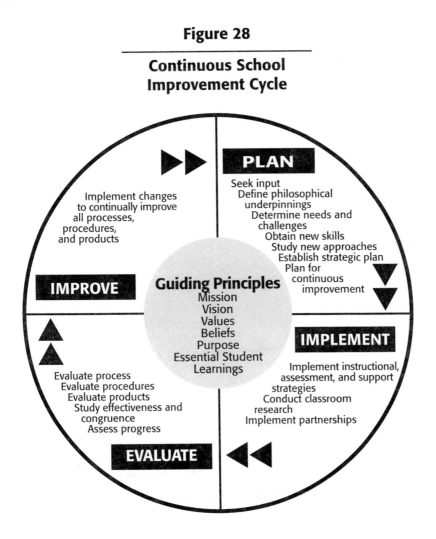

PLAN

Begin the Process of School Improvement

The process of school improvement begins when the entire school community, or a subgroup of the school community, determines that current processes can be improved. This "opportunity" is often revealed in the form of a crisis, although many "excellent" schools begin the process when they recognize the possibilities for improvement. Other schools are able to begin the process at the invitation of a business or corporation offering assistance to schools in their geographic area, and some begin when the process is mandated by administration or some regulatory agency. However it is first initiated, the process officially begins when staff commit to rethinking the way they do business.

Define the Needs and Challenges

Understanding what needs to change is the first step in planning for improvement. Participation from all factions of the school community—students, teachers, classified staff, parents, business representatives, neighbors—can help ensure a comprehensive view of future issues, challenges, and needs. Data about all elements of the school's operation and their impact should be gathered to better understand the school's strengths and weaknesses and to determine pressing issues. Perceptions of the learning environment from all perspectives of the school community and data such as demographics, current and future needs, and trends must be gathered to thoroughly understand what needs to change. The thoroughness of this part of the planning process influences the entire improvement process.

Philosophical Underpinnings

The most important component in the school improvement process is the establishment and maintenance of a shared vision—the same visual image of what is to be accomplished is held by all members of the school community. The shared vision is built from a set of collective values and beliefs that represent individual personal values and beliefs within the school community—beliefs about the purpose of school, in general, and the purpose and mission of this particular school. The vision also encompasses what students are expected to know and be able to do by the time they leave the learning organization. These are often called essential student learnings or student learning standards. The combination of these elements—as they are manifested in the guiding principles—is the foundation of the school and school improvement process.

Establish a Plan for Change

To ensure that the commitment to change the manner in which the school does business is actually carried out—to lead to real change for students—it is imperative to establish a plan for studying new approaches, building skills, conducting meetings, communicating, and integrating recommendations for new approaches into one overall recommendation.

Establish Structure for Change

Continuously improving schools must have in place a flexible leadership infrastructure that takes into account the root causes of problems and keeps in mind the philosophical underpinnings of the organization. This leadership infrastructure must enhance communication and support shared decision making as it studies approaches to meeting the needs of its clients.

Identify Pressing Issues

In order to identify areas that need to be improved, an analysis of the pressing issues is conducted using an approach designed to assess the root causes of problems based upon data the school has collected.

Build Skills for Change

When the plan for change is approved, skill-building training begins to support the change. The training might include building skills in team building, understanding the process of change, effective team strategies, shared decision making, conducting effective meetings, time management, consensus building, strategic planning, and continuous improvement and evaluation. With these new skills, teams are established to study the different approaches to achieving the school vision.

This professional development training will continue indefinitely. As staff study new approaches, professional development training clarifies if a particular approach is desirable and if it will meet the needs of the students. Even after the overall school plan is established and the skills required of the school community are determined, comprehensive, ongoing professional development continues to be a major component that supports the school improvement effort.

Study New Approaches

Based upon the major vision, study teams divide the work of researching different approaches to meeting the academic, social, and emotional needs of their students. While conducting this research, it is important for study teams to communicate with each other as much as possible. Often leadership teams act as conduits for information sharing. A process by which study teams make official recommendations at the conclusion of their research efforts should be included in the plan for change. The recommendation of each study team is then integrated into one overall recommendation that is congruent with the philosophical underpinnings and is hypothesized to overcome the pressing issues of the school.

Plan for Implementation

After the overall recommendation is approved by staff, a strategic plan for implementing the recommendation is developed. The strategic plan consists of an itemization of the action to be taken, the person responsible for the action being implemented, due date, and timelines. Included in the action to be taken is professional development training for staff to upgrade their skills to implement innovative instructional techniques and a plan for continuous improvement and evaluation. When the strategic plan is complete, staff reviews, approves, and commits to its implementation.

Establish Structure for Implementation

Now a structure is established to coordinate, implement, and support the strategic plan. Teams "built around" the vision will implement the plan in ways that reflect grade levels, subject areas, learning families or academies, and must establish steps for implementation that are congruent with the vision and overall strategic plan. Each team communicates its plan to the full staff.

. . . .

IMPLEMENT

Implement New Strategies

The ultimate goal in school improvement is to develop a learning organization that will help students learn what they need to know to function as productive citizens in the future. Teachers must understand and use a variety of instructional and assessment strategies. They must be able to adjust these strategies to meet the needs of their students. They must be able to assess the impact of their actions on students, and they must be able to help students become motivated learners and self assessors.

Implementation Support Strategies

Schools committed to continuously improving their processes and comprehensively implementing the school vision would do well to adopt implementation support strategies at the teacher level. These strategies might include any kind of peer collaboration such as peer coaching—the pairing of teachers to work together to establish plans, observe each other implementing specific elements, and to provide feedback to each other. They might also include collaborative teacher research—establishing hypotheses and studying the impact of the specific implementation efforts, and working with staff-developed rubrics for accountability and direction in implementation that indicate where the whole staff and individual teachers are in the implementation process. Failure to build in support strategies is one of the most common reasons plans do not get implemented.

Implement Partnerships

Schools continuously improving to meet the future needs of students establish partnerships with businesses, the community, and parents to enhance student learning of real-world applications. The implementation of partnerships is planned in support of the school's philosophical underpinnings to enhance instructional strategies.

· ·

EVALUATE

Evaluate

A continuously improving learning organization uses evaluation to understand the impact and effectiveness of its actions to ensure the congruence and synergy of the elements of its vision, and to determine how well the new strategies have been implemented, with the overall goal of improving processes, products, and procedures in an ongoing fashion. Figure 29 outlines evaluation questions based upon school improvement process activities. Purpose, desired outcome, and possible approaches are included in the chart to help focus the questions. Figure 29 (4 pages) follows.

· ·

Figure 29

**Evaluation Questions
Outline, page 1**

	ACTIVITY	PURPOSE	OUTCOME	EVALUATION QUESTIONS	APPROACH
P L A N	Seek input from students, parents, business, and community.	Make sure all clients of the school have input into defining the current and future needs of students and the school.	Commitment of school community to work together to rethink how student needs will be met in the future. Ownership of the process.	What constituencies need to be involved? Who is involved? Is the involvement representative of all constituencies? Does everyone feel they are truly involved and have a say? Is there a commitment to study new approaches to meeting student needs? Does each person understand his or her role?	Questionnaires to potential constituents; review rosters; interviews.
	Define the philosophical underpinnings of the organization.	Values and beliefs provide the context behind the mission, vision, purpose of school, and outcomes, and serve as guides for the improvement efforts.	A shared purpose, mission, and clear outcomes built from the values and beliefs of the school community so everyone has the same understanding of and motivation for the change. A shared vision to establish the same visual image of what is to be accomplished.	Were individuals' values, beliefs, and opinions sought, understood, and respected? Are the values and beliefs of the individuals congruent? Do they represent what the individuals actually believe? Are they shared? How were shared values and beliefs established? Was the sharing accomplished in such a way that individuals were not "talked out" of their personal values and beliefs, or did the shared vision emerge from the personal? Is the mission an accurate representation of the purpose of the school? Is it built on the values and beliefs of the individuals of the school community? Is it a clear, compelling, and proactive goal that can serve to unify and challenge the organization? Can outsiders understand it with little explanation? Do insiders have a precise understanding of it? Does the vision describe what the school will be like when the mission is achieved? Is the vision congruent with the values and beliefs of the school community? Does it bring the mission to life? Is the vision truly shared? Was the vision built from personal visions and meeting the future needs of students? Are all individuals committed to the vision?	Facilitated group meeting or training sessions; questionnaires; interviews.

Figure 29

**Evaluation Questions
Outline, page 2**

PLAN

ACTIVITY	PURPOSE	OUTCOME	EVALUATION QUESTIONS	APPROACH
Determine the needs and challenges of the students, community, and the school.	Understand current and future needs of students, the community, and the school to focus on school improvement efforts on preparing students for the future within the context.	Clear understanding of the clients, their needs, root causes of problems, the impact of current processes on the clients, and identification of essential student learnings.	Who are the students, parents, teachers, administrators? What are their needs? What are their skills? How effective are current processes in meeting student needs from every constituent's perspective and from existing school data? Who are the future students? What will they face in the future? How do they learn best? What are the overall challenges, needs, pressing issues, and/or opportunities? What are the root causes of the problems and challenges? What is the current process of schooling? How effective is it in meeting the overall challenges and needs? What does the school want students to know and be able to do when they leave? What are the elements of school that must be changed? How are all of these understandings communicated to everyone in the school community?	Needs assessment survey: student, teacher, parent questionnaires, existing data; review of literature, flowchart of current processes.
Establish plan for school improvement.	Analyze needs, challenges, and current structure to plan an approach to studying and sustaining improvement.	A decision-making structure/ comprehensive data-based plan for developing a strategic action plan for systemic school improvement.	Given the needs, challenges, pressing issues, and identified student outcomes, is the plan and structure for study and day-to-day decision making appropriate? Is each structure congruent with the philosophical underpinnings of the organization? What information needs to be tracked for improvement? Does the new study and decision-making structure sufficiently represent all points of view? Does the structure allow for effective communication with all members of the school community?	Analyses of data, including current processes; review of literature; brainstorming.
Build skills for change.	Obtain new skills that will allow the school community to work in ways different from current processes and structures.	Abilities to share decisions; work in teams; build consensus; communicate; run efficient meetings; plan; and continuously improve operations.	What skills are present in the school community and needed for individuals to work together to establish a new structure to share in decision making and studying new approaches to meeting the needs of students? How are current skills assessed and new skills obtained? How effective is the training received for building new skills? Is the training appropriate and sufficient? How will new skills be monitored, supported, and implemented? How effective are individual, team, and staff interactions that require use of these new skills? How can they be improved?	Interviews; facilitated meetings; literature reviews; questionnaires; brainstorming.

Figure 29

**Evaluation Questions
Outline, page 3**

	ACTIVITY	PURPOSE	OUTCOME	EVALUATION QUESTIONS	APPROACH
P L A N	Study new approaches to meeting the needs of students.	Understand how students in this school learn, and new approaches for ensuring student success that leads to recommendations for new ways of operating to meet student needs.	Well-researched recommendations for the systemic improvement of every aspect of the school, based on the comprehensive study of pressing issues and how students learn that will lead to a strategic plan for implementation.	Is each study team comprised of representative members of the community? Are the teams effective in their study of new approaches? Do all team members participate? Is there consensus? Is the study in-depth or cursory? Are the items being considered for implementation potentially effective in meeting the needs of this student population, or do they represent the latest fad? Is the communication within and between teams appropriate, sufficient, and effective? Is the plan for study appropriate, effective, and efficient? Are the timelines for study sufficient? Do teams offer sufficient rationale for why they believe their recommendations will work?	Team meetings; questionnaires; interviews; review of the literature; visits to other schools.
	Develop an overall strategic plan for school improvement.	Establish a comprehensive strategic plan that integrates the in-depth research of the study teams and guides the implementation of the new approach throughout the period.	A strategic plan that will lead to the congruent and articulated implementation of new structures, strategies, and their continuous improvement, congruent with the mission, vision, and outcomes.	Is the decision-making body appropriate for integrating the study team recommendations? Is everybody aware of the approach to be used? Do they understand how to provide input to the process? Are they committed to the implementation of the integrated plan? Does the strategic plan have a comprehensive list of tasks to be implemented, skills needed for implementation, timelines, responsible persons, and due dates? Is the plan challenging, yet doable? Does the plan reflect the latest research on effective implementation strategies? Does the strategic plan appropriately reflect the intent of the study team recommendations, as well as the outcomes and philosophical underpinnings of the school? Does the plan provide a clear and efficient method of implementing the vision? Will the plan really lead to change that can be sustained? Is there more than one school plan?	Interviews; facilitated meetings; literature reviews; questionnaires; brainstorming; review of plan.
	Establish a structure to implement the plan and vision.	Establish a structure for implementation and decision making congruent with the strategic plan and vision.	Appropriate teams and effective decision-making structure are established to implement the overall strategic plan.	Are the teams appropriate for implementing the vision? Do all members understand their roles and responsibilities? Does each team have a plan and have they identified student outcomes? Are consensus-building and communication strategies used appropriately and effectively? Does each team understand how to run effective and efficient meetings? Do appropriate support, monitoring, skill-building, and accountability components exist for implementing the vision? Are they effective?	Team meetings; questionnaires; interviews; review of the literature.

Figure 29

**Evaluation Questions
Outline, page 4**

	ACTIVITY	PURPOSE	OUTCOME	EVALUATION QUESTIONS	APPROACH
IMPLEMENT	Implement new strategies.	To achieve student outcomes and realize the vision, new strategies, defined in the strategic plan must be implemented, not merely adopted.	A vision congruent with the mission of the school is implemented in every aspect of the organization. Student outcomes are achieved and the school becomes a true learning organization.	Is the structure effective for implementing the strategic plan? For decision making? What elements are most effective? What elements are least effective? Is communication effective for teams and full staff? Is professional development training for implementing the vision appropriate, ongoing, supportive, and effective? Are new strategies really being implemented? Are the new strategies appropriate? Is there enough support and accountability? What is the impact of implementation on staff, teachers, students, administrators, parents, community? Is everyone informed of implementation strategies and expected outcomes? Are partnerships appropriate and effective? What are the benefits of the new strategies?	Team meetings; questionnaires; interviews; review of the literature; data analysis.
EVALUATE	Evaluate.	Analyze the intent and implementation of all processes, procedures, and products with respect to the philosophical underpinnings of the organization.	Understanding of the impact and effectiveness of implemented processes, procedure and products on students and other members of the school community.	Does a real learning organization exist? Is there an understanding of implementation through leverage points? Is communication effective in every element of the organization and across elements? Are all elements of the organization congruent with the mission, vision, values, beliefs, and outcomes? How can any or each of the elemnts be improved? Why are some things not improving? What elements impact other elements? Is there a clear understanding of the interrelationships of the elements? What is the status of the pressing issues? Were the root causes and serious problems effectively attended to? Is the vision implemented? Can the vision be implemented within the current structure?	Interviews; questionnaires; data analysis; observations.
IMPROVE	Continuously improve.	Act on the results and information obtained through the ongoing evaluation process to continuously improve the organization.	An organization that is sensitive to the impact of its actions on its clients, and is capable of data-based decision making and implementing change for improvement.	Based on the evaluation report recommendations, what changes need to be made to improve operations? What processes need to change to ensure the school community that the vision is being implemented? What elements of the vision need to change based on new information received while implementing the vision? Does the mission, vision, and purpose need to be revisited and improved? Does the school community understand the interrelationship of elements and on this basis know how changing one element will impact other elements? What is the impact of the changes made?	Interviews; questionnaires; data analysis; observations.

171

IMPROVE

Continuously Improve

A continuously improving learning organization understands the impact each element has upon the other. In conjunction with evaluation data, the learning organization determines what to improve and makes those improvements on an ongoing basis. Continuous improvement is an unending process.

Systems Thinking

Combining systems thinking with continuous improvement and evaluation, the learning organization looks to understand the interactions, the interrelationships, and the congruence of the interdependent elements that form the complex whole. At the core of this reflection is the desire for individuals within the learning organization to see how their actions impact others and the overall school improvement effort.

> *Vision without systems thinking ends up painting lovely pictures of the future with no deep understanding of forces that must be mastered to move from here to there ... Systems thinking makes understandable the subtlest aspect of the learning organization—a new way individuals perceive themselves and their world.*
>
> Peter Senge

The school portfolio, with its measurement criteria, makes it easy to apply the concepts of systems thinking. Leafing through the descriptions, evidence, and assessments in the portfolio, one is able to recognize incongruences, identify next steps, and determine how to leverage components to make the process more efficient and improve current operations.

Charts that depict an assessment on each continuum give an excellent overview of progress while the set of charts give a comprehensive profile of the overall effort. Figures 30, 31, and 32 profile three schools' assessments on the *Education for the Future Initiative* Continuous Improvement Continuums.

Figure 30 consists of seven bar charts that represent School A's ratings on the seven *Education for the Future Initiative* Continuous Improvement Continuums. The ratings were taken in September and June of their second year of working on systemic school improvement—their first year using the continuums. Even though it is easy for outsiders to think they can make assumptions about the school's progress from these charts, only the school staff are in the position to make judgments. What follow are highlights of staff discussion of the charts and their progress.

Figure 30

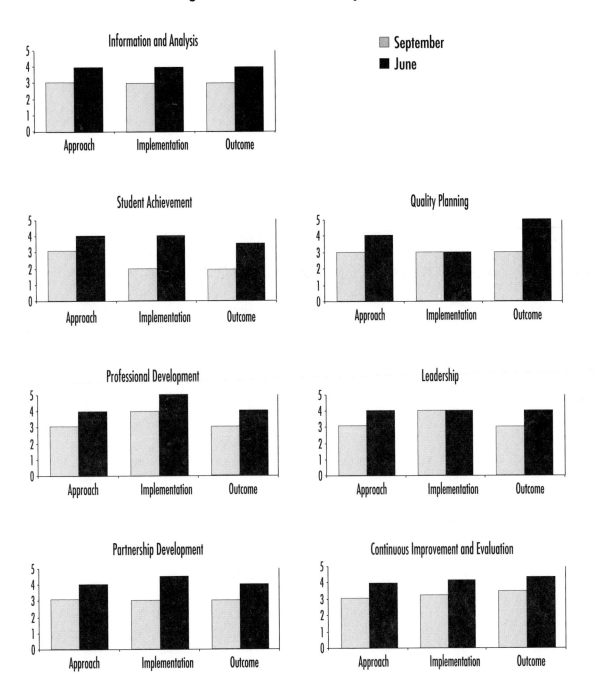

School A's Ratings on the Continouous Improvement Continuums

Each time staff made an assessment, the reflections enabled them to lay out steps to move up in *approach* on every continuum. They consequently moved up the continuums in *implementation* and *outcome* in all but two instances. In Leadership and Quality Planning, *implementation* remained at the same level. By the end of the year, staff felt that they were working much harder in Professional Development than the *outcome* they were receiving. They truly implemented their approach to Leadership to obtain the outcome they wanted.

- **Information and Analysis**. Staff conducted numerous surveys, utilized them within their school improvement process, and through the year were able to use and benefit from gathering and analyzing data about their processes.

- **Student Achievement**. Initially *implementation* lagged behind *approach*. Staff analyzed and took action on questionnaire data related to Student Achievement. They found students had clearly outlined what they liked and what they wished were different about the school—insightful perceptions that helped teachers make changes that resulted in an increase in *outcome* in June.

- **Quality Planning**. This summary rating reflects a school that learned the impact of a comprehensive strategic quality plan. During this year, the school went from what they thought was a good plan to one comprehensive school plan that clearly reflected the vision, delineating timelines and steps to the vision. Staff felt, and the chart shows, that the benefits outweighed the effort made, indicated by the June *outcome* rating—a full two steps above the *implementation* rating. The plan enabled staff to see what each of them needed to do to move the process along and, most significantly, parents and community members were able to see how they could contribute. They rallied around the improvement effort.

- **Professional Development**. This is a category that staff felt they learned most about. Staff thought that they were moving ahead quite nicely with their long-term professional development training commitments. However, when they looked at what they were doing within the context of their strategic plan and Student Achievement, they could see that they needed to revisit their implementation strategies to enable them to get the outcome they wanted.

+ **Leadership**. Staff felt that they were implementing shared decision making at a high level at the beginning of the year. They were able to realize higher levels in *approach* and *outcome* after roles and responsibilities were clarified at the time they revisited their vision.

+ **Partnership Development**. It was easy for staff to see the impact of this continuum on all other continuums and vice versa. At the beginning of the year, staff established a partnership plan. By the middle of the year, community members became a part of the leadership team, and helped staff identify student learning standards and propose real-world experiences for students. Anytime the school wanted to do something different they began by surveying parents and the community for their opinions which resulted in better decision making and support throughout the community.

+ **Continuous Improvement and Evaluation**. During this year staff learned how to evaluate every aspect of their school improvement process and make changes on the basis of the information received. Quality improvements resulted. A major improvement was in their vision. Until they began to evaluate their actions, they hadn't realized that they did not have a true shared vision.

+ **Overall**. Staff were pleased with their progress during the year in all areas but one—Professional Development. As a result, an action team was created to analyze the situation. Before the strategic plan had been created, staff had a seven-year professional development plan that focused one year on math, another English, and so on. The team determined that an implementation support component, coupled with combined integrated instruction and assessment training, would leverage their time and energy. The team recommended that staff utilize peer coaching to support the implementation of the combination.

In overview, School A's charts profile a staff that has a shared vision, is committed to continuous improvement, and is proficient at laying out steps to make what they do even better.

Figure 31 is a profile of a school, School B, that "started wrong." Figure 32, is a profile of School C which became unfocused and subsequently returned to the process of school improvement. School B began the process of school improvement when a corporation in its city offered to support its efforts. The school staff was motivated by the discretionary dollars offered by the corporation. By the end of the fourth year there was nothing to show for their efforts or for the thousands of dollars that had passed through their hands except

Figure 31

School B's Ratings on the Continouous Improvement Continuums

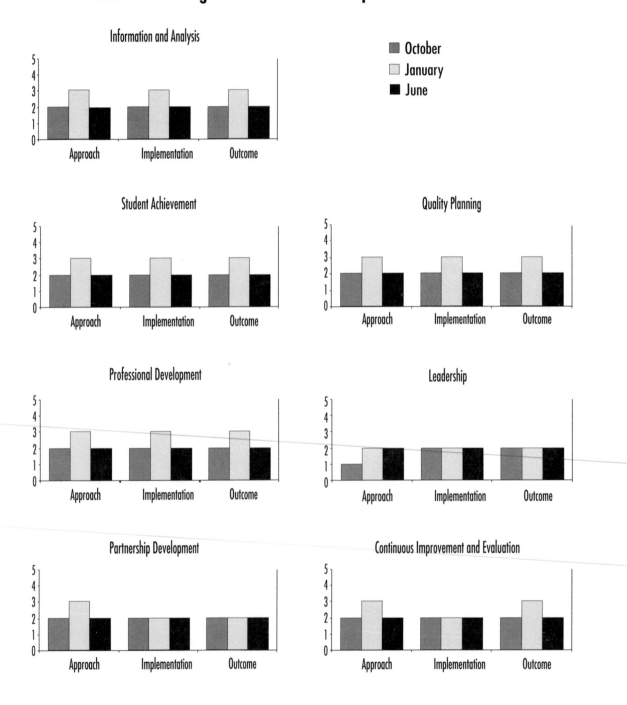

antiquated technology. As the school began its fifth year, its corporate sponsor asked them to assess where they were on the *Education for the Future Initiative* Continuous Improvement Continuums. After reviewing the results, the corporation connected the school with an external change agent with strengths in continuous improvement and evaluation. With the help and lead of the external change agent, the school was able to move up in almost every continuum by the middle of the year. The external change agent helped staff construct, distribute, and analyze surveys about the school. Analyses made clear what elements were not congruent. In addition to the fact that the staff had no faith in the principal, they also lacked a shared vision, a strategic plan, and no real leadership structure. Analyses showed that staff had no base on which to build a shared vision—staff values and beliefs about children, learning, teaching, the purpose of school, and leadership varied greatly. Previously staff had not understood why they were working so hard to implement shared decision making and not getting anywhere. They heard the principal express support vocally for shared decision making, but in fact she was vehemently opposed to the concept and her actions tended to undermine what staff were trying to do.

Depressed by the reality of their squelched efforts, School B staff did not work to implement the analyses during the spring semester. Thus, their ratings reverted to October levels.

The corporate representatives met with staff to find out what they could do to help the school get back on track for the benefit of the children who were not receiving a continuum of learning that would prepare them for the world of work. After a lengthy discussion with the corporate partners and the superintendent (who refused to replace the principal), staff decided that it would be impossible for them to continue in the partnership.

Figure 32 shows the profile of School C, a large inner-city middle school in its third year of school improvement and first year of conducting self-assessments on the *Education for the Future Initiative* Continuous Improvement Continuums. In October, staff basically concentrated their efforts on getting ready for a State Department of Education program review that was to take place at the end of March. They did what they needed to do to do well on the review. They sent out questionnaires, set up a school plan related to one subject area, and sent their faculty to professional development training in the areas that related to the program review. In January, they analyzed questionnaire results, but for the most part did little toward their systemic school improvement efforts. They began using and seeing the benefits of data and a comprehensive school plan. The charts of

Figure 32

School C's Ratings on the Continouous Improvement Continuums

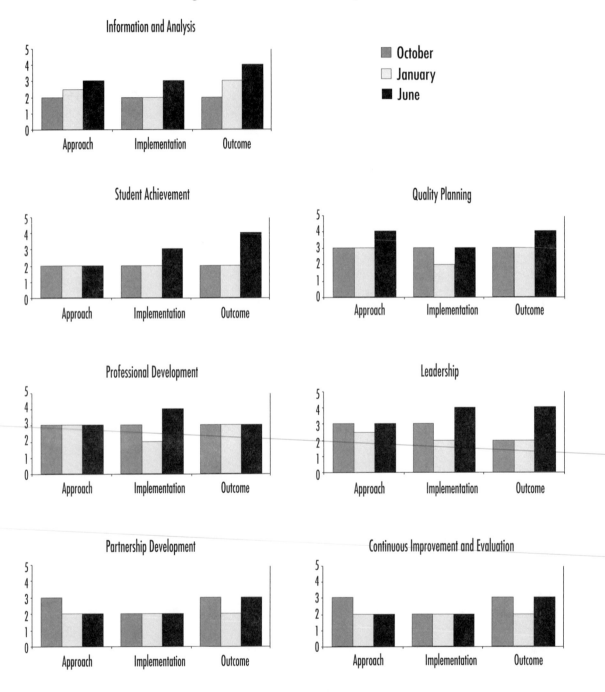

School C's continuum summary graphically show how progress stopped during the program review that focused on one subject area and resumed when it was over.

What it Looks Like

When we work with schools on continuous schoolwide improvement, we must take schools from wherever they are and establish or refocus them on their guiding principles. The process will look different and begin differently for every school.

Let's pick up where Paul Jones Elementary left off in Chapter 4.

Teachers of Paul Jones Elementary School had pressure from the school board and their community to increase student achievement scores. They tried to "restructure" for two years—to no avail. They had absolutely nothing to show for their efforts.

They also thought they were doing the best they could possibly do with the population with which they had to work. They had students coming directly from Mexico, many having never experienced school—even 12 year olds. Many families took their students out of the classrooms to move to Arizona for part of the year—just when they were making progress! In addition, many of these families stayed in Mexico after Christmas, often not returning until February. The teachers became frustrated with having to limit classroom activities to videos for the few students who were in classes during the month of January.

When they began to gather data for their "restructuring" efforts, it became evident that it would be very difficult to meaningfully disaggregate student achievement scores when the scores were already in the 2nd percentile and when 86 percent of the population was of one ethnicity. Questionnaire results did not show anything significant. The teachers were again asked what they thought the purpose of the school was. They answered that the purpose of this K-6 school was to prepare students for middle school. When asked if they knew how well they were doing with regard to their purpose, they all looked a little bewildered. It was recommended that they send a group of teachers to the middle school and the high school to understand how well they were doing with respect to their purpose.

Six teachers visited the feeder middle school and then the high school. They returned in tears. They found the following:

- *Many of their former students were already dropping out of school by the 7th grade.*
- *Only a few graduated from high school.*

- *Every student who was not fluent in English was tracked in a bilingual or special education program. They were, perhaps, never going to learn English and never going to become "mainstream."*
- *The tracked students were never allowed to work on computers or take career opportunity or college-bound classes.*
- *Basically every student who was not fluent in English was treated like, and considered, a "throw away kid."*

The teachers were beginning to see how they had contributed to limiting their students' options and opportunities. The discussion that followed led them to immediately agree that the purpose of the school was to prepare students to be anything they wanted to be in the future. Their number one goal became ensuring that every student articulating from Paul Jones Elementary School could speak, read, and write in English.

The teachers turned to Education for the Future Initiative staff for guidance. They asked, "how do we achieve our number one goal of ensuring English fluency?" They were told to look very carefully at current practices. In other words, how were they currently teaching students to speak, read, and write English? They analyzed their processes and results. The teachers found that by following the national standard of 20 minutes of English instruction to Spanish-speaking students each day, 35 out of 985 students moved into English-speaking classrooms each year. In fact, they found that they had been using the same processes and were netting the same results for almost five years. They groaned in sad embarrassment. If only they'd known this little formula five years ago.

Immediately teachers asked, "what if we begin providing 40 minutes of English instruction a day?" They tried it and, equally important, they measured it as soon as they could. The results: more than twice the number of students moved into English-speaking classrooms—in the first semester.

Staff also took a hard look at all offerings of the school and who their clients were. Teachers admitted that they had been blaming the kids and the parents for the lack of progress. They knew they needed to provide a more nurturing and inviting learning environment for both. With 86 percent of their clientele gone in January, they decided they could easily change their school calendar to gain a whole month's instruction. This was just the beginning.

In a short period of time, many wonderful things started to happen:

- *Student achievement increased in all areas.*

- *Parent education classes were offered and very well attended.*

- *Approximately 250 parents showed up for every School Improvement meeting.*

- *Families stopped migrating!!! Fathers would go to Arizona, but families stayed because, for the first time ever, they felt like they belonged to a community and to a school.*

- *In the Spring of 1995, students in a 4th grade transitional class sent a quilt to the Education for the Future Initiative office. They called it "The Dreams of Children Quilt." Each of the students made a block that illustrated what they would like to be when they grow up, and each student wrote a note explaining why they wanted to be what they wanted to be. Then they wrote, "thank you for helping our school give us the opportunity to dream and providing us with options in life. "*

A shared vision paints the picture of what a school wants to create. Self-assessments on rubrics and comprehensive continuous improvement and evaluation allow a school to see what they have created. Systems thinking allows teachers to see beyond the four walls of their classroom and it reveals how the individuals in the school have created what they currently have, and how each participant fits into the big picture.

Assessing Your School's Continuous Improvement and Evaluation

Table 8 is the Continuous Improvement and Evaluation Continuum. Using the sections in the continuum, as well as the paraphrased descriptions that follow, assess your school's *approach*, *implementation* and *outcome* with respect to Continuous Improvement and Evaluation.

Which statement below best describes your school's *approach* to Continuous Improvement and Evaluation?

. . . .

Approach

1. No attempt is made to plan for change, implement change, evaluate, or improve. The culture of the school does not support goal setting.

2. Although there is no attempt to plan for overall change or to look at the components of a school as interrelated parts, the staff and administration do try to find solutions to the perceived problems of the school.

3. The school has begun to use a continuous improvement model of planning, implementing, evaluating, and improving for some components of the school.

4. The school plans, implements, evaluates, and continually works to improve all components of the school. The staff understands the interrelationship between parts of the system and, therefore, makes sure that all parts are working together to help students move forward along a continuum of learning.

5. A rigorous process of continuous improvement, using data-based evaluation to drive improvement, is used throughout the school by staff and administrators. The entire school improvement effort is focused on the achievement of all students along a continuum of learning.

Your assessment _____ Date _____

Which statement below best describes your school's *implementation* of Continuous Improvement and Evaluation?

· ·

Implementation

1. The school operates day-to-day, with teachers and administrators reacting individually to problems as they arise.

2. Changes, which are made in response to specific problems, tend to be superficial because they are not based on root causes, and do not take into account how the different aspects of the system impact each other.

3. Data, including client perceptions, are used to plan, implement, and evaluate the effectiveness of changes which have been made at the school level. Ongoing evaluation is used for further school improvement. The school's operational system is examined as a whole.

4. The continuous improvement process—plan, implement, evaluate, and improve—is evident in all classrooms throughout the school, as well as the school as a whole. Teachers use the process to improve instructional strategies and to prevent student failure.

5. Continuous improvement and evaluation is a way of life for every member of the school organization. Teachers use student feedback and performance data on an ongoing basis to reassess and refine teaching strategies. The entire school organization is focused on supporting teacher efforts to improve student performance along a comprehensive learning continuum.

Your assessment _____   Date _____

Which statement below best describes your school's *outcome* with respect to Continuous Improvement and Evaluation?

· ·

Outcome

1. In the face of poor student achievement, individuals blame each other or "the system." Because the school's problems are viewed as inevitable, the same mistakes are made again and again.

2. There are little, if any, positive long-term results from the changes which were undertaken. The staff is surprised by new problems which arise from the failure to understand how the elements of the system are related to each other.

3. Student performance improves and fewer students fail as a result of the improvement process. The school is able to maintain positive results because it is continually reassessing based on data and fine-tuning the changes it has made to all the components of the school.

4. Student performance improvements are evident throughout the school and for all subgroups. Teachers are skilled at using data to assess and improve teaching strategies and to prevent individual student failures.

5. Every student achieves along a continuum of learning. The entire school is an effective learning organization, focused on continually improving student performance. Strategies and practices which do not serve this end are replaced through the *plan, implement, evaluate,* and *improve* process.

Your assessment _____   Date _____

Table 8

Continuous Improvement and Evaluation

	ONE	TWO	THREE	FOUR	FIVE
APPROACH	Neither goals nor strategies exist for the evaluation and continuous improvement of the school organization or for elements of the school organization.	The approach to continuous improvement and evaluation is problem solving. If there are no problems, or if solutions can be made quickly, there is no need for improvement or analyses. Changes in parts of the system are not coordinated with all other parts.	Some elements of the school organization are evaluated for effectiveness. Some elements are improved on the basis of the evaluation findings.	All elements of the school's operations are evaluated for improvement and to ensure congruence of the elements with respect to the continuum of learning students experience.	All aspects of the school organization are rigorously evaluated and improved on a continuous basis. Students, and the maintenance of a comprehensive learning continuum for students, become the focus of all aspects of the school improvement process.
IMPLEMENTATION	With no overall plan for evaluation and continuous improvement, strategies are changed by individual teachers and administrators only when something sparks the need to improve. Reactive decisions and activities are a daily mode of operation.	Isolated changes are made in some areas of the school organization in response to problem incidents. Changes are not preceded by comprehensive analyses, such as an understanding of the root causes of problems. The effectiveness of the elements of the school organization, or changes made to the elements, is not known.	Elements of the school organization are improved on the basis of comprehensive analyses of root causes of problems, client perceptions, and operational effectiveness of processes.	Continuous improvement analyses of student achievement and instructional strategies are rigorously reinforced within each classroom and across learning levels to develop a comprehensive learning continuum for students and to prevent student failure.	Comprehensive continuous improvement becomes the way of doing business at the school. Teachers continuously improve the appropriateness and effectiveness of instructional strategies based on student feedback and performance. All aspects of the school organization are improved to support teachers' efforts.
OUTCOME	Individuals struggle with system failure. Finger pointing and blaming others for failure occurs. The effectiveness of strategies is not known. Mistakes are repeated.	Problems are solved only temporarily and few positive changes result. Additionally, unintended and undesirable consequences often appear in other parts of the system. Many aspects of the school are incongruent, keeping the school from reaching its vision.	Evidence of effective improvement strategies is observable. Positive changes are made and maintained due to comprehensive analyses and evaluation.	Teachers become astute at assessing and in predicting the impact of their instructional strategies on individual student achievement. Sustainable improvements in student achievement are evident at all grade levels, due to continuous improvement.	The school becomes a congruent and effective learning organization. Only instruction and assessment strategies that produce quality student achievement are used. A true continuum of learning results for all students.

Items That Might Be Found In the Continuous Improvement and Evaluation Section of the School Portfolio

The following are appropriate items for inclusion in this section:

- School's assessment on the Continous Improvement and Evaluation Continuous Improvement Continuum
- Plans for evaluation
- Plans for continuous improvement
- Summary assessments on all continuous improvement continuums
- Accomplishments for the year
- Analysis of progress
- Plans for improvement
- Analysis of what needs to happen to move to the next steps in the continuum

Continuous Improvement and Evaluation Questions

The following questions are designed to help you think about what your school has in evidence of where you are with regard to Continuous Improvement and Evaluation.

What do you have for documentation for the Continuous Improvement and Evaluation section of your school portfolio?

What other things do you need to gather and document in the Continuous Improvement and Evaluation section?

What are your next steps with staff with respect to Continuous Improvement and Evaluation?

Coupling the school portfolio process with a measurement device such as the *Education for the Future Initiative* Continuous Improvement Continuums has proven to be an effective ongoing monitoring system that promotes systemic change. This nonthreatening and positive approach enables schools to move beyond merely adopting innovations and new strategies to actually implementing them. When properly used, the portfolio approach helps to create and maintain a shared vision and leads to the successful creation of a comprehensive learning organization.

Chapter 11

PUTTING IT ALL TOGETHER

In the preceding chapters, the intent behind the *Education for the Future Initiative* Continuous Improvement Continuums was described, as was the documentation and materials one might include in a school portfolio using these criteria. This chapter brings the focus back to the logistics of creating, updating, and maintaining the school portfolio and managing the school improvement effort. The first part of this chapter discusses the role and benefits of having a school coach who supports the improvement efforts, and is followed by a section addressing methods for updating and maintaining the school portfolio. The chapter continues with common questions school personnel ask when developing their own school portfolios and school improvement efforts. The chapter concludes with a set of questions designed to think through the process of updating and maintaining a school portfolio.

This year I was elected as the school site council coordinator. I was reluctant to take this on, seeing it as the "bagel and fruit" coordinator for inservice training. . . . Now that we have begun developing a school portfolio, using the Education for the Future Initiative Continuous Improvement Continuums, I feel that maybe I can make a difference toward coordinating all of our school efforts toward one goal that is known to all teachers. I find myself eager to get to work to try it all out. It's given me a little faith— I don't want to lose it.

Jackie Davis Martin

School Coach

There is nothing more valuable to the school improvement process than another pair of eyes, especially in the form of a dedicated school coach or external change agent whose priority is your school's success. School personnel who have utilized quality school coaches have realized changes they thought might only be part of a dream.

> *The real voyage of discovery consists not in seeking new landscapes, but in seeing with new eyes.*
>
> Marcel Proust

Schools need help with the logistics of the school improvement process. A school coach can help staff do the things they need to do while helping them internalize the knowledge and skills needed to sustain change after the coach leaves. Coaches who are not involved at the same level of detail as school personnel are able to see the big picture and ask questions that can clarify ideas and approaches.

The most effective school coaches are individuals with no vested personal interests in the current operations and processes of the schools and who are driven by and committed to the purposes for the change—increased student achievement and schools that prepare their students for work in the 21st Century. An ideal coach is creative, flexible, and capable of thinking about schools and school processes in new ways; capable of stimulating and causing change; capable of assisting with the translating of the vision into action; and, is a good listener and synthesizer of information. Effective school coaches understand continuous improvement and measurement and are able to help school personnel learn how to measure progress and change. Ideally, school coaches are also effective resource brokers.

School coaches must have credibility within the school, be knowledgeable of the school's rules, teachers, cultures, climates, and group processes, and thoughtful about the improvement process. Specifically, they must be able to—

- help the school plan for systemic change by guiding the synthesis of diverse subplans into one cohesive school plan that reflects the consensus of thought and provides a focus for everyone
- reinforce, explain, and model, focusing on achieving the school plan, conducting effective meetings, and facilitating consensus decisions
- assist school personnel in becoming proficient at data-based decision making and working with a driving purpose
- help define and support school principals in new leadership roles as keepers of the vision

- support teachers in new leadership roles as decision makers and researchers

- assist schools in analyzing and utilizing measures of process impact to be able to answer questions like: How well are our current processes meeting our clients' needs? How can we continually improve our operations to continually meet our clients' needs?

- help staff think beyond currently defined boundaries and how to make all the pieces congruent and focused on the school vision

- ask questions to help staff clarify their thinking

- coach and model for teachers and administrators how to communicate with one another, how to work in collaboration to focus their efforts on children, and how to let others help them do the things they have begun

- remind teachers and administrators of the difference between a condition and a problem. A condition is something they cannot change. A problem is something they do have the power to change—keep them using their time effectively by working on the things they can change

- assure school personnel that asking for assistance and guidance is a sign of intelligent strength and not of weakness

Updating and Maintaining the School Portfolio

Before staff actually begin the process of creating their school portfolio, it often seems to be an overwhelming task. With a few simple steps, however, it becomes obvious what evidence they need to collect, and where it goes, once they—

- identify the sections they want to use
- create an outline which details what they currently have and things they still need for each section
- conduct their assessments using a measurement tool such as the *Education for the Future Initiative* Continuous Improvement Continuums

It is a real spirit booster when school staff first see their hard work with students reflected in a finished school portfolio. The usefulness of the portfolio in getting grants, showing to visitors, and using as a basis for accreditation is obvious; however, the portfolio has the potential to be far more than a public relations document. When used well, it is an ongoing tool for assessing progress toward the school's vision and goals and helping everyone understand what steps need to be taken to move ahead.

Leni von Blanckensee,
Education for the Future
Initiative Associate

As the evidence is pulled together into one document, how the pieces work together also becomes obvious. This is, of course, one of the reasons for creating the school portfolio in the first place—to document, reflect, and continuously improve the alignment of all parts of the learning organization. When elements are documented and assessed, they start to change, and steps needed to move ahead become clear.

On the first writing, staff will find elements that are obviously out of alignment with the vision. A plan for bringing them into alignment can be created quickly while writing the portfolio. Larger elements that need work, such as the vision and action plan, will require whole staff attention and definition beyond the first year. This early phase of school portfolio writing is very exciting. Everyone senses the opportunity for change and can begin to picture a new scenario.

For schools that have already embarked on a systemic change process, the school portfolio offers two powerful features. First, the school portfolio organizes the documentation involved in any systemic change process—one place to keep all evidence that will be used to measure total program quality and progress toward the school vision and goals. Second, the school portfolio provides for comprehensive measurement of processes and data analyses—a critical part that is most often missing in systemic change processes.

Updating the School Portfolio

When the school portfolio is written, bound, and on display, staff have a sense of pride in their finished product. In fact, most cannot imagine operating their school without one. However, the job is far from over. When a new self-assessment is completed and new test scores arrive, the discussion about what to do with this new "stuff" begins. Although staff may have had conversations about updating and maintaining the portfolio when it was being developed, the process of maintaining and updating may be different when confronted with the reality of the new "stuff" in front of them.

Just like the newness of the school portfolio can be exciting, the updating of the school portfolio does not have to be a difficult and tedious undertaking. The key is to plan early for updating and maintenance to ensure a smooth process. Recommendations to this end include the following:

+ Establish indices so everyone knows which sections will be rewritten each year, which sections will have subsections that get added annually, and which sections accumulate information on a regular basis.

+ Clarify what will be added when.

+ Determine who is going to do the work.

+ Set up an archival process.

<u>Establish Indices</u>

If clear indices were not established when the portfolio was first developed, it is one of the first things to do in the first update. In fact, the first update will clarify the indices needed. Your major sections might be congruent with the *Education for the Future Initiative* Continuous Improvement Continuums. Adding subsections that identify major elements of each section will help organize the school portfolio for maintenance over the years. An example index follows which illustrates the point (see Figure 33).

Figure 33

Sample School Portfolio Index

Introduction

Overview of the School Portfolio

Information and Analysis
  The School*
    Location
    Community
    Students
    Teachers
    Administration
  Student Questionnaire Results
    Year 1
    Year 2
    Year 3
  Teacher Prediction of Student
  Questionnaire Results
    Year 1
    Year 2
    Year 3
  Teacher Questionnaire Results
    Year 1
    Year 2
    Year 3
  Parent Questionnaire Results
    Year 1
    Year 2
    Year 3
  Standardized Test Results
  Authentic Assessment Results
  Analysis of Information & Analysis
    Year 1
    Year 2
    Year 3

Student Achievement
  Year 1
  Year 2
  Year 3

Quality Planning
  Year 1
  Year 2
  Year 3

Professional Development
  Year 1
  Year 2
  Year 3

Leadership
  Year 1
  Year 2
  Year 3

Partnership Development
  Parents
  Business
  Community

Continuous Improvement and Evaluation
  Ratings on the Continuous
  Improvement Continuums (CIC)
    Year 1
    Year 2
    Year 3

---

* A lot of this information is found in most "School Accountability Report Cards." While it is an excellent beginning, make sure it is accurate and useful in its form for inclusion here.

Identify What Will Be Added When

What and when to add to the school portfolio depends upon the type and purpose of the evidence and information being gathered. Staff should outline how evidence will be treated and when it will be updated to ensure that others will understand the timeline. A system directly within the school portfolio, e.g., subsections in the indices, can be helpful in clarifying what will be added when.

School staff seldom rewrite their entire school portfolio each year. While the exception and not the rule, some sections do lend themselves to being rewritten each year, e.g., context of the school, its enrollment, and the demographics of its population. These are sections that the school will want to have ready for use at all times. They are the boilerplates for grants, state and regional reviews, and for federal program reporting. It is also a section that blends historical data with current data.

Other sections likely to be rewritten each year are the subsections reporting student achievement results. The school will want to work with historical charts in order to follow cohorts of students over time to track increases in student achievement. As new scores are added, new charts must be created to replace the outdated charts.

The frequency of adding new material to the school portfolio varies from section to section. Most sections will probably need to be added to once or twice a year. For example, questionnaire results will likely be added once a year, and self-assessments on the *Education for the Future Initiative* Continuous Improvement Continuums will likely be added twice a year.

Since the portfolio documents the school's continuous improvement process and progress, and since continuous improvement is an ongoing process not a year-end activity, relevant newspaper articles and other evidence need to be added as they become available. An example of a section that might need to be updated on an ongoing basis is the school plan. As things are accomplished and new information is obtained with respect to implementing the school vision, the plan should be updated to reflect the progress and changes.

When implementing a system for updating the school portfolio, it is important to remember that one of the original purposes of the school portfolio is to create one document that describes the school and can be used for multiple purposes. Be sure to keep those purposes in mind and the objectives clear throughout the updating process.

Determine Who is Going to Do the Work

Staff will have to decide who takes the lead in updating the school portfolio. In many cases, the school improvement coordinator or the principal takes responsibility for updating the portfolio. That does not mean that they do all the work. It just means that they take the lead and may delegate parts to different teams or individuals in the school who would then be responsible for making sure that the portfolio is up to date for major events such as open houses, program reviews, and important visitors.

Set Up an Archival Process

The school portfolio will eventually hold all historical data, analytical data, and other evidence important to the school. Consequently, the physical size of your portfolio can become very big and too cumbersome to handle. It is recommended that you establish an annual process to archive the old evidence that may no longer be current but still of value to keep.

Your old evidence may have historical significance in the years ahead. Your old statistical data will serve to cement the school's progress and growth as you look back in time. Create charts that consolidate data over time and write up summaries of events that occurred during the year. This process makes the collection of a lot of additional evidence unnecessary. You might choose to add adjunct binders that hold charts and other supporting material.

Maintaining the School Portfolio

One process that will involve most, if not all, staff members in the maintenance of the school portfolio is to set up a School Portfolio Maintenance Vine (see Figure 34). Set up the vine by agreeing on who the School Portfolio Vine Keeper will be. It should be an energetic, dynamic, respected, and not-afraid-to-ask staff member. This person may or may not be the principal. Next, all staff members are divided into small groups or "vines." Staff members should be grouped based upon interests in particular sections of the school portfolio, collegiality, access to one another, break times, early birds, late workers, proximity, and any other criteria which bring people together.

The Vine Leaders will coordinate maintenance activities with the School Portfolio Vine Keeper. Each Vine Leader will have staff members in its vine, and each staff member will be responsible for collecting or writing specific pieces of evidence. The Vine Leaders as well as the Vine Keeper must actively participate in this process. By keeping in communication with her/his staff members, the Vine Leaders will make sure that the target dates for collecting all evidence will be met.

The success of each vine depends upon how well each member meets their responsibilities for data collection evidence. Once the Vine Leaders collect all the evidence, they will meet with the Vine Keeper to update the school portfolio.

Figure 34

SCHOOL PORTFOLIO MAINTENANCE VINE

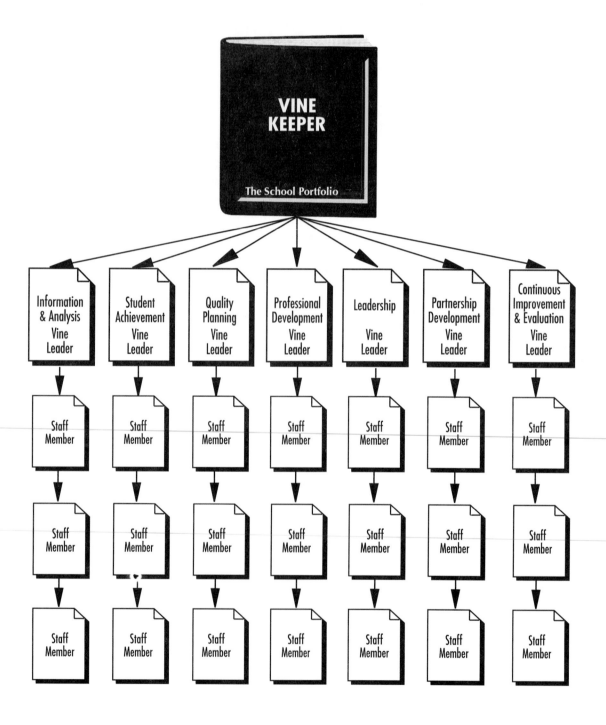

Another tool which is useful for maintaining the school portfolio is the School Portfolio Update Worksheet. Staff use this worksheet to think through the updating of the portfolio sections when they conduct their assessments on the *Education for the Future Initiative* Continuous Improvement Continuums (see Figure 35 below).

Figure 35

School Portfolio Update Worksheet

Portfolio Section _____

What has been done?	Has it shown growth? Or non-growth?	Measured by what evidence?

Frequently Asked Questions Related to Creating, Updating, and Maintaining the School Portfolio

How does one get started creating a school portfolio?

The steps recommended for creating a comprehensive school portfolio for school improvement include the following:

- Locate a large binder for storing the information. (Add an attractive cover page that displays the school logo or an image of the school's vision.)

- Determine, as staff, who will manage the logistics.

- Develop, as a staff, a systematic management system that specifies what goes into the portfolio and how often it will be monitored and updated.

- Establish criteria for monitoring processes, progress, and products.

- Set up the binder with dividers based on the *Education for the Future Initiative* Continuous Improvement Continuums, or other criteria you have chosen.

- Take a baseline assessment of your school on each of the criteria or continuums.

- Gather and organize all information described in Chapters 4 through 10 that exists about the school.

> *The more we develop a sensitivity to systems, the more we define our role in managing the system... the intent becomes one of understanding movement based on a deep respect for the web of activity and relationships that comprise the system.*
>
> Margaret Wheatley

- Determine items that will need to be constructed, issues that need to be discussed and planned with the entire school community, and list actions required for moving ahead on the continuums.

- Determine additional information required to describe the school's uniqueness.

- Begin writing a narrative that tells the story of your school, its vision, and its progress.

- Make sure the organization of your school portfolio will allow for many uses (i.e., grants, state reviews, regional accreditation, etc.).

What should go into a school portfolio?

The preceding chapters describe the items to consider for inclusion in a school portfolio for the specific categories of Information and Analysis, Student Achievement, Quality Planning, Professional Development, Leadership, Partnership Development, and Continuous Improvement and Evaluation. If other categories are adopted, much of the same evidence probably will be used, but may be arranged in a different order.

In general, it is best to start each category with a description of where the school rated itself when the school improvement process began, the vision for the category, what the school is doing to reach the vision, progress to date, and plans for improvement. The continuum assessments and descriptions can help organize each chapter. Most of these descriptions will set the baseline, or boilerplate, for the portfolio. In fact, it is expedient to establish descriptions to which one can *add* easily, so that the sections do not need to be rewritten each time items are added. Periodic updating of the text might be necessary, but hopefully only to add new information and not to rewrite. Overall, the intent is to document the evolution of change and ongoing assessments for synthesis and reflection.

Evidence needed for each category becomes apparent from descriptions of progress and from the criteria on which the assessment of progress is made. For example, if the school's shared decision-making structure has evolved from a team structure that has been *studying* different approaches to increasing student achievement to a team structure to *implement* the study teams' recommendations, it would be appropriate to document the make-up of the study teams, how they were formed, their roles and responsibilities, their recommendations, and their current status. How and why the study teams evolved into implementation teams should also be detailed. A schematic chart or description of the different team structures can display how the teams evolved and work together.

The documentation of evidence will be important whenever trouble shooting becomes necessary, and is important as a reference. Wherever possible, actual evidence should be included, such as questionnaire results, budgets, newspaper clippings, and where appropriate, actual student work that demonstrates changes in achievement.

What is meant by evidence?

In the context of the school portfolio, evidence can be described as documentation which shows the current status of the school with respect to elements of schoolwide improvement. It can address a specific section of a portfolio or demonstrate that action was taken. Student achievement results are evidence of the impact of school processes and are considered documentation for a school portfolio. Evidence such as a new parent-school partnership, a new business partnership, or a group of teachers who attended inservice on building classroom web pages should also be documented in the school portfolio.

What happens when items can go in two or more places?

Many times you will find that an item of evidence or a description could fit into two or more places within the portfolio. Because all school elements are interrelated, many items and descriptions can fit and appear in more than one section quite easily. If the evidence appears in one category or chapter, you can still write about it in another category or chapter. For example, historical student achievement data logically fit in both the Information and Analysis and the Student Achievement chapters. One could decide to show the information once or twice, talk about it in both places, just show and talk about it in one place, or show it in one place and talk about it in another. Part of the decision should be made based upon where it helps the reader most.

Should there be rules established for what goes in the portfolio and when it is updated?

Staff will need to establish rules or processes for putting information into the school portfolio so that it does not become a storage bin for everything that the school does. Some schools concentrate on the descriptions at the beginning of each chapter, and include specific evidence referenced in the descriptions as well as those implied in the measurement criteria.

Many schools review portfolio text and evidence when they conduct their self-assessments on the *Education for the Future Initiative* Continuous Improvement Continuums—two times each year. That way they can use the portfolio to help determine where they are, to reflect on and set goals based upon the information, and to update the portfolio to reflect progress since the previous assessment. In some schools, the portfolio is updated on an annual basis. Unfortunately, some of these schools find that information they want to include at the end of the year cannot be located. Most find that the task of updating once a year is much more arduous than taking a continuous updating approach. Also, updating on an ongoing basis helps to make the portfolio a real living resource.

How long should evidence be kept in the portfolio?

The answer to this question depends upon the evidence, how the portfolio is updated and maintained, and staff preference. In most cases, as soon as the evidence can be described in text form, or replaced by more current evidence, the old evidence can be discarded or archived. For example, student achievement results are evidence that your school would want to leave in the portfolio all year for reference. As new data are obtained, a new chart with historical information can replace the previous chart. Professional development plans and schedules are established for the year. The actual plan for a past year can be reduced to a paragraph describing the goals and accomplishments of that year. Other evidence, like previous years' questionnaire results, might remain in the portfolio where it first appeared, or it might be moved to another volume or an appendix for occasional access, or it might be incorporated into another year's graph.

Who actually does the writing of a school portfolio?

This depends upon your school. If at all possible, try to look at the school portfolio effort as something that also meets other needs. For example, if you have someone in charge of grants at the school and they are released from other duties to work on grant applications, perhaps that person could write parts of the portfolio, especially the initial parts that can also be used as boilerplates for grant writing. If one person is not identified to do the writing, different staff members or teams might take responsibility for specific sections. If a team is writing a state or regional review, they could be establishing the beginnings of a school portfolio.

Where should the school portfolio be kept?

The school portfolio should be kept in a location where it is safe, kept intact, and where everyone in the school has access to it—especially the leadership team who will find the information contained in it necessary and helpful for decision making. It is preferable to have at least three copies of the portfolio accessible and available to parents and community members to read; one for the teachers' workroom, one copy for a coffee table in the welcoming area of the school, and one in the principal's office which would be available to respond to requests for information by the district office or to show visitors or potential partners. Some district offices also keep a copy of each of their schools' portfolios.

Who is responsible for the school portfolio?

A school portfolio is a comprehensive document that reflects everything there is to know about the school. Every staff member should be aware of its contents, understand its purpose and uses, assist with its creation and updating, and know where it is located so that it can be used whenever it is needed. If having a school portfolio is new for the school, staff will need to identify a person, or group of persons, to be responsible for its organization, development, and updating. The coordinator for the school's improvement efforts, the principal, or both, typically assume responsibility for the portfolio.

How do we know where we are on the continuums, and how do we know if we are where we say we are?

Staff have to be the ultimate judge of where the school is on the *Education for the Future Initiative* Continuous Improvement Continuums assessment criteria; however, evidence included in the portfolio will help to make the determination. Discussions held while reaching consensus on the assessments clarify where staff are collectively. It may be easiest to determine where the school is not. As the school progresses with the school improvement process, and as staff get more practice conducting the assessments, it becomes easier to know where the school is on any of the continuums.

Only six of us are working on change in our math program. Can we use a portfolio?

The beauty of the school portfolio is its flexibility. Different kinds of schools and programs can use it effectively for their specific needs. In fact, much of the text could be the same. Most grants want to understand the context of the program, so information and analysis and the overall design of the school and plan are appropriate.

How can we start if we have no money or no release time?

If you are overwhelmed by all of the questionnaire data and information that you need to gather to produce a meaningful portfolio, and if you have no money or release time, start with what you have. For example, most school districts can easily provide historical, school-level student achievement data. Make these data into graphs or, better yet, have students make the graphs. If that still seems like a burden, then start by listening to the kids—ask them what they like about school; what they wish were different. Then, at staff meetings, compare notes with colleagues. In fact, staff meetings are a good place to begin the dialogue about what staff really want to collect and how it can be gathered. Also, check with the district, county, or regional offices of education for assistance in processing and collecting data. It might be that some of the data have already been collected. In some states, state or county departments of education provide data to download—check their websites.

The important thing is to focus on what you can do. Once you get started, you will find that using a school portfolio (with criteria for assessment, such as the *Education for the Future Initiative* Continuous Improvement Continuums) will help staff use their limited time more effectively. It will enable staff to do one data collecting task that can be used for multiple purposes without adding to the workload.

It is highly recommended that you connect with a school coach or an external change agent who can assist your school with the school portfolio and school improvement process.

Who interprets the data?

Staff, perhaps with students, community members, or a school coach are the ones who ultimately have to make sense out of the data. Sometimes it is necessary to bring someone in from the outside—someone with some data analysis skills—to look at the data objectively. Every school is encouraged to find an external change agent who can coach the school through the improvement process and help with the synthesis of data. Someone external to the process can often see things that people directly involved in making change cannot see.

What software programs do you recommend for developing a school portfolio?

Standard wordprocessing programs can be used to input and update school portfolio text. Tables, such as the evaluation table in Chapter 10, can be created with wordprocessing programs. Graphics and charts can easily be inserted within the text. For making charts, spreadsheet analyses, and for data-based information, locate a good high-end spreadsheet program with database and chart-making capabilities. Make sure the programs you choose are user friendly so that these tools do not keep you from doing what you want to do with the school portfolio. Also check on the programs your district uses so, if there are data available, you will have the appropriate program at the school.

How do we go about getting regional accreditation to accept this process in lieu of the current process?

Certainly using a school portfolio with rubrics similar to the *Education for the Future Initiative* Continuous Improvement Continuums, or similar ones, can be as comprehensive, if not more, than some regional or state review processes. The benefit of using the portfolio is that it utilizes one comprehensive school plan which can be used for many different applications and processes. Review the accrediting agency's requirements and think through how the school portfolio could meet both entities' needs. Write and send an analysis of the similarities and advantages of using the school portfolio to the accrediting agency. Visit or call to talk through the options. These agencies are generally very receptive to "experimental" approaches. Who knows? When they see the power of the school portfolio, they may adopt it as their preferred approach.

Why is updating important?

When updating of the school portfolio is warranted to reflect progress based upon actual evidence, the portfolio greatly enriches that reflection. It helps everyone understand where the gaps are, what changes are needed so all parts of the organization can be congruent with the vision, and what each person's role is in moving forward to reach the vision. It is not only a record of what the school has done, but also a map that helps the school understand how to get to its desired destination.

Using a school portfolio with assessment criteria for school improvement will help everyone in the school understand their part in moving the school to a vision. The chosen assessment criteria can form the structure of the school portfolio. The discussion around the criteria are excellent beginning words for a new portfolio. While each school portfolio will be unique, it is important that the portfolio be an evolving document that reflects the assessment of the staff rather than an individual, and that it be accessible to everyone in the school community. Plan for the maintenance of your school portfolio from the beginning. Design your portfolio around how you want to update it. You may want to have yearly dividers behind each section of the portfolio for ease in updating information and finding it later. Some schools write summaries each year and weed out some of the old evidence. Others keep old evidence as a way of tracking progress, while others will rewrite the sections. Any way is fine. Staff will begin to see the value of the portfolio when the long-term information is included.

Putting It All Together Questions

Who is, or can be, your school coach?

Who will be responsible for creating your school portfolio?

How will the school portfolio be updated and maintained?

Who will be responsible for updating and maintaining the school portfolio?

Who will be responsible for keeping your school portfolio?

How will it be organized and how will what goes in it be determined?

These *Education for the Future Initiative* Continuous Improvement Continuums, adapted from the Malcolm Baldrige Award Program for Quality Business Management, provide an authentic means for measuring schoolwide improvement and growth. In conjunction with a school portfolio, schools use these continuums as a vehicle for ongoing self-assessment. They use the results of the assessment to acknowledge their accomplishments, to set goals for improvement, and to keep school districts and partners apprised of the progress they have made in their school improvement efforts.

Appendix
A

CONTINUOUS IMPROVEMENT CONTINUUMS

The *Education for the Future Initiative* Continuous Improvement Continuums are a type of rubric that represents the theoretical flow of systemic school improvement. The continuums are made up of seven key, interrelated, and overlapping components of systemic change—Information and Analysis, Student Achievement, Quality Planning, Professional Development, Leadership, Partnership Development, and Continuous Improvement and Evaluation.

The continuums are made up of seven key, interrelated, and overlapping components of systemic change

Understanding the Continuums

These rubrics, extending from *one* to *five* horizontally, represent a continuum of expectations related to school improvement with respect to an *approach* to the continuum, *implementation* of the approach, and the *outcome* that results from the implementation. A *one* rating, located at the left of each continuum, represents a school that has not yet begun to improve. *Five*, located at the right of each continuum, represents a school that is one step removed from "world class quality." The elements between *one* and *five* describe how that continuum is hypothesized to evolve in a continuously improving school. Each continuum moves from a reactive mode to a proactive mode—from fire fighting to prevention. The *five* in *outcome* in each continuum is the target.

Vertically, the *approach, implementation,* and *outcome* statements, for any number *one* through *five,* are hypotheses. In other words, the *implementation* statement describes how the *approach* might look when implemented, and the *outcome* is the "pay-off" for implementing the approach. If the hypotheses are accurate, the outcome will not be realized until the approach is actually implemented.

Using the Continuums

The most valuable way to use the continuums is to have all staff rate the school together. First have each member of the staff make their personal rating of where they feel the school as a whole is on each continuum. Take a quick count of how many feel this school is a *one* in *approach* to Information and Analysis, a *two*, and so on. If all staff agree on the same number, record the number and rationale, and move on. If there is a discrepancy, ask for discussion. The discussion clarifies what is happening schoolwide with respect to the continuum. The goal is to get a number that represents the rating that everyone can live with. The discussion and documentation of next steps are more important than the actual number that results. The ultimate goal is to make all aspects of the school consistent and congruent with the vision. Assessing your school on the Continuous Improvement Continuums at least twice each year is recommended.

> *The ultimate goal is to make all aspects of the school consistent and congruent with the vision*

Using these continuums will enable you and your school to stay motivated, to shape and maintain your shared vision, and assist with the continuous improvement of all elements of your school.

Remember that where your school is at any time is where it is. The important thing is what you do with this information. Continuous improvement is a never-ending process which, when used effectively and for the right purpose, will ultimately lead your school toward providing a quality program for all children.

Information & Analysis

	ONE	TWO	THREE	FOUR	FIVE
APPROACH	Data or information about student performance and needs are not gathered in any systematic way; there is no way to determine what needs to change at the school, based on data.	There is no systematic process, but some teacher and student information is collected and used to problem-solve and establish student learning standards.	School collects data related to student performance (e.g., attendance, achievement) and conducts surveys on student, teacher, and parent needs. The information is used to drive the strategic quality plan for school change.	There is systematic reliance on hard data (including data for subgroups) as a basis for decision making at the classroom level as well as at the school level. Changes are based on the study of data to meet the needs of students and teachers.	Information is gathered in all areas of student interaction with the school. Teachers engage students in gathering information on their own performance. Accessible to all levels, data are comprehensive in scope and an accurate reflection of school quality.
IMPLEMENTATION	No information is gathered with which to make changes. Student dissatisfaction with the learning process is seen as an irritation, not a need for improvement.	Some data are tracked, such as dropout rates and enrollment. Only a few individuals are asked for feedback about areas of schooling.	School collects information on current and former students (e.g., student achievement and perceptions), analyzes and uses it in conjunction with future trends for planning. Identified areas for improvement are tracked over time.	Data are used to improve the effectiveness of teaching strategies on all student learning. Students' historical performances are graphed and utilized for diagnostics. Student evaluations and performances are analyzed by teachers in all classrooms.	Innovative teaching processes that meet the needs of students are implemented to the delight of teachers, parents, and students. Information is analyzed and used to prevent student failure. Root causes are known through analyses. Problems are prevented through the use of data.
OUTCOME	Only anecdotal and hypothetical information is available about student performance, behavior, and satisfaction. Problems are solved individually with short-term results.	Little data are available. Change is limited to some areas of the school and dependent upon individual teachers and their efforts.	Information collected about student and parent needs, assessment, and instructional practices are shared with the school staff and used to plan for change. Information helps staff understand pressing issues, analyze information for "root causes," track results for improvement.	An information system is in place. Positive trends begin to appear in many classrooms and schoolwide. There is evidence that these results are caused by understanding and effectively using data collected.	Students are delighted with the school's instructional processes and proud of their own capabilities to learn and assess their own growth. Good to excellent achievement is the result for all students. No student falls through the cracks. Teachers use data to predict and prevent potential problems.

Table A-2

Student Achievement

	ONE	TWO	THREE	FOUR	FIVE
APPROACH	Instructional and organizational processes critical to student success are not identified. Little distinction of student learning differences is made. Some teachers believe that not all students can achieve.	Some data are collected on student background and performance trends. Learning gaps are noted to direct improvement of instruction. It is known that student learning standards must be identified.	Student learning standards are identified and a continuum of learning is created throughout the school. Student performance data are collected and compared to the standards in order to analyze how to improve learning for all students.	Data on student achievement are used throughout the school to pursue the improvement of student learning. Teachers collaborate to implement appropriate instruction and assessment strategies for meeting student learning standards articulated across grade levels. All teachers believe that all students can learn.	School makes an effort to exceed student achievement expectations. Innovative instructional changes are made to anticipate learning needs and improve student achievement. Teachers are able to predict characteristics impacting student achievement and to know how to perform from a small set of internal quality measures.
IMPLEMENTATION	All students are taught the same way. There is no communication with students about their academic needs or learning styles. There are no analyses of how to improve instruction.	Some effort is made to track and analyze student achievement trends on a schoolwide basis. Teachers begin to understand the needs and learning gaps of students.	Teachers study effective instruction and assessment strategies to increase their students' learning. Student feedback and analysis of achievement data are used in conjunction with implementation support strategies.	There is a systematic focus on the improvement of student learning schoolwide. Effective instruction and assessment strategies are implemented in each classroom. Teachers support one another with peer coaching and/or action research focused on implementing strategies that lead to increased achievement.	All teachers correlate critical instructional and assessment strategies with objective indicators of quality student achievement. A comparative analysis of actual individual student performance to student learning standards is utilized to adjust teaching strategies to ensure a progression of learning for all students.
OUTCOME	There is wide variation in student attitudes and achievement with undesirable results. There is high dissatisfaction among students with learning. Student background is used as an excuse for low student achievement.	There is some evidence that student achievement trends are available to teachers and are being used. There is much effort, but minimal observable results in improving student achievement.	There is an increase in communication between students and teachers regarding student learning. Teachers learn about effective instructional strategies that will meet the needs of their students. They make some gains.	Increased student achievement is evident schoolwide. Student morale, attendance, and behavior are good. Teachers converse often with each other about preventing student failure. Areas for further attention are clear.	Students and teachers conduct self-assessments to continuously improve performance. Improvements in student achievement are evident and clearly caused by teachers' and students' understandings of individual student learning, linked to appropriate and effective instructional and assessment strategies. A continuum of learning results. No students fall through the cracks.

Table A-3

Quality Planning

	ONE	TWO	THREE	FOUR	FIVE
APPROACH	No quality plan or process exists. Data are neither used nor considered important in planning.	The staff realizes the importance of a mission, vision, and one comprehensive action plan. Teams develop goals and timelines, and dollars are allocated to begin the process.	A comprehensive school plan to achieve the vision is developed. Plan includes evaluation and continuous improvement.	One focused and integrated schoolwide plan for implementing a continuous improvement process is put into action. All school efforts are focused on the implementation of this plan that represents the achievement of the vision.	A plan for the continuous improvement of the school, with a focus on students, is put into place. There is excellent articulation and integration of all elements in the school due to quality planning. Leadership team ensures all elements are implemented by all appropriate parties.
IMPLEMENTATION	There is no knowledge of or direction for quality planning. Budget is allocated on an as-needed basis. Many plans exist.	School community begins continuous improvement planning efforts by laying out major steps to a shared vision, by identifying values and beliefs, the purpose of the school, a mission, vision, and student learning standards.	Implementation goals, responsibilities, due dates, and timelines are spelled out. Support structures for implementing the plan are set in place.	The quality management plan is implemented through effective procedures in all areas of the school. Everyone knows what she/he needs to do, and when it needs to be done to accomplish the school goals.	Schoolwide goals, mission, vision, and student learning standards are shared and articulated throughout the school and with feeder schools. The attainment of identified student learning standards is linked to planning and implementation of effective instruction that meets students' needs.
OUTCOME	There is no evidence of comprehensive planning. Staff work is carried out in isolation. A continuum of learning for students is absent.	The school community understands the benefits of working together to implement a comprehensive continuous improvement plan.	There is evidence that the school plan is being implemented in some areas of the school. Improvements are neither systematic nor integrated schoolwide.	A schoolwide plan is known to all. Results from working toward the quality improvement goals are evident throughout the school.	Evidence of effective teaching and learning results in significant improvement of student achievement attributed to quality planning at all levels of the school organization. Teachers understand and share the school mission and vision, the impact and importance of quality planning, and accountability.

Table A-4

Professional Development

	ONE	TWO	THREE	FOUR	FIVE
APPROACH	There is no professional development. Teachers, principals, and staff are seen as interchangeable parts that can be replaced.	The "cafeteria" approach to professional development is used, whereby individual teachers choose what they want to take, without regard to an overall school plan.	The school plan and student needs are used to target appropriate professional development for all employees. Staff is inserviced in relevant instructional and leadership strategies.	Professional development and data-gathering methods are used by all teachers and are directed toward the goals of continuous improvement. Teachers have ongoing conversations about student achievement research. Other staff members receive training in their roles.	Leadership and staff continuously improve all aspects of the school structure through an innovative and comprehensive continuous improvement process that prevents student failures. Professional development is appropriate for implementing the vision, supportive, collegial, effective, systemic, and ongoing. Traditional teacher evaluations are replaced by collegial coaching and action research focused on student learning standards.
IMPLEMENTATION	Teacher, principal, and staff performance is controlled and inspected. Performance evaluations are used to detect mistakes.	Teacher professional development is sporadic and unfocused, lacking an approach for implementing new procedures and processes. Some leadership training begins to take place.	Teachers are involved in year-round quality professional development. The school community is trained in shared decision making, team building concepts, and effective communication strategies.	Teachers, in teams, continuously set and implement student achievement goals. Leadership considers these goals and ensures appropriateness of professional development. Teachers utilize effective support approaches as they implement new instruction and assessment strategies.	Teams passionately support each other in the pursuit of quality improvement at all levels. Teachers make bold changes in instruction and assessment strategies focused on student learning standards and student learning styles. A teacher as action researcher model is implemented. Staffwide conversations focus on systemic reflection and improvement.
OUTCOME	No professional growth and no performance improvement. There exists a high turnover rate of employees. Attitudes and approach filter down to students.	The effectiveness of professional development is not known or analyzed. Teachers feel helpless about making schoolwide changes.	Teachers, working in teams, feel supported and begin to feel they can make changes. Evidence shows that shared decision making works.	A collegial school is evident. Effective classroom strategies are practiced, articulated schoolwide, and are reflective of professional development aimed at ensuring student achievement.	True systemic change and improved student achievement result because teachers are knowledgeable of and implement effective teaching strategies for individual student learning styles, abilities, and situations. Teachers are sensitive to and apply approaches that work best for each student.

Table A-5

Leadership

	ONE	TWO	THREE	FOUR	FIVE
APPROACH	Principal as decision maker. Decisions are reactive to state, district, and federal mandates.	A shared decision making structure is put into place and discussions begin on how to achieve a school vision. Most decisions are focused on solving problems and are reactive.	Leadership team is committed to continuous improvement. Leadership seeks inclusion of all school sectors and supports study teams by making time provisions for their work.	Leadership team represents a true shared decision making structure. Study teams are reconstructed for the implementation of a comprehensive continuous improvement plan.	A strong continuous improvement structure is set into place that allows for input from all sectors of the school, district, and community, ensuring strong communication, flexibility, and refinement of approach and beliefs. The school vision is student focused, based on data and appropriate for school/ community values, and meeting student needs.
IMPLEMENTATION	Principal makes all decisions, with little or no input from teachers, the community, or students. Leadership inspects for mistakes.	School values and beliefs are identified; the purpose of school is defined; a school mission and student learning standards are developed with representative input. A structure for studying approaches to achieving student learning standards is established.	Leadership team is active on study teams and integrates recommendations from the teams' research and analyses to form a comprehensive plan for continuous improvement within the context of the school mission. Everyone is kept informed.	Decisions about budget and implementation of the vision are made within teams, by the principal, by the leadership team, and by the full staff as appropriate. All decisions are communicated to the leadership team and to the full staff.	The vision is implemented and articulated across all grade levels and into feeder schools. Quality standards are reinforced throughout the school. All members of the school community understand and apply the quality standards. Leadership team has systematic interactions and involvement with district administrators, teachers, parents, community, and students about the school's direction.
OUTCOME	Decisions lack focus and consistency. There is little staff buy-in. Students and parents do not feel they are being heard. Decision-making process is clear and known.	The mission provides a focus for all school improvement and guides the action to the vision. The school community is committed to continuous improvement. Quality leadership techniques are used sporadically.	Leaders are seen as committed to planning and quality improve-ment. Critical areas for improvement are identified. Faculty feel included in shared decision making.	There is evidence that the leadership team listens to all levels of the organization. Implementation of the continuous improvement plan is linked to student learning standards and the guiding principles of the school. Teachers are empowered.	Site-based management and shared decision making truly exists. Teachers understand and display an intimate knowledge of how the school operates. Teachers support and communicate with each other in the implementation of quality strategies. Teachers implement the vision in their classrooms and can determine how their new approach meets student needs and leads to the attainment of student learning standards.

Table A-6

Partnership Development

	ONE	TWO	THREE	FOUR	FIVE
APPROACH	There is no system for input from parents, business, or community. Status quo is desired for managing the school.	Partnerships are sought, but mostly for money and things.	School has knowledge of why partnerships are important and seeks to include businesses and parents in a strategic fashion related to student learning standards for increased student achievement.	School seeks effective win-win business and community partnerships and parent involvement to implement the vision. Desired outcomes are clearly identified. A solid plan for partnership development exists.	Community, parent, and business partnerships become integrated across all student groupings. The benefits of outside involvement are known by all. Parent and business involvement in student learning is refined. Student learning regularly takes place beyond the school walls.
IMPLEMENTATION	Barriers are erected to close out involvement of outsiders. Outsiders are managed for least impact on status quo.	A team is assigned to get partners and to receive input from parents, the community, and business in the school.	Involvement of business, community, and parents begins to take place in some classrooms and after school hours related to the vision. Partners begin to realize how they can support each other in achieving school goals. School staff understand what partners need out of the partnership.	There is a systematic utilization of parents, community, and businesses schoolwide. Areas in which the active use of these partnerships benefits student learning are clear.	Partnership development is articulated across all student groupings. Parents, community, business, and educators work together in an innovative fashion to increase student learning and to prepare students for the 21st Century. Partnerships are evaluated for continuous improvement.
OUTCOME	There is little or no involvement of parents, business, or community at large. School is a closed, isolated system.	Much effort is given to establishing partnerships. Some spotty trends emerge, such as receiving donated equipment.	Some substantial gains are achieved in implementing partnerships. Some student achievement increases can be attributed to this involvement.	Gains in student satisfaction with learning and school are clearly related to partnerships. All partners benefit.	Previously non-achieving students enjoy learning, with excellent achievement. Community, business, and home become common places for student learning, while school becomes a place where parents come for further education. Partnerships enhance what the school does for students.

Table A-7

Continuous Improvement and Evaluation

	ONE	TWO	THREE	FOUR	FIVE
APPROACH	Neither goals nor strategies exist for the evaluation and continuous improvement of the school organization or for elements of the school organization.	The approach to continuous improvement and evaluation is problem solving. If there are no problems, or if solutions can be made quickly, there is no need for improvement or analyses. Changes in parts of the system are not coordinated with all other parts.	Some elements of the school organization are evaluated for effectiveness. Some elements are improved on the basis of the evaluation findings.	All elements of the school's operations are evaluated for improvement and to ensure congruence of the elements with respect to the continuum of learning students experience.	All aspects of the school organization are rigorously evaluated and improved on a continuous basis. Students, and the maintenance of a comprehensive learning continuum for students, become the focus of all aspects of the school improvement process.
IMPLEMENTATION	With no overall plan for evaluation and continuous improvement, strategies are changed by individual teachers and administrators only when something sparks the need to improve. Reactive decisions and activities are a daily mode of operation.	Isolated changes are made in some areas of the school organization in response to problem incidents. Changes are not preceded by comprehensive analyses, such as an understanding of the root causes of problems. The effectiveness of the elements of the school organization, or changes made to the elements, is not known.	Elements of the school organization are improved on the basis of comprehensive analyses of root causes of problems, client perceptions, and operational effectiveness of processes.	Continuous improvement analyses of student achievement and instructional strategies are rigorously reinforced within each classroom and across learning levels to develop a comprehensive learning continuum for students and to prevent student failure.	Comprehensive continuous improvement becomes the way of doing business at the school. Teachers continuously improve the appropriateness and effectiveness of instructional strategies based on student feedback and performance. All aspects of the school organization are improved to support teachers' efforts.
OUTCOME	Individuals struggle with system failure. Finger pointing and blaming others for failure occurs. The effectiveness of strategies is not known. Mistakes are repeated.	Problems are solved only temporarily and few positive changes result. Additionally, unintended and undesirable consequences often appear in other parts of the system. Many aspects of the school are incongruent, keeping the school from reaching its vision.	Evidence of effective improvement strategies is observable. Positive changes are made and maintained due to comprehensive analyses and evaluation.	Teachers become astute at assessing and in predicting the impact of their instructional strategies on individual student achievement. Sustainable improvements in student achievement are evident at all grade levels, due to continuous improvement.	The school becomes a congruent and effective learning organization. Only instruction and assessment strategies that produce quality student achievement are used. A true continuum of learning results for all students.

Appendix
B

STAFF-DEVELOPED RUBRICS

Figure B-1

Frank Paul School:
Brain Compatible Education Rubric

LEVEL ONE

Physical & Social Values of Environment

- Responsibility to authority is the most important value
- Social development and interaction is based on external rewards and consequences
- The environment is agitated
- Teacher uses loud colors to display items on the bulletin board
- Students sit in rows

Curriculum

- Subject areas and specific skills are taught in isolation
- Curriculum is textbook driven and teacher centered

Instructional Strategies

- Textbook and lecture driven
- Students working in isolation

Assessment

- Publishers' tests are used

Outcomes

- Students do not see connections between school and real life and do not understand the interrelationships among concepts common to various subject areas
- Students are teacher-dependent, passive, authority complacent
- Students tend not to self-initiate

Frank Paul School: Brain Compatible Education Rubrics, written by: Vickie Hogan, ITI Coach, Frank Paul School; Jackie Munoz, Restructuring Coordinator, Frank Paul School; Jenne Herrick, Bilingual Education Director, Alisal Union School District; Victoria Bernhardt, Executive Director, Education for the Future Initiative; Mid-California Science Improvement Program (MCSIP) Coaches and Mentors ©1994

Frank Paul School:
Brain Compatible Education Rubric

LEVEL TWO

Physical & Social Values of Environment

- Responsibility to authority is the most important value
- Classroom has calming colors, music, plants, and potpourri
- Students sit in clusters with individual access to work tools
- Yearlong theme and life skills are posted

Curriculum

- Teacher provides for real-life experiences
- The curriculum content is aligned with district guidelines
- Teacher designs a yearlong theme, key points, and inquiries for classroom use which integrate the three areas of science for at least one component of the theme
- Teacher includes math and science skills essential to the teaching of at least the one component
- Teacher models and teaches the absence of threat elements as part of the curriculum: life skills, lifelong guidelines, decision making, triune brain, multiple intelligences, written procedures and directions
- Teacher meets with a professional or peer coach who supports the implementation of ITI in the classroom

Instructional Strategies

- Teacher implements a theme-based brain compatible program for at least five hours a week
- Teacher predominately uses real-life, immersion, hands-on experiences
- Teacher implements collaborative learning strategies
- Teacher uses varied instructional strategies such as agendas, direct instruction, mind mapping, discovery process, etc.
- Adequate time is allowed to let students complete their work
- Limited choices are introduced through inquiries, supplies, time, doing now or doing it later

Assessment

- Post-lesson processing about academic or collaborative experiences
- Use of selected inquiries to assess mastery of key points in such forms as projects, presentations, and some traditional tests
- Teacher selects work for portfolio folder

Outcomes

- Students respond positively to enriched environment by participating in all classroom activities, when there is trust and absence of threat
- Students are actively participating in the classroom by not being absent, being on time, staying on task, actively listening, responding to teachers' questions, collaborative interactions, and making connections between the classroom and real life
- Students do not put others down
- Students' behavior is absent of threat

Figure B-3

Frank Paul School: Brain Compatible Education Rubric

LEVEL THREE

Physical & Social Values of Environment

- Students are beginning to take responsibility for own behavior through the use of the life skills
- Classroom has calming colors, music, plants, and potpourri
- The calmness of the teacher's voice contributes to a settled classroom environment
- Students are beginning to work in cooperative clusters with individual access to work tools
- Yearlong theme and life skills are posted

Curriculum

- Teacher refines the theme and adds at least one additional content area, key points, and inquiries for at least two components of the theme for the year
- Teacher includes supporting math and language skills which are necessary to the teaching of science
- 50% of science curriculum is planned and implemented
- Absence of threat elements are refined and reinforced
- Teacher will be supported with implementation by working with a peer or professional coach

Instructional Strategies

- Teacher implements ITI for at least ten hours a week
- Teacher uses "being there" experiences to make learning real for students
- Teacher engages students in solving problems in a cooperative manner
- Teacher consistently allows choices for students through presentations—discoveries, explorations, key points, inquiries based on knowledge of the theory of multiple itelligence and Bloom's Taxonomy

Assessment

- Post-lesson about academic or collaborative experiences
- Use of selected inquiries to assess mastery of key points in such forms as projects, presentations, and some traditional tests
- Student/teacher selects work for showcase portfolio
- Assessment of social skills as referred to under absence of threat

Outcomes

- Students are self-directed during ITI implementation
- Students are able to solve problems in a collaborative way
- Students can make connections between what is learned in science and at least one content area to real life
- Students master and apply social skills in school and outside of the classroom
- Students begin to demonstrate the use of life skills

Frank Paul School:
Brain Compatible Education Rubric

LEVEL FOUR

Physical & Social Values of Environment

- Self-responsibility and self-initiated engagement are the most important values
- Classroom has calming colors, music, plants, and potpourri
- The calmness of the teacher's voice contributes to a settled classroom environment
- Students are working in cooperative clusters with individual access to work tools
- Yearlong theme and life skills are posted

Curriculum

- Teacher refines the yearlong theme and integrates all three areas of science and at least two other content areas, key points, inquiries for at least 50% of the curriculum for the year
- Curriculum is based predominately on visible locations which provide "being there" experiences and connections with the real world
- Curriculum is designed to enhance pattern-seeking and program building
- The three sciences are integrated for at least 75% of the time
- Curriculum for collaborative assignments is specifically designed for group work

Instructional Strategies

- Teacher implements integrated thematic instruction for at least ten to fifteen hours a week
- Teacher utilizes explorations and discoveries to make learning real for students
- Students make choices about how they master the key points; including assisting in the development of inquiries
- Learning experiences are predominately based on real life immersion and hands-on of real things
- Collaboration is regularly used whenever it would enhance pattern seeking and program building
- Teacher introduces peer and cross-age tutoring to students
- Teacher introduces the idea of outcomes to students

Assessment

- Implementing culminating performances chosen by the teacher that demonstrate mastery and application of key points
- Students can judge their performance through academic and social skills
- Students select work for showcase portfolio
- Student/parent/teacher conferences led by the student

Outcomes

- Students take control of their learning and act in a self-directed manner for the entire day
- Students demonstrate more shared leadership while doing collaborative activities
- Peer and cross-age tutoring is being explored
- Students can make connections between what is learned in science and at least two other content areas to real life
- Students participate in the design and evaluation of outcomes
- Students demonstrate life skills throughout the day

Figure B-5

Frank Paul School:
Brain Compatible Education Rubric

LEVEL FIVE*
Physical & Social Values of Environment
• The sense of responsibility for others and the feeling of the community are the most important values • Classroom has calming colors, music, plants, and potpourri • The calmness of the teacher's voice contributes to a settled classroom environment • Students are working in cooperative clusters with individual access to work tools • Yearlong theme is evident throughout classroom environment and life skills are an integral part of the class
Curriculum
• Teacher develops and implements a yearlong theme which integrates the three science areas, all content areas, key points, and inquiries for the entire year • 100% of science curriculum is planned
Instructional Strategies
• Teacher implements integrated thematic instruction all day, all year • Collaborative groupings for students • Students make choices about the inquiries they do • Students help in the selection of key points and take part in writing inquiries
Assessment
• Culminating performances chosen by the student that demonstrate mastery and application of key points • Performance task assesses original, creative, and problem-solving thinking • Students/peers self-assessment • Students select best work for showcase portfolio • Ongoing student/teacher assessment conferences with the use of rubrics • Student/teacher/parent interaction and conferences about portfolio
Outcomes
• Students participate in the design and evaluation of outcomes • Students take control of their learning and act in a self-directed manner for the entire day • Students demonstrate more shared leadership while doing collaborative activities • Students participate in peer and cross-age tutoring • Students can connect what they are learning in school to real life • Students can creatively solve real-life problems through interrelating and connecting what they have learned in various subject areas and the real world • Students use life skills as the basis for interacting with others

(*Level Five was developed for older learners.)

Appendix C

SCHOOL IMPROVEMENT PROCESS

Figure C-1

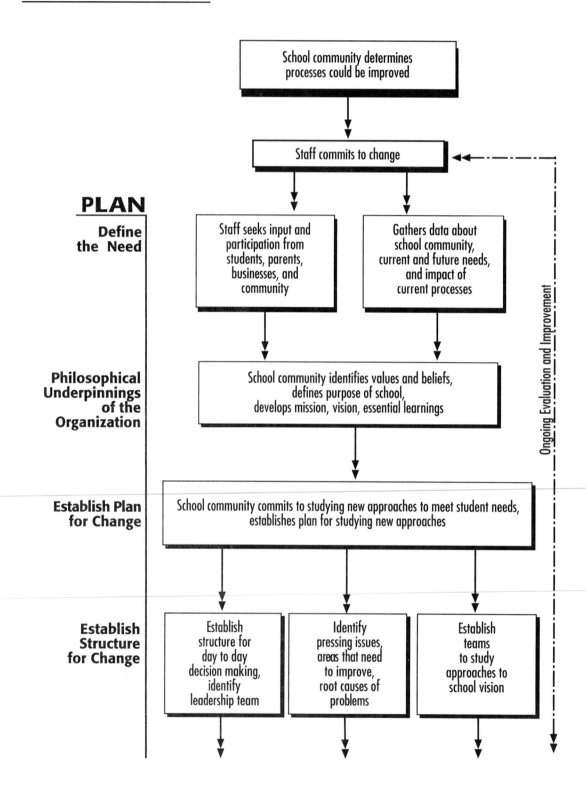

Figure C-2

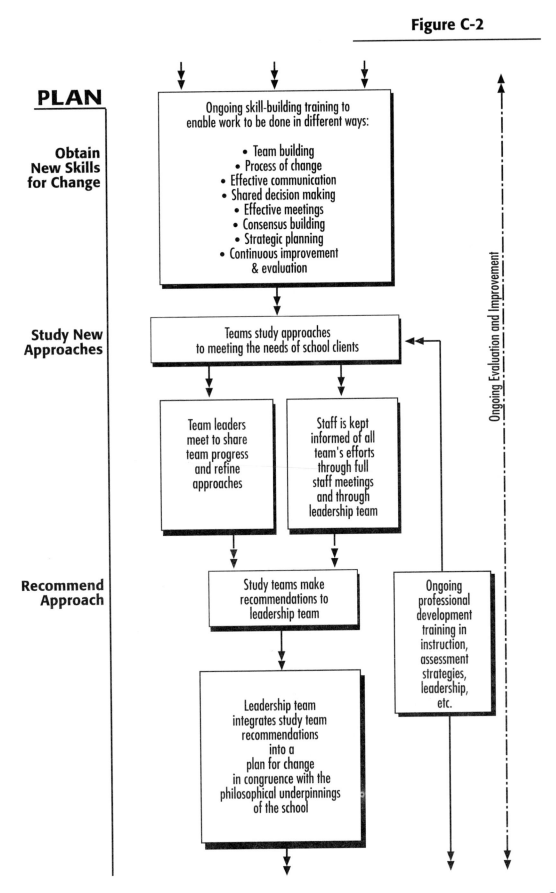

PLAN

**Obtain
New Skills
for Change**

Ongoing skill-building training to
enable work to be done in different ways:

- Team building
- Process of change
- Effective communication
- Shared decision making
- Effective meetings
- Consensus building
- Strategic planning
- Continuous improvement
& evaluation

**Study New
Approaches**

Teams study approaches
to meeting the needs of school clients

Team leaders
meet to share
team progress
and refine
approaches

Staff is kept
informed of all
team's efforts
through full
staff meetings
and through
leadership team

**Recommend
Approach**

Study teams make
recommendations to
leadership team

Ongoing
professional
development
training in
instruction,
assessment
strategies,
leadership,
etc.

Leadership team
integrates study team
recommendations
into a
plan for change
in congruence with the
philosophical underpinnings
of the school

Ongoing Evaluation and Improvement

Figure C-3

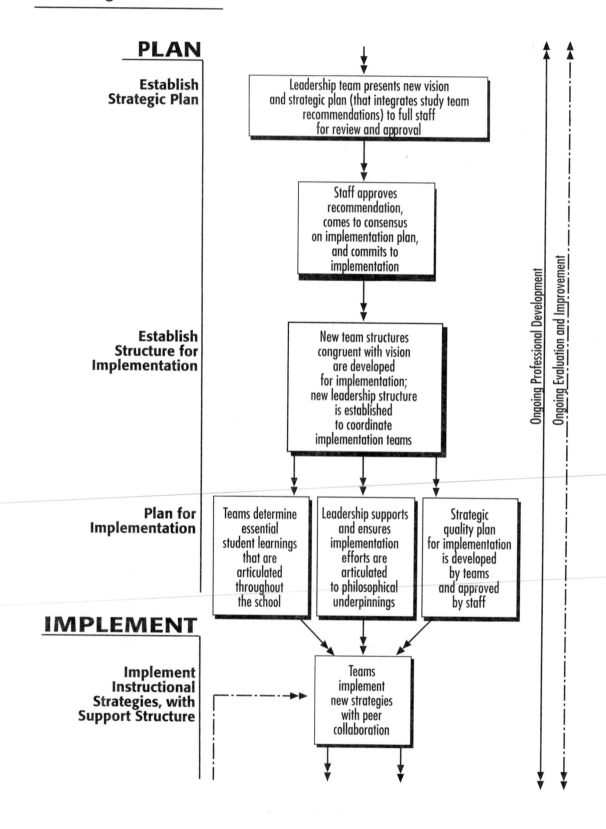

Figure C-4

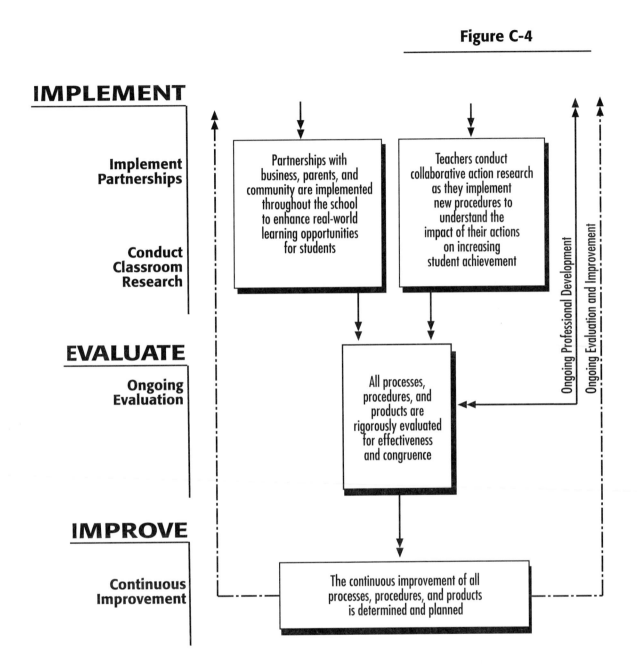

IMPLEMENT

Implement Partnerships

Conduct Classroom Research

Partnerships with business, parents, and community are implemented throughout the school to enhance real-world learning opportunities for students

Teachers conduct collaborative action research as they implement new procedures to understand the impact of their actions on increasing student achievement

EVALUATE

Ongoing Evaluation

All processes, procedures, and products are rigorously evaluated for effectiveness and congruence

Ongoing Professional Development

Ongoing Evaluation and Improvement

IMPROVE

Continuous Improvement

The continuous improvement of all processes, procedures, and products is determined and planned

Appendix D

SAMPLE QUESTIONNAIRES

On the pages that follow are student, teacher, and parent questionnaires that schools working with *Education for the Future Initiative* have used since 1991. We offer them here as examples of questionnaires that work.

Please note that they cannot be copied and scanned as they are right now. One would need to set them up to be scanned, or to be administered on line. To see suggestions for questionnaire design, administration, and analysis, refer to the companion book, Bernhardt, V., *Data Analysis for Comprehensive Schoolwide Improvement*, (1998), Appendix A.

Figure D-1

Student Questionnaire
Grade 1-6   Page 1

students

I AM IN:
- ○ First Grade
- ○ Second Grade
- ○ Third Grade
- ○ Fourth Grade
- ○ Fifth Grade
- ○ Sixth Grade

I AM: (Darken all that apply.)
- ○ African-American
- ○ American Indian
- ○ Asian
- ○ Caucasian
- ○ Hispanic
- ○ Other: _____

I AM: Boy ○
          Girl ○

Strongly Disagree   Disagree   Neutral   Agree   Strongly Agree

When I am at school, I feel:

	Strongly Disagree	Disagree	Neutral	Agree	Strongly Agree
I belong.	1	2	3	4	5
I am safe.	1	2	3	4	5
I have fun learning.	1	2	3	4	5
I like this school.	1	2	3	4	5
This school is good.	1	2	3	4	5
I have freedom at school.	1	2	3	4	5
I have choices in what I learn.	1	2	3	4	5
My teacher treats me with respect.	1	2	3	4	5
My teacher cares about me.	1	2	3	4	5
My teacher thinks I will be successful.	1	2	3	4	5
My teacher listens to my ideas.	1	2	3	4	5
My principal cares about me.	1	2	3	4	5
My teacher is a good teacher.	1	2	3	4	5
My teacher believes I can learn.	1	2	3	4	5
I am recognized for good work.	1	2	3	4	5
I am challenged by the work my teacher asks me to do.	1	2	3	4	5
The work I do in class makes me think.	1	2	3	4	5
I know what I am supposed to be learning in my classes.	1	2	3	4	5
I am a good student.	1	2	3	4	5
I can be a better student.	1	2	3	4	5
Very good work is expected at my school.	1	2	3	4	5
I behave well at school.	1	2	3	4	5
Students are treated fairly by teachers.	1	2	3	4	5
Students are treated fairly by the principal.	1	2	3	4	5
Students are treated fairly by the people on yard duty.	1	2	3	4	5
Students at my school treat me with respect.	1	2	3	4	5
Students at my school are friendly.	1	2	3	4	5
I have lots of friends.	1	2	3	4	5
I have support for learning at home.	1	2	3	4	5
My family believes I can do well in school.	1	2	3	4	5
My family wants me to do well in school.	1	2	3	4	5

What do you like about this school?

What do you wish were different at this school?

What do you wish I would have asked you about your school?

Figure D-3

Student Questionnaire
High School   Page 1

High School Student Questionnaire

Please complete this form using a No. 2 pencil.
Be sure to completely darken the circle that best corresponds
to your thoughts about the following statements.
Thank you!

	Strongly Disagree	Disagree	Neutral	Agree	Strongly Agree
I feel safe at this school	1	2	3	4	5
I feel like I belong at this school	1	2	3	4	5
I feel challenged at this school	1	2	3	4	5
I have opportunities to choose my own projects	1	2	3	4	5
I understand how to apply what I learn at school to real-life situations	1	2	3	4	5
I feel like I am in charge of what I learn	1	2	3	4	5
Teachers encourage me to assess the quality of my own work	1	2	3	4	5
This school is preparing me well for what I want to do after high school	1	2	3	4	5
I assess my own work	1	2	3	4	5
I am treated with respect by teachers	1	2	3	4	5
I am treated with respect by school administrators	1	2	3	4	5
I am treated with respect by campus supervisors	1	2	3	4	5
I am treated with respect by the office staff	1	2	3	4	5
I am treated with respect by other students at this school	1	2	3	4	5
The people most responsible for what I learn are my teachers	1	2	3	4	5
The work at this school is challenging	1	2	3	4	5
I find what I learn in school to be relevant to real life	1	2	3	4	5
I feel successful at school	1	2	3	4	5
The person most responsible for what I learn is myself	1	2	3	4	5
School is fun here	1	2	3	4	5
I like this school	1	2	3	4	5
I think this is a good school	1	2	3	4	5
I like the students at this school	1	2	3	4	5
Students at this school like me	1	2	3	4	5
I like to learn	1	2	3	4	5
Doing well in school makes me feel good about myself	1	2	3	4	5
I am doing my best in school	1	2	3	4	5
Students at this school have opportunities to learn from each other	1	2	3	4	5
Students at this school have opportunities to learn about each other	1	2	3	4	5
Participating in extracurricular activities is important to me	1	2	3	4	5
Students at this school respect other students who are different than they are	1	2	3	4	5

© *Education for the Future Initiative (1997) San Francisco: Pacific Bell Foundation*

Figure D-4

Student Questionnaire
High School   Page 2

My teachers:

	Strongly Disagree	Disagree	Neutral	Agree	Strongly Agree
expect students to do their best	1	2	3	4	5
expect me to do my best	1	2	3	4	5
are understanding when students have personal problems	1	2	3	4	5
set high standards for achievement in their classes	1	2	3	4	5
help me gain confidence in my ability to learn	1	2	3	4	5
have confidence in me	1	2	3	4	5
know me well	1	2	3	4	5
listen to my ideas	1	2	3	4	5
care about me	1	2	3	4	5
make learning fun	1	2	3	4	5
are excited about the subject they teach	1	2	3	4	5
give me individual attention when I need it	1	2	3	4	5
challenge me to do better	1	2	3	4	5

I am ready for the real world in reference to:

	Strongly Disagree	Disagree	Neutral	Agree	Strongly Agree
my ability to write	1	2	3	4	5
my ability to read	1	2	3	4	5
my ability with mathematics	1	2	3	4	5
my ability to present information	1	2	3	4	5
my technology skills	1	2	3	4	5

In my classes, time is spent:

	Strongly Disagree	Disagree	Neutral	Agree	Strongly Agree
listening to the teacher talk	1	2	3	4	5
in whole-class discussions	1	2	3	4	5
working in small groups	1	2	3	4	5
reading	1	2	3	4	5
answering questions from a book or worksheet	1	2	3	4	5
working on projects or research	1	2	3	4	5
doing work that I find meaningful	1	2	3	4	5
using computers	1	2	3	4	5

I work well when:

	Strongly Disagree	Disagree	Neutral	Agree	Strongly Agree
I am working on projects or research	1	2	3	4	5
the teacher is leading a discussion with the whole class	1	2	3	4	5
I am working in a small group	1	2	3	4	5
I am working by myself	1	2	3	4	5

Figure D-5

Student Questionnaire
High School   Page 3

What do you like about this school?

What do you wish were different at this school?

What do you wish I would have asked you about your school?

Student Demographic Data

I am: (darken all that apply)
- ○ African-American
- ○ American Indian
- ○ Asian
- ○ Caucasian
- ○ Filipino
- ○ Hispanic/Latino
- ○ Middle Eastern
- ○ Pacific Islander
- ○ Other _____

I am a:
- ○ Freshman
- ○ Sophomore
- ○ Junior
- ○ Senior

I am a:
- ○ Female
- ○ Male

I participate in: (darken all that apply)
- ○ Athletics (includes cheerleading and Flag Team)
- ○ School clubs
- ○ Instrumental music
- ○ Vocal music
- ○ Drama
- ○ Speech/Debate
- ○ Not connected to any school club or regular extracurricular activity

I came to this school:
- ○ This year
- ○ Last year
- ○ Year before last
- ○ Three years ago

Immediately after graduation, I plan to:
- ○ go to a 2-year community college
- ○ go to a 4-year college
- ○ enter a training or apprenticeship program
- ○ get a full-time job
- ○ join the military
- ○ get married
- ○ other _____

Figure D-6

**Staff Questionnaire
Page 1**

Education for the Future *Staff Survey*

*Please darken the circle that best describes your beliefs and feelings,
using the rating scale to the right.*

Rating scale: Strongly Disagree (1), Disagree (2), Neutral (3), Agree (4), Strongly Agree (5)

I feel:

	1	2	3	4	5
like I belong at this school	○	○	○	○	○
that staff care about me	○	○	○	○	○
that learning can be fun	○	○	○	○	○
that learning is fun at this school	○	○	○	○	○
recognized for good work	○	○	○	○	○
intrinsically rewarded for doing my job well	○	○	○	○	○

I work with people who:

	1	2	3	4	5
treat me with respect	○	○	○	○	○
listen if I have ideas about doing things better	○	○	○	○	○

My administrator:

	1	2	3	4	5
treats me with respect	○	○	○	○	○
is an effective instructional leader	○	○	○	○	○
facilitates communication effectively	○	○	○	○	○
supports me in my work with students	○	○	○	○	○
supports shared decision making	○	○	○	○	○
allows me to be an effective instructional leader	○	○	○	○	○
is effective in helping us reach our vision	○	○	○	○	○

I have the opportunity to:

	1	2	3	4	5
develop my skills	○	○	○	○	○
think for myself, not just carry out instructions	○	○	○	○	○

I love:

	1	2	3	4	5
working at this school	○	○	○	○	○
seeing the results of my work with students	○	○	○	○	○

I work effectively with:

	1	2	3	4	5
special education students	○	○	○	○	○
limited English-speaking students	○	○	○	○	○
an ethnically/racially diverse population of students	○	○	○	○	○
heterogeneously grouped classes	○	○	○	○	○
low-achieving students	○	○	○	○	○
I believe that every student can learn	○	○	○	○	○

I believe student achievement can increase through:

	1	2	3	4	5
hands-on learning	○	○	○	○	○
effective professional development related to our vision	○	○	○	○	○
integrating instruction across the curriculum	○	○	○	○	○
thematic instruction	○	○	○	○	○
cooperative learning	○	○	○	○	○
multi-age classrooms	○	○	○	○	○
student self-assessment	○	○	○	○	○
authentic assessment	○	○	○	○	○
the use of computers	○	○	○	○	○
the use of varied technologies	○	○	○	○	○
providing a threat-free environment	○	○	○	○	○
close personal relationships between students and teachers	○	○	○	○	○

Figure D-7

Staff Questionnaire
Page 2

	Strongly Disagree	Disagree	Neutral	Agree	Strongly Agree

I believe student achievement can increase through: (continued)

addressing student learning styles	1	2	3	4	5
effective parent involvement	1	2	3	4	5
partnerships with business	1	2	3	4	5
teacher use of student achievement data	1	2	3	4	5

The instructional program at this school is challenging	1	2	3	4	5
The school provides an atmosphere where every student can succeed	1	2	3	4	5
Quality work is expected of all students at this school	1	2	3	4	5
Quality work is expected of me	1	2	3	4	5
Quality work is expected of all the adults working at this school	1	2	3	4	5
The vision for this school is clear	1	2	3	4	5
The vision for this school is shared	1	2	3	4	5
We have an action plan in place which can get us to our vision	1	2	3	4	5
This school has a good public image	1	2	3	4	5

I think it is important to communicate often with parents	1	2	3	4	5
I communicate with parents often about their child's progress	1	2	3	4	5
I communicate with parents often about class activities	1	2	3	4	5

Morale is high on the part of:

teachers	1	2	3	4	5
students	1	2	3	4	5
support staff	1	2	3	4	5
administrators	1	2	3	4	5

I am clear about what my job is at this school	1	2	3	4	5
I feel that others are clear about what my job is at this school	1	2	3	4	5

Items for teachers and instructional assistants only:

The student outcomes for my class(es) are clear to me	1	2	3	4	5
The student outcomes for my class(es) are clear to my students	1	2	3	4	5
Teachers in this school communicate with each other to make student learning consistent across grades	1	2	3	4	5
Learning is fun in my classroom	1	2	3	4	5
I love to teach	1	2	3	4	5

For each item, please check the description that applies to you. Demographic data, which is used for summary analysis, will not be reported if individuals can be identified.

I am a(n):
- ○ classroom teacher
- ○ instructional assistant
- ○ certificated staff (other than a classroom teacher)
- ○ classified staff (other than an instructional assistant)

Ethnicity: (darken all that apply)
- ○ African-American
- ○ Asian
- ○ Caucasian
- ○ Latino/Hispanic
- ○ Other _____

Gender:
- ○ Male
- ○ Female

Items for teachers only:

I teach:
- ○ primary grades
- ○ upper elementary grades
- ○ middle school grades
- ○ high school grades (9-10)
- ○ high school grades (11-12)

I have been teaching:
- ○ 1-3 years
- ○ 4-6 years
- ○ 7-10 years
- ○ 11 years, or more

I am part of a formal teaching team:
- ○ Yes   ○ No

Figure D-8

Parent Questionnaire
Page 1

parents

Please complete this form for your family.
Please use a No. 2 pencil and completely
darken the circles. Thank you!

	Strongly Disagree	Disagree	Neutral	Agree	Strongly Agree
I feel welcome at my child's school.	①	②	③	④	⑤
I am informed about my child's progress.	①	②	③	④	⑤
I know what my child's teacher expects of my child.	①	②	③	④	⑤
My child is safe at school.	①	②	③	④	⑤
My child is safe going to and from school.	①	②	③	④	⑤
There is adequate playground supervision during school.	①	②	③	④	⑤
There is adequate supervision before and after school.	①	②	③	④	⑤
The teachers show respect for the students.	①	②	③	④	⑤
The students show respect for other students.	①	②	③	④	⑤
The school meets the social needs of the students.	①	②	③	④	⑤
The school meets the academic needs of the students.	①	②	③	④	⑤
The school expects quality work of its students.	①	②	③	④	⑤
The school has an excellent learning environment.	①	②	③	④	⑤
I know how well my child is progressing in school.	①	②	③	④	⑤
I like the school's report cards/progress report.	①	②	③	④	⑤
I respect the school's teachers.	①	②	③	④	⑤
I respect the school's principal.	①	②	③	④	⑤
Overall, the school performs well academically.	①	②	③	④	⑤
The school succeeds at preparing children for future work.	①	②	③	④	⑤
The school has a good public image.	①	②	③	④	⑤
The school's assessment practices are fair.	①	②	③	④	⑤
My child's teacher helps me to help my child learn at home.	①	②	③	④	⑤
I support my child's learning at home.	①	②	③	④	⑤
I feel good about myself as a parent.	①	②	③	④	⑤
I enjoy being a parent.	①	②	③	④	⑤

Number of Children in This School:
① ② ③ ④ ⑤ ⑥ ⑦ ⑧ ⑨

Number of Children in Household:
① ② ③ ④ ⑤ ⑥ ⑦ ⑧ ⑨

Children's Grades:
○ Kindergarten
○ First
○ Second
○ Third
○ Fourth
○ Fifth
○ Sixth
○ Seventh
○ Eighth

My Native Language Is:
○ Chinese
○ Eastern European
○ English
○ Japanese
○ Korean
○ Spanish
○ Vietnamese
○ Other

Ethnic Background:
(Darken all that apply)
○ African-American
○ American Indian
○ Asian
○ Caucasian
○ Hispanic
○ Other

© *Education for the Future Initiative (1997) San Francisco: Pacific Bell Foundation*

Figure D-9

Parent Questionnaire
Page 2

What are the strengths of your child's school?

What needs to be strengthened at your child's school?

What would make the school better?

Comments:

The references used in this book along with other resources that will assist busy school administrators and teachers in continuously improving appear below, categorized by topic for easy perusal.

REFERENCES AND RESOURCES

Mapping the Route to Education Excellence

Action Research

American Heritage Electronic Dictionary, Houghton-Mifflin, 1995.

Berliner, D.C. & Casanova, U. (1993). *Putting research to work in your school.* New York, NY: Scholastic, Inc.

Sagor, R. (March 1991). Collaborative action research: a report from Project LEARN. *Educational Leadership.* 48, 6:6-10.

Sagor, R. (April 1995). Overcoming the one-solution syndrome. *Educational Leadership.* 52, F:24-27.

Change Process

Fullan, M. (1993). Innovation, reform, and restructuring strategies. In G. Cawelti (Ed.) *Challenges and achievements of American education: 1993 yearbook of the Association for Supervision and Curriculum Development.* Alexandria, VA: Association for Supervision and Curriculum Development.

Fullan, M. G. (1993). *Change Forces: Probing the depths of educational reform.* Bristol, PA: Falmer.

Fullan, M. G., with Stiegelbauer, S. (1991). *The new meaning of educational change.* New York, NY: Teachers College Press.

Glickman, C. D. (1993). *Renewing America's schools: A guide for school-based action.* San Francisco, CA: Jossey-Bass Publishers.

Rigden, D. (1994). *Sustaining change in school: A role for business.* New York, NY: Council for Aid to Education, Inc.

Waterman, R. H. (1990). *Adhocracy: The power to change.* Knoxville, TN: Whittle Direct Books.

Continuous Improvement

Deming, W. E. (1993). *The new economics for industry, government, education*. Cambridge, MA: Massachusetts Institute of Technology Center for Advanced Engineering Study.

Deming, W. E. (1993). *Out of crisis*. Cambridge, MA: Massachusetts Institute of Technology Center for Advanced Engineering Study.

Mann, N. R. (1989). *The keys to excellence: The story of the Deming philosophy*. Los Angeles, CA: Prestwick Books.

Scherkenbach, W. (1991). *Deming's road to continual improvement*. Knoxville, TN: SPC Press, Inc.

Effective Meetings

Doyle, M. & Straus, D. (1993). *How to make meetings work*. New York, NY: Berkeley Publishing Group.

Frank, M. (1989). *How to run a successful meeting in half the time*. New York, NY: Simon and Schuster.

Leadership and Organization Development

Bernhardt, V. L. (1998). *Data analysis for comprehensive schoolwide improvement*. Larchmont, NY: Eye on Education, Inc.

Covey, S. R. (1991). *Principle-centered leadership*. New York, NY: Fireside.

Deal, T. & Peterson, K. (1994). *The leadership paradox: Balancing logic and artistry in school*. San Francisco, CA: Jossey-Bass, Inc.

National LEADership Network Study Group on Restructuring Schools, U.S. Department of Education. (1991). *Developing leaders for restructuring schools: New habits of mind and heart*. Washington, D.C.: United States Department of Education.

National LEADership Network Study Group on Restructuring Schools, U.S. Departmenzt of Education. (1993). *Toward quality in education: The leader's odyssey*. Washington, D.C.: United States Department of Education.

Neal, R. G. (1991). *School based management: A detailed guide for successful implementation*. Bloomington, IN: National Educational Service.

Patterson, J. L. (1993). *Leadership for tomorrow's schools*. Alexandria, VA: Association for Supervision and Curriculum Development.

Prasch, J. (1990). *How to organize for school-based management*. Alexandria, VA: Association for Supervision and Curriculum Development.

Schein, E. H. (1992). *Organizational culture and leadership.* San Francisco, CA: Jossey-Bass, Inc.

Sergiovanni, T. J. (1991). *The principalship: A reflective practice perspective.* Second edition. Boston: Allyn and Bacon.

Learning Organizations

Costa, A. & Kallick, B. (1995). *Shifting the assessment paradigm: The role of assessment in the learning organization.* Alexandria, VA: Association for Supervision and Curriculum Development.

Senge, P. (1990). *The fifth discipline: The art & practice of the learning organization.* New York, NY: Doubleday Currency.

Senge, P. (1994). *The fifth discipline fieldbook: Strategies and tools for building a learning organization.* New York, NY: Doubleday Currency.

Partnerships

Asche, J. A. (1993). *Finish for the future: Exemplary partnerships for school dropout prevention.* Alexandria, VA: National Association of Partners in Education, Inc.

Ban, J. R. (1993). *Parents assuring student success (PASS): Achievement made easy by learning together.* Bloomington, IN: National Educational Service.

Henderson, A. T. & Berla, N. (Ed.). (1994). *A new generation of evidence: The family is critical to student achievement.* Washington, D.C.: National Committee for Citizens in Education.

Karwin, T. (1992). *Beyond the handshakes: An examination of university-school collaboration.* Long Beach, CA: California Academic Partnership Program.

Melaville, A. I. & Blanik, M. J. (1993). *Together we can; A guide for crafting a profamily system of education and human services.* Washington, D.C.: United States Department of Education.

Rigden, D. (1992). *Business and the schools: A guide to effective programs.* New York, NY: Council for Aid to Education, Inc.

Rioux, J. W. & Berla, N. (1993). *Innovations in parent & family involvement.* Princeton Junction, NJ: Eye on Education, Inc.

Professional Development

Covey, S. R. (1989). *The 7 habits of highly effective people: Powerful lessons in personal change.* New York, NY: Fireside.

Cawelti, G. (Ed.). (1993). *Challenges and achievements of American education: 1993 yearbook of the Association for Supervision and Curriculum Development.* Alexandria, VA: Association for Supervision and Curriculum Development.

Dufor, R. (1991). *The principal as staff developer.* Bloomington, IN: National Educational Service.

Glasser, W. (1993). *The quality school teacher: A companion volume to the quality school.* New York, NY: HarperCollins Publishers.

Hargreaves, A. & Fullan, M. G. (1992). *Understanding teacher development.* New York, NY: Teachers College Press.

Joyce, B. (Ed.). (1990). *Changing school culture through staff development.* Alexandria VA: Association for Supervision and Curriculum Development.

Little, J. W. (Fall 1982). Norms of collegiality and experimentation: Workplace conditions of school success. *American Educational Research Journal.* 19, 3:325-340.

Quality Management

Barker, J. (1993). *Discovering the future: The business of paradigms.* New York, NY: HarperBusiness.

Dobyns, L. & Crawford-Mason, C. (1991). *Quality or else: Revolution in world business.* New York, NY: Houghton Mifflin.

Drucker, P. (1993). *Innovation and entrepreneurship: Practice and principles.* New York, NY: HarperBusiness.

Peters, T. (1987). *Thriving on chaos: A handbook for a management revolution.* New York, NY: HarperPerrenial.

Townsend, P. L. with Gebhardt, J. E. (1990). *Commit to quality.* New York, NY: John Wiley & Sons, Inc.

School Improvement

Barth, R. S. (1990). A personal vision of a good school. *Phi Delta Kappan.* March. pp. 512-516.

Berliner, D.C. & Biddle, B.J. (1995). *The manufactured crisis: Myths, fraud, and the attack on America's public schools.* Reading, MA: Addison-Wesley Publishing Company.

California High School Task Force. (1992). *Second to none: A vision of the new California high school.* Sacramento, CA: California Department of Education.

Editors of Education Week Newspaper. (1993). *From risk to renewal: Charting a course for reform.* Washington, D.C.: Editorial Projects in Education.

Elmore, R. F., & Associates. (1990). *Restructuring schools: The next generation of educational reform.* San Francisco, CA: Jossey-Bass Publishers.

Elementary Grades Task Force. (1992). *It's elementary! Elementary grades task force report.* Sacramento, CA: California Department of Education.

Gardner, H., & Boix-Mansilla, V. (February 1994). Teaching for understanding: Within and across the disciplines. *Educational Leadership.* 51, 5:14-18.

Hargreaves, A., Earl, L., & Ryan, J. (1996). *Schooling for change: Reinventing education for early adolescents.* New York: Falmer Press.

Hill, J. (1992). *The new American school: Breaking the mold.* Lancaster, PA: Technomic Publishing Company, Inc.

Joyce, B., Wolf, J., & Calhoun, E. (1993). *The self-renewing school.* Alexandria VA: Association for Supervision and Curriculum Development.

Lezotte, L.W. (1997). *Learning for all.* Okemos, MI: Effective Schools Products, Ltd.

Lezotte, L. & Jacoby, B. (1990). *A guide to the school improvement process based on effective school research.* Okemos, MI: Effective Schools Products, Ltd.

Lezotte, L. & Jacoby, B. (1992). *Sustainable school reform: The district context for school improvement.* Okemos, MI: Effective Schools Products, Ltd.

Murphy, J. & P. Hallinger. (Eds.). (1993). *Restructuring schooling: Learning from ongoing efforts.* Newbury Park, CA: Corwin Press, Inc.

National Governors' Association. (1994). *Transforming education: Overcoming barriers.*

Olsen, L. (1994). *The unfinished journey: Restructuring schools in a diverse society.* San Francisco, CA: California Tomorrow.

Reavis, C. A. & Griffith, H. (1992). *Restructuring schools: Theory and practice.* Lancaster, PA: Technomic Publishing Company, Inc.

Schmoker, M. (1996). Results: *The key to Continuous School Improvement.* Alexandria, VA: Association for Supervision and Curriculum Development.

Sergiovanni, T. J. & Moore, J. H. (Eds.). (1989). *Schooling for tomorrow: Directing reforms to issues that count.* Needham Heights, MA: Simon & Schuster.

Wiles, J. W. (1993). *Promoting change in schools.* New York, NY: Scholastic Inc.

Strategic Planning

Barth, R. S. (1993). Coming to a vision. *Journal of Staff Development*, 14 (1), 1-9.

Bean, W. (1993). *Strategic planning that makes things happen: Getting from where you are to where you want to be.* Amherst, MA: HRD Press, Inc.

Collins, C. C. & Porras, J. I. (1991). Organizational Vision and Visionary Organizations. *California Management Review Reprint Series.* Fall. pp. *30-51.*

Lodish, R. (1992). Developing a mission statement. *NAESP*, 10 (4).

Student Achievement

Clewell, B. C., Anderson, B. T., & Thorpe, M. E. (1992). *Breaking the barriers: Helping female and minority students succeed in mathematics and science.* San Francisco, CA: Jossey-Bass Inc.

Elmore, R. F., & Fuhrman, S. (Eds.). (1994). *The governance of curriculum.* Alexandria, VA: Association for Supervision and Curriculum Development.

Glasser, W. (1992). *The quality school: Managing students without coercion.* New York, NY: HarperCollins Publishers.

Hoover, J. J. (1991). *Classroom applications of cognitive learning styles.* Boulder, CO: Hamilton Publications.

Kovalik, S. with Olsen, K. D. (1992). *Integrated thematic instruction: The model.* Village of Oak Creek, AZ: Susan Kovalik & Associates.

McClanahan, E., & Wicks, C. (1993). *Future force: Kids that want to, can, and do!* Glendale, CA: Griffin Publishing.

Teacher Evaluation

Manning, R. (1988). *The teacher evaluation handbook: Step-by-step techniques and forms for improving instruction.* Englewood Cliffs, NJ: Prentice Hall.

McLean, G., Damme, S., & Swanson, R. (Eds.). (1990). *Performance appraisal: Perspectives on a quality management approach.* Alexandria, VA: American Society for Training and Development.

Teams

Larson, C . E. & F. M. J. LaFasto. (1989). *Team work.* Newbury Park, CA: Sage Publications.

Maeroff, G.I. (1993). Building teams to rebuild schools. *Phi Delta Kappan.* 74, 7:512-519.

Morley, C.L. (1994). *How to get the most out of meetings*. Alexandria, VA: Association for Supervision and Curriculum Development.

Quick, T. L. (1992). *Successful team building*. New York, NY: AMACOM.

Scholtes, P. R., et. al. (1988). *The team handbook*. Madison, WI: Joiner Associates Inc.

Wellins, R. S., W. C. Byham, & J. M. Wilson. (1991). *Empowered teams*. San Francisco, CA: Jossey-Bass.

Time Management

Covey, S. R., Merrill, A. R. & Merrill, R. R. (1994). *First things first: To live, to love, to learn, to leave a legacy*. New York, NY: Simon & Schuster.

Robbins, A. (1991). *Awaken the giant within*. New York, NY: Fireside.

Total Quality Management and Education

Byrnes, M., Cornesky, R. & Byrnes, L. (1992). *The quality teacher: implementing total quality management in the classroom*. Bunnell, FL: Cornesky & Associates Press.

Langford, D. P. *Total quality learning*. P.O. Box 80133, Billings, MT.

McCormick, B. L. (1991). *Quality & education: Critical linkages*. Princeton Junction, NJ: Eye on Education, Inc.

Schargel, F. (1994). *Transforming education through total quality management: A practitioner' guide*. Princeton Junction, NJ: Eye on Education.

Schmoker, M. J., & R. B. Wilson. (1993). *Total quality education: Profiles of schools that demonstrate the power of Deming's management principles*. Bloomington, IN: Phi Delta Kappa Educational Foundation.

Spanbauer, S. J. (1992). *A quality system for education*. Milwaukee, WI: ASQC Quality Press.

Trucker, S., Oddo, F., and Brassard, M. (1993). *The educators' companion to the memory jogger plus+*. Methuen MA. GOAL/QPC.

Total Quality Management Tools

Brassard, M. (1989). *The memory jogger plus+: Featuring the seven management and planning tools*. Methuen, MA: GOAL/QPC.

Lynch, R. & Werner, T. (1992). *Continuous improvement: Teams & tools*. Atlanta, GA: QualTeam, Inc.

McCloskey, L., & Collett, D. (1993). *A primer guide to total quality management.* Methuen, MA: GOAL/QPC.

Sashkin, M. & Kiser, K. (1993). *Putting total quality management to work: What TQM means, how to use it & how to sustain it over the long run.* San Francisco, CA: Berrett-Koehler Publishers.

INDEX